CHILD VICTIMS

CHILD VICTIMS

Crime, Impact, and Criminal Justice

JANE MORGAN
and
LUCIA ZEDNER

CLARENDON PRESS · OXFORD
1992

Oxford University Press, Walton Street, Oxford OX2 6DP

Oxford New York Toronto
Delhi Bombay Calcutta Madras Karachi
Petaling Jaya Singapore Hong Kong Tokyo
Nairobi Dar es Salaam Cape Town
Melbourne Auckland
and associated companies in
Berlin Ibadan

Oxford is a trade mark of Oxford University Press

Published in the United States
by Oxford University Press, New York

British Library Cataloguing in Publication Data
Data available

Library of Congress Cataloging in Publication Data
Morgan, Jane.
Child victims: crime, impact, and criminal justice / Jane Morgan
and Lucia Zedner.
Includes bibliographical references and index.
1. Children—England—Crimes against.   2. Victims of crimes—
England.   I. Zedner, Lucia.   II. Title.
HV6250.4.C48M67   1992   362.88'083—dc20   91–30454

ISBN 0–19–825699–X
ISBN 0–19–825700–7 (pbk.)

Typeset by Hope Services (Abingdon) Ltd
Printed in Great Britain by
Biddles Ltd
Guildford & King's Lynn

Preface

Children as victims of crime have hitherto attracted only limited academic attention. Interest in child victimization has focused exclusively on child abuse and, since the 1970s, child sexual abuse in particular. There is no systematic information available about children who are victims of other crimes. Neither is there any information about the experiences of children who are victims of all crime within the criminal justice system, their interaction with the professionals of that system—the police, lawyers, court officials—and the response of the social and welfare agencies to child victims. By contrast to the growing attention to adult victims, children are a comparatively neglected theme.

The present study of the victimization of children and young people under the age of 17 is an attempt to correct this omission.[1] It examines the extent and nature of offences against children, and explores the impact of the entire range of crimes on child victims. It then looks at the possible sources of help, ranging from the criminal justice system, through the social and welfare agencies, statutory, professional, and voluntary. It looks in particular at those agencies which already offer assistance to child victims, as well as those that have the potential to do so. Finally it examines the perceptions of children and their families of the help which they sought or were offered to aid their recovery from the impact of victimization.

The research was carried out at the Centre for Criminological Research, University of Oxford, on behalf of the Home Office. A considerable number of organizations and individuals materially helped us in our field-work. Their assistance made the research not merely productive but genuinely interesting and stimulating. Amongst the organizations who helped us, we must particularly mention the Police Authorities in Thames Valley and Bedfordshire, who allowed us access to their personnel and police files and records: without their co-operation the research could not have been carried out. We are

[1] For the sake of simplicity, we have chosen to refer generally to all those up to the age of 17 as children instead of repeating the cumbersome phrase 'children and young persons' throughout the book.

especially grateful to the Chief Constables of these forces and the Chief Superintendents in the field-work areas—Chief Superintendent John Goodenough of 'B' Division in Thames Valley and Chief Superintendents Prickett and Spalding in 'D' and 'C' Division of Bedfordshire respectively.

We would like to thank Victim Support, who facilitated access to Victim Support Schemes nationally and, in particular, the management committees and key personnel of the Victim Support Schemes in both Oxford and Bedfordshire who allowed us full access to the schemes' records and permitted us to interview their staff and volunteers. A special debt of gratitude is owed to the co-ordinators, Elizabeth Duff and Joanna Fenstermacher, in Oxford, and to Alan Doughty, the county Director in Bedfordshire and the area co-ordinators, Guy Pollock, Margaret Doughty, Enid Ingrey, and Sue Hudspith. Mention should also be made of the management committees and key personnel in the six other Victim Support Schemes we visited outside the field-work areas, who generously gave their time and expressed their views during long interviews. Helen Reeves, Anne Viney, and Jane Cooper of the national headquarters of Victim Support have been particularly helpful to us throughout. Lengthy discussions with them served to encourage us and played an important role in the development of the study in so far as it relates to Victim Support. We also thank the Secretary of the Criminal Injuries Compensation Board, David North, for discussing criminal injuries compensation with us. Finally, it should not be forgotten that a major part of this research could not have been carried out had it not been for the co-operation of the many children and families who agreed to share their experiences with us. To all of them we express our sincere thanks.

The study was commissioned by the Home Office Research and Planning Unit. We are grateful to Mrs Mary Tuck and Mr Roy Walmsley for their support and to Dr Lorna Smith and Dr Tim Newburn, our liaison officers, who were always on hand to advise and assist us at all stages of the study. We also had the benefit of advice from a distinguished consultative committee which was chaired by Roy Walmsley and included Dr Lorna Smith and Dr Tim Newburn. The other members were: Professor Juliet Cheetham of Stirling University; Dr David Jones of the Park Hospital for Children, Oxford; Harry Blagg of Lancaster University; Michele Elliott of Kidscape; Katherine Byrne of Westminster Social Services; Anne

Viney of Victim Support; Chief Superintendent Anthony Kilkerr of the Metropolitan Police; Dr Barbara Ely of the Department of Health; Jonathan Potts of 'C4' Division of the Home Office; and Dr Roger Hood, Reader in Criminology at the University of Oxford and Director of the Centre for Criminological Research. Joyce Plotnikoff, who was originally employed as a research fellow on the project, has been of considerable assistance. We are indebted to her invaluable research and thank her warmly for all her work.

We are grateful to our colleagues at the Centre for their moral support and to the administrator, Mrs Sylvia Littlejohns, who has been of particular assistance throughout. Jackie Neate helped to organize the field-work and Heather Clark typed the original report for the Home Office, while Helen Rhind of the London School of Economics also provided much valuable research assistance in preparing the manuscript. We thank them warmly.

The manuscript greatly benefited from the careful reading of Professor Sir Henry Phelps Brown and Professor Kenneth Morgan. Above all, Dr Roger Hood, the Director of the Centre, helped us through the various stages and took a great interest in the work throughout. To him we owe a considerable debt of gratitude. Of course, none of the people or institutions listed here is in any way responsible for the views expressed in this book, or for any errors of fact or interpretation that doubtless remain.

Our final thanks must be personal—to our families for their forbearance and encouragement while this book was being written.

J.M.
L.Z.

Contents

1

Introducing Child Victims: The Problem of Child Abuse

Responding to Victims of Crime

Since the 1970s there has been a growing interest, both nationally and internationally, in victims of crime. Indeed, the past twenty years have seen the emergence both of victim studies and of services for victims.[1] During this period the nature of victimization and its extent have received widespread publicity.[2] A great deal is now known about the effects of crime on victims, the needs that may arise from victimization, and the reaction of various agencies to those needs. There has been a growing recognition that the legal response and intervention by helping professions may make a significant contribution to the overall impact of crime. As a result, demands have been made for the criminal justice system to be more sensitive to the needs and rights of victims. In 1990 the government published a *Victim's Charter*, which suggests that more should be done to help the victim. It sets out for the first time how victims of crime should be treated and what they are entitled to expect from the criminal justice system.[3]

These developments are of relatively recent origin. Since the nineteenth century, criminal justice practitioners and criminologists

---

[1] J. Shapland *et al.*, *Victims in the Criminal Justice System* (Aldershot, 1985); M. Maguire and C. Corbett, *The Effects of Crime and the Work of Victims Support Schemes* (Aldershot, 1987); R. I. Mawby and M. L. Gill, *Crime Victims: Needs, Services and the Voluntary Sector* (London, 1987); E. A. Fattah (ed.), *From Crime Policy to Victim Policy* (London, 1986); M. Maguire and J. Pointing (eds.), *Victims of Crime: A New Deal?* (Milton Keynes, 1988); S. Walklate, *Victimology: The Victim and the Criminal Justice Process* (London, 1989).

[2] G. C. Barclay (ed.), *A Digest of Information on the Criminal Justice System*, Home Office Research and Statistics Department (London, 1991), 13. In 1988, 1 in 5 of the population were the victims of one or more crimes.

[3] Home Office, *Victim's Charter: A Statement of the Needs and Rights of Victims of Crime* (London, 1990).

have been preoccupied with offenders as part of a general search for explanations of criminal behaviour or for ways of preventing reoffending through rehabilitation and training. The victim, by contrast, has played a lesser role. Other than a source of information or a potential witness in court proceedings, he or she has not occupied centre stage as a major performer. Gradually, however, victims have gained the attention of both criminologists and makers of criminal justice policy, who have come to recognize that victims have substantial rights and needs to which the system should respond. This change has come about as a result of a number of factors. Growing scepticism about the potential of punishment to deter or to rehabilitate has induced pessimism about the very purpose of the criminal justice system. In contrast, new empirical research ranging from national victimization or crime surveys to small scale, in-depth qualitative studies of specific types of victim or particular areas has produced a wealth of new data on the extent and nature of victimization. There has also been a burgeoning of work on fear of crime and perceptions of risk; on the psychological and financial effects of crime; and on victims' consequent needs.[4] The growth of welfare consumerism, which has prompted users of public services to lobby for greater responsiveness and better services from the State, has drawn attention to victims and has led to criticism of the ways in which they are treated by the police and the courts.[5] These criticisms have led to suggestions for improving policies and procedures for victims and identified new, more positive functions for the criminal justice system not least in providing for compensation, mediation, and reparation.

In the 1980s a variety of well-organized pressure groups set up specifically to assist, or campaign on behalf of, victims were influential in forming a climate of opinion more sympathetic to their needs and

---

[4] M. Hough and P. Mayhew, *The British Crime Survey: First Report*, Home Office Research Study, No. 76 (London, 1983); M. Hough and P. Mayhew, *Taking Account of Crime: Key Findings from the 1984 British Crime Survey*, Home Office Research Study, No. 85 (London, 1985); P. Mayhew *et al.*, *The 1988 British Crime Survey*, Home Office Research Study, No. 111 (London, 1989); T. Jones *et al.*, *The Islington Crime Survey: Crime, Victimization and Policing in Inner-City London* (London, 1986); Shapland *et al.*, *Victims in the Criminal Justice System*; Maguire and Corbett, *The Effects of Crime and the Work of Victims Support Schemes*; Mawby and Gill, *Crime Victims*; Fattah, *From Crime Policy to Victim Policy*; Maguire and Pointing (eds.), *Victims of Crime: A New Deal?*; Walklate, *Victimology*.

[5] National Association of Victims Support Schemes, *The Victim in Court: Report of a Working Party* (London, 1988).

rights.[6] They called for greater sensitivity to the plight of victims and emphasized the need for the agencies coming into contact with them to take their interests into consideration. Largely as a result of their campaigning activities, the victim is no longer the 'forgotten actor' in the criminal justice process. The Press, television, and radio now frequently carry features relating to victimization. Similarly, criminal justice, welfare, and health professionals are beginning to take seriously the impact of their activities upon the victim and to consider how they might improve their response. To what degree this arises from a genuine concern for the plight of the victim, out of disillusionment with their capacity to ameliorate the impact of crime, or simply from the public relations advantage to be gained from victim-centred policies is open to debate.

Politicians, too, have begun to recognize the broad-based public sympathy for victims across the political spectrum.[7] The victim is seen as a 'safe' subject with popular appeal on whom to focus the politician's humanitarianism. On the political left, it has been recognized that victims (for example, on housing estates) are very often those who can least afford to suffer the losses inflicted by crime and that aid to victims should, therefore, form a natural extension of existing national insurance arrangements. On the political right, concern about victims has been presented as reflecting the caring face of the 'law and order' lobby. In addition, they see aid to voluntary organizations such as Victim Support as congruent with the search for restructuring a lost community, the desire to promote 'active citizenship', and the qualities of the good neighbour—not to mention reducing expenditure by central government.

Certainly the voluntary sector has been most prominent in the provision of specialist, non-financial support.[8] Help for specific groups of victims has been developed by voluntary organizations such as Rape Crisis Centres for victims of rape and sexual assault and by women's refuges for victims of domestic violence. A more general service for a much wider range of victims has been generated by the

---

[6] M. Maguire, and J. Shapland, 'The "Victims Movement" in Europe', in A. J. Lurigio *et al.*, *Victims of Crime: Problems, Policies and Programs* (Newbury Park, Calif., 1990).

[7] A. Phipps, 'Ideologies, Political Parties, and Victims of Crime', in Maguire and Pointing (eds.), *Victims of Crime*.

[8] Mawby and Gill, *Crime Victims*; M. L. Gill and R. I. Mawby, *Volunteers in the Criminal Justice System* (Milton Keynes, 1990).

rapid development of Victim Support.[9] This began life as a local voluntary organization established first in Bristol in 1974 in recognition of the fact that victims had needs which were not being met by the criminal justice system. In the decade since the formation of the National Association of Victims Support Schemes, now Victim Support, the annual number of referrals has grown to over 400,000 and at the start of the 1990s there were over 350 schemes affiliated to the national organization covering most of England and Wales.[10] Over 10,000 volunteers were involved. Each scheme is run by a management committee composed of representatives of relevant professions— the Probation Service, Social Services, the police, and the local volunteers bureau. The key person in every scheme is the co-ordinator, who is responsible for ensuring that referrals of victims are received, and for allocating visits to the volunteers. Schemes lay emphasis on personal contact, upon 'reaching out' to victims rather than leaving it to them to ask for help, and upon establishing contact as soon as possible after the offence. Reliant largely upon the work of unpaid volunteers, the schemes seek to provide a sympathetic 'listening' ear for the fears, distress, and anger which many victims need to express.

The government has been active in providing funds for Victim Support Schemes and in establishing the Criminal Injuries Compensation Scheme. In 1985–6 it granted £126,000 to Victim Support Schemes in order to support the work of volunteers in giving help to victims. By 1988–9 £2.5 million had been made available to Victim Support by government funding. By 1989–90 total funding approached £4 million.[11] In addition, as early as 1964, financial aid to victims was introduced by the government when it established the Criminal Injuries Compensation Board (CICB) to administer an *ex gratia* scheme with the duty to compensate fairly all those who suffer personal injuries directly attributable to a crime of violence.[12] The

[9] P. Rock, *Helping Victims of Crime: The Home Office and the Rise of Victim Support in England and Wales* (Oxford, 1990).

[10] Victim Support (formerly the National Association of Victims Support Schemes) enforces a measure of uniformity through its constitution. Schemes are only affiliated if they fulfil certain requirements regarding management committee representation, volunteer training, etc.

[11] Home Office, *Crime, Justice and Protecting the Public*, Cm. 965 (London, 1990), 3; J. Russell, *Home Office Funding of Victim Support Schemes: Money Well Spent?*, Home Office Research and Planning Unit Paper, No. 58 (London, 1990); Barclay (ed.), *A Digest of Information on the Criminal Justice System*, 21.

[12] See *Annual Reports* of the Criminal Injuries Compensation Board; P. Duff 'Criminal Injuries Compensation and Violent Crime', *Criminal Law Review* (1987),

scheme was placed on a statutory footing by the 1988 Criminal Justice Act.[13] Applications to the CICB (including Scotland) have risen from 22,000 in 1979–80 to 53,650 in 1989–90 and the number of awards made in the same period increased from 17,500 to 27,800.[14]

In 1973 the government introduced compensation orders, which may be made by both Crown and magistrates courts, and may involve the payment of a specified amount of money by the offender via the court to the victim. An order may be made in respect of a victim who has suffered personal injury, loss, or damage as a result of an offence. Under the Criminal Justice Act 1988 the courts are obliged to give reasons for not ordering compensation to those who are eligible.[15] In 1989 113,600 compensation orders were made to victims at magistrates courts (12,800 at the Crown Court) and the average amount of compensation was £139 (£924 in the Crown Court). The publication of the *Victim's Charter* in 1990, which spells out what victims are entitled to expect and the help available to them, underlines the government's continued commitment to helping victims. Statements such as these represent a notable confirmation of changing attitudes towards victims in the period since the 1970s.

In all this, however, there is very little mention of children as victims of crime. The victimization of children is seen solely in terms of child abuse, physical and sexual. In the criminal justice system allegations of child abuse are treated in a different way from other types of allegation made by, or on behalf of, children or adults. The overriding factor in the treatment of children who are victims of child abuse is that the best interests of the child shall be served and the welfare of the child shall be paramount. The term 'child abuse' is used to describe acts which may fail to be recorded as crime, and such cases may be diverted out of the criminal justice process into civil child protection proceedings. As a result, interest and concern about child victimization has developed largely outside a criminological framework and has become the preserve of social workers, child care

---

219–30; T. Newburn, *The Settlement of Claims at the Criminal Injuries Compensation Board*, Home Office Research Study, No. 112 (London, 1989).

[13] D. Miers, 'The Criminal Justice Act: The Compensation Provisions', *Criminal Law Review* (1989), 32—42.

[14] Barclay (ed.), *A Digest of Information on the Criminal Justice System*, 13.

[15] Over 108,000 offenders were ordered to pay compensation by the court in 1988; the average amount was £118 in magistrates courts and £1,140 in the Crown Court. Home Office, *Crime, Justice and Protecting the Public*, 3.

professionals, and social policy-makers. Much of the earlier criminological debate on victims passed children by.

The Problem of Child Abuse

At the beginning of the 1990s child abuse, physical and sexual, is now seen to be a serious social problem. Since the 1960s there has been increasing recognition of the extent of physical abuse of children within the home and the consequent needs of its victims.[16] Until the latter part of the 1980s, however, there was comparatively little public concern about the existence of sexual abuse. Professionals took the complacent, perhaps post-Freudian, view that if a child reported a sexual encounter it must be a fantasy. Many reasons have been given for this delay in recognizing the fact of child sexual abuse. It is rarely a life-and-death issue. There are few, if any, external signs when a child has been abused in this way. Children tend not to disclose what is happening to them at the time. They may have been threatened into remaining silent, they may be afraid to tell in case they are removed from their families, or they may not expect to be believed. In the 1980s, the assumption that children do not tell the truth about sexual abuse was challenged by both child psychologists and psychiatrists as well as by the growing number of incest survivors' groups and women's groups, which have allowed women to reveal their childhood experiences for the first time.[17] However, it was not until the launch of Childline, a telephone helpline for children, on television in 1986 that child sexual abuse came to be seen as a serious social problem.

This interest in child abuse has spawned a large body of research and voluminous publication of its findings, including at least one journal devoted solely to the subject, *The International Journal of Child Abuse and Neglect*. It is now more readily accepted that children are unlikely to lie about being abused, that child sexual abuse is

[16] C. M. Lee (ed.), *Child Abuse: A Reader and Sourcebook* (Milton Keynes, 1978); N. Parton, *The Politics of Child Abuse* (Basingstoke, 1985); P. Dale *et al.*, *Dangerous Families: Assessment and Treatment of Child Abuse* (London, 1986); R. Calam and C. Franchi, *Child Abuse and its Consequences* (Cambridge, 1987); D. Jones *et al.*, *Understanding Child Abuse*, 2nd edn. (Basingstoke, 1987); Violence Against Children Study Group, *Taking Child Abuse Seriously* (London, 1990).

[17] D. P. H. Jones and M. McQuiston, *Interviewing the Sexually Abused Child* (London, 1988), 9–15; G. S. Goodman, 'The Child Witness: Conclusions and Future Directions for Research and Legal Practice', *Journal of Social Issues*, 40(2) (1984), 157–75.

probably far more prevalent than previously thought, and that it may occur in families across the social spectrum. The wealth of data now available provides resounding evidence of the fact that child sexual abuse has considerable effects on its victims, both in the immediate and in the longer term; that it is exploitative and destructive; and that it causes a great deal of suffering, pain, and distress, particularly when a person whom the child has trusted, such as the child's father, is the offender. Its long-term effects may include depression, lack of self-esteem, and difficulties with personal relationships.[18]

Despite this outburst of concern, statistics in this area have never been easy to obtain. Moreover, recent research has drawn attention to the fact that there is no agreed definition of child sexual abuse upon which to base an estimate of its incidence,[19] although the one most often quoted is that of Schechter and Roberge: 'The involvement of dependent, developmentally immature children and adolescents in sexual activities that they do not fully comprehend, and are unable to give informed consent to and that violate the social taboos of family roles.'[20] This definition does not discriminate between acts committed within the family and by outsiders. It also includes 'non-contact' abuse, such as indecent exposure, as well as contact abuse such as anal or genital rape.

There are no reliable national statistics for reported child abuse. In 1990 a survey of 109 local authorities in England showed that on average local authorities registered 3.6 children per thousand as being at risk of abuse (39,200 in England as a whole). A seventh of these were registered because of concern about sexual abuse. The Department of Health gave figures for the year ending 31 March 1990 of about 43,900 children in Child Protection Registers.[21] Baker and Duncan in 1985 estimated that 12 per cent of girls and 8 per cent of boys under the age of 16 had been abused, using the definition: 'any

---

[18] D. Finkelhor (ed.), *A Sourcebook on Child Sexual Abuse* (London, 1986); P. B. Mrazek and C. H. Kempe (eds.), *Sexually Abused Children and their Families* (New York, 1987); C. Bagley and K. King, *Child Sexual Abuse: The Search for Healing* (London, 1990).

[19] D. P. H. Jones and J. Melbourne McGraw, 'Reliable and Fictitious Accounts of Sexual Abuse to Children', *Journal of Interpersonal Violence*, 2(1) (1987), 27–45.

[20] M. D. Schechter and L. Roberge, 'Sexual Exploitation', in R. E. Hefler and C. H. Kempe (eds.), *Child Abuse and Neglect: The Family and the Community* (Cambridge, Mass., 1986), quoted in D. P. H. Jones and McQuiston, *Interviewing the Sexually Abused Child*, 1.

[21] S. Conroy *et al.*, *Investigating Child Sexual Abuse: A Study of a Joint Initiative* (London, 1990), 8; Dept of Health, 'Provisional Feedback' (1991).

sexual exploitation between an adult and a child, whether by coercion or with consent'.[22] These figures may be an underestimation. In North America reported rates range from 6 per cent to 62 per cent for females and from 3 per cent to 31 per cent for males.[23]

Concern about child abuse is not new. Historical evidence shows that it was clearly identified as a social problem by the late Victorian period and that concern continued to build up throughout the twentieth century.[24] Social policy-makers and growing numbers of welfare professionals drew attention to the plight of children and their vulnerability to neglect and to abuse within the family. The family was held uniquely responsible for the socialization of its offspring.[25] Abuse and neglect represented a clear failure of the family to fulfil its required role.

A major contributing factor in the development of concern about child abuse was the growing recognition of childhood and of children as separate, vulnerable beings with distinct needs.[26] Over the second half of the nineteenth century the steady decline in infant mortality, diminishing opportunities for child labour, and the growth of elementary schooling in Western Europe all led to the extension of the notion of childhood as forming a distinct phase in life. It is arguable that effective concern about abuse of children originated in the United States of America, in part perhaps a symptom of the involvement of women in social reform in the decades after the Civil War. It was there that the first society for the prevention of cruelty to children was founded in New York in 1871. It was set up largely as a result of publicity about the case of Mary Ellen Wilson, who had been appallingly ill-treated by her adoptive parents. She was only rescued after a judge interpreted the word 'animal', under laws against cruelty to animals, to include children. The furore surrounding her case led directly to the New York Society for the Prevention of Cruelty to

---

[22] A. W. Baker and S. P. Duncan, 'Child Sexual Abuse: A Study of Prevalence in Great Britain', *Child Abuse and Neglect*, 9 (1985), 457–67.

[23] Finkelhor (ed.), *A Sourcebook on Child Sexual Abuse*.

[24] M. May, 'Violence in the Family: A Historical Perspective', in J. P. Martin (ed.), *Violence in the Family* (London, 1978); H. Ferguson, 'Rethinking Child Protection Practices: A Case for History', in Violence Against Children Study Group, *Taking Child Abuse Seriously*; Parton, *The Politics of Child Abuse*.

[25] J. Donzelot, *The Policing of Families: Welfare versus the State* (London, 1979).

[26] P. Ariès, *Centuries of Childhood* (London, 1962); I. Pinchbeck and M. Hewitt, *Children in English Society*, i (London, 1969); E. Shorter, *The Making of the Modern Family* (London, 1976); P. Thane, 'Childhood in History', in M. King (ed.), *Childhood, Welfare and Justice* (London, 1981), 6–25.

Children (SPCC)'s being provided with police powers to place agents in the city's magistrates courts in order to investigate cases of destitute, neglected, or wayward children. By the turn of the century, the SPCC was a highly active force, patrolling city slums and fighting battles to gain custody over abused children and to send their parents to prison.

In Britain, the National Society for the Prevention of Cruelty to Children (NSPCC) was founded on the model of its American counterpart, significantly, more than twenty years after the formation of the RSPCA.[27] It, too, was successful in its campaigns to draw attention to the plight of abused children and was highly influential in bringing about the Prevention of Cruelty to, and Better Protection of, Children Act 1889, which made child cruelty and neglect a specific criminal offence for the first time.[28] Other campaigning organizations such as the London Society for the Protection of Young Females, the National Vigilance Association, and the Salvation Army were also instrumental in drawing attention to the abuse of children, particularly the sexual abuse of young girls.[29] The particular fear that young girls were being sold into prostitution generated a major 'moral panic' fuelled by the crusading Liberal journalist W. T. Stead, editor of *The Pall Mall Gazette*, who, in his articles on 'The Maiden Tribute of Modern Babylon', reported buying a young girl ostensibly for the purposes of prostitution. In response to this public outcry, the Criminal Law Amendment Act 1885 raised the age of consent for sexual intercourse to 16 years, thus providing the basis of late twentieth-century criminal law on sexual assault outside the family. The Act failed, however, to provide adequate protection for sexual abuse within the family: where the girl had passed the age of 16 the law could not be applied retrospectively to punish continuing incest.

In the 1880s the NSPCC and the National Vigilance Association combined to wage a campaign to make incest amongst adults a criminal offence on the grounds that such intercourse had almost always first started before the girl had reached the age of consent.

[27] The Society for the Prevention of Cruelty to Children was founded in Liverpool at a meeting for the Royal Society for the Prevention of Cruelty to Animals; the National Society (NSPCC) received its royal charter in 1895. L. G. Housden, *The Prevention of Cruelty to Children* (London, 1955); Parton, *The Politics of Child Abuse*, ch. 2.

[28] The Act made it an offence for an adult (over the age of 16) in charge of any girl under 16 years or any boy under 14 years to ill-treat, neglect, or injure them in any way likely to cause them harm or ill health.

[29] E. J. Bristow, *Vice and Vigilance: Purity Movements in Britain since 1700* (Dublin, 1977).

Their efforts led eventually to the passing of the 1908 Punishment of
Incest Act, which made sexual relations between people within the
family a crime for the first time.[30] The main impetus behind this Act
was a desire to protect girls from the sexual attentions of their adult
male relatives, particularly in the overcrowded slums of urban areas.
Those campaigning in the cause of 'social purity' were joined in a
vocal coalition by the growing numbers of middle-class women who
had espoused the cause of social feminism.[31] In 'child-saving', middle-
class women, intent on expanding their sphere of social activity,
found a respectable outlet for their energies which was nevertheless
consistent with their conventional, 'maternal' role.[32] Thus the growth
of social feminism at the end of the nineteenth century was an
additional factor in drawing public attention to the problem of child
abuse and neglect.

Whilst the early impetus to 'child-saving' was founded on concern
about the welfare of children, a distinct shift in emphasis is discernible
around the turn of the century. Partly as a result of public outcry over
the poor quality of recruits for enlistment in the army during the Boer
War (1899–1902) there was a growing concern about the health of the
race and the need to prevent its physical, intellectual, and moral
degeneration.[33] Often this had powerful imperialist or even racialist
overtones. The Eugenics Movement, which drew support across the
political spectrum, sought to improve the quality of future offspring
and focused attention on the health and welfare of children generally.
It saw in incest the particular risk of producing children liable to be
physically feeble or of weak intellect. The family was a key source of
moral and physical welfare: legislation such as the Punishment of
Incest Act 1908 was as much concerned with the 'policing of families'

---

[30] V. Bailey, and S. Blackburn, 'The Punishment of Incest Act 1908: A Case Study
of Law Creation', *Criminal Law Review* (1979), 708–18.

[31] O. Banks, *Faces of Feminism: A Study of Feminism as a Social Movement* (Oxford,
1981).

[32] A. M. Platt, *The Child Savers: The Invention of Delinquency* (Chicago, Ill., 1969);
F. K. Prochaska, *Women and Philanthropy in Nineteenth Century England* (Oxford,
1980); B. C. Pope, 'Angels in the Devil's Workshop', in R. Bridenthal *et al.* (eds.),
Becoming Visible: Women in European History (Boston, Md., 1979); M. Vicinus, *A
Widening Sphere: Changing Roles of Victorian Women* (Bloomington, Ind., 1977).

[33] M. Freeden, 'Eugenics and Progressive Thought: A Study in Ideological Affinity',
Historical Journal, 22(3) (Sept. 1979), 645–72; M. Freeden, *The New Liberalism: An
Ideology of Social Reform* (Oxford, 1986); R. Soloway, 'Counting the Degenerates: The
Statistics of Race Deterioration in Edwardian England', *Journal of Contemporary
History*, 17(1) (Jan. 1982), 137–64.

as with the protection of children from abuse.[34] The fact that step-daughters were not protected by the Act underlines the fact that it was primarily feeble genes rather than abuse which the legislators sought to prevent.

Arguably, a more important, and certainly more enduring, reason for concern about child abuse and neglect was the growing anxiety about the problem of juvenile delinquency. Increasingly at the beginning of the twentieth century attention focused on the relationship between good parentage and good citizenship; between abuse and delinquency.[35] The fear that the abused or neglected child would grow up to be a juvenile delinquent promoted the development of a preventive penology which sought to intervene at an early stage in the child's life.[36] Where the family was seen to break down, the State sought to assume responsibility in its place. Under the auspices of the juvenile court, civil care proceedings empowered the State to take control over children who were seen to be in need of protection, whether as victims or as offenders.

The Juvenile Justice System

Since the beginning of the twentieth century, the principles and philosophy underlying the treatment of juveniles who were either victims of abuse and neglect or 'in trouble' as offenders has been that the welfare of the child should be the primary consideration. The Children and Young Persons Act 1933 s. 44(1) stated that

Every court in dealing with a child or young person who is brought before it, either as an offender or other wise, shall have regard to the welfare of the child or young person and shall in a proper case take steps for removing him from undesirable surroundings, and for securing that proper provision is made for his education and training.

This principle has been endorsed in subsequent legislation on juvenile justice. It forms the first of three principles which are to guide a court when making decisions about a child under the Children Act 1989.

---

[34] Donzelot, *The Policing of Families*.

[35] V. Bailey, *Delinquency and Citizenship: Reclaiming the Young Offender 1914–1948* (Oxford, 1987); A. Morris and H. Giller, *Understanding Juvenile Justice* (London, 1987).

[36] R. Dingwall *et al.*, *The Protection of Children: State Intervention and Family Life* (Oxford, 1983), ch. 11.

The legal framework for the treatment of children who are abused or who offend is set out in the Children and Young Persons Act 1933 and the Children and Young Persons Act 1969. A separate forum for proceedings, the juvenile court, with a more sensitive and informal approach than the adult court and whose procedures give special recognition to the vulnerability and special needs of children, was set up under the Children Act of 1908.[37] Significantly this court was given jurisdiction over both deprived and delinquent juveniles. Barely distinguishing between these two categories of 'problem children', the court combined both civil and criminal functions to fulfil both preventive and remedial roles. Subsequently, a series of government inquiries were commissioned to explore the relationship between provision for the welfare of children and the control of juvenile delinquency. Of these, the Molony Committee 1927 and the Curtis Committee 1946 were the most significant. These generated a number of important legislative measures designed primarily to deal with the problem of the juvenile and young offender but which recognized that much delinquency was the product of abuse and neglect.

In 1956 the Ingleby Committee inquired into the operation of the juvenile court and considered whether local authorities should be given new powers and duties to prevent or forestall the suffering of children through neglect in their own homes. More than any previous report it argued strongly for recognition of similarities between the needs of neglected and of delinquent children. It insisted that the overriding principle when dealing with them should be that their welfare and best interests should be served. The apotheosis of this view was marked by the passing of the Children and Young Persons Act 1969, acclaimed at the time as the triumph of 'welfarism'.[38] At the beginning of the 1990s the principles underlying the court's treatment

---

[37] A. Morris and M. McIsaac, *Juvenile Justice? The Practice of Social Welfare* (London, 1978), 10.

[38] This reached its height in the 1960s when the philosophy of 'welfarism' was in the ascendant. The Labour government's White Paper *The Child, the Family and the Young Offender* (Cmd. 2742, London, 1965) was critical of the fact that the juvenile court procedures were almost identical to those of the adult criminal courts. It proposed replacing the juvenile court with local family councils. Due to predictable opposition from vested interests, these proposals got nowhere. For a full discussion see A. E. Bottoms, 'On the Decriminalization of English Juvenile Courts', in R. Hood (ed.), *Crime, Criminology and Public Policy* (London, 1974). For comparisons with the Scottish Juvenile Justice system see S. McCabe and P. Treitel, *Juvenile Justice in the United Kingdom: Comparisons and Suggestions for Change* (London, 1984); Morris and McIsaac, *Juvenile Justice?*; and F. M. Martin *et al.*, *Children Out of Court* (Edinburgh, 1981).

of children in need of protection remain the same—the overriding principles for the courts when dealing with them should be that their welfare and best interests should be served.[39]

'Welfare' in Action

A definition of the welfare approach has been provided by Michael King:

The welfare approach is founded upon an ethos of enlightened concern arising from advances in the behavioural sciences which supposedly enable experts to assess and meet the needs of children and thus entitle them to take or influence a wide range of decisions over what should happen to children who, for one reason or another, come to the attention of state authorities.[40]

Indeed, these legislative developments and the growth and nurture of the philosophy of 'welfare' cannot be separated from the emergence of a growing army of welfare professionals such as social workers and child psychologists in the first half of the twentieth century. Their working philosophy was based on the premiss that delinquency and child abuse were the outcome of the same problems: family and environmental circumstances and broken and unhappy homes. It was through studying and helping the parents that further harm could be prevented. Care proceedings were intended to provide protection to children at risk, but they were no less a means of minimizing the risk of their becoming future delinquents. But while framed in the language of welfarism and protection, the reponse of removing children from their parents and taking them into care had a punitive quality which has not gone unnoticed by historians and sociologists. Modern interpretations of the history of the treatment of juveniles often emphasize the social-control motives of the philanthropic and humanitarian founders of the juvenile justice system.[41]

---

[39] For a full discussion of the Juvenile Justice System see Morris and Giller, *Understanding Juvenile Justice*.

[40] M. King, 'Welfare and Justice', in M. King (ed.), *Childhood, Welfare and Justice: A Critical Examination of Children in the Legal and Childcare Systems* (London, 1981), 105.

[41] See esp. D. Garland, *Punishment and Welfare: A History of Penal Strategies* (Aldershot, 1985); R. Harris and D. Webb, *Welfare, Power and Juvenile Justice: The Social Control of Delinquent Youth* (London, 1987); S. Asquith, 'Justice, Retribution and Children', in A. Morris and H. Giller, *Providing Criminal Justice For Children* (London, 1983), 7–18.

It was for other reasons, however, that during the 1970s and 1980s the way in which welfare was interpreted by those in the juvenile justice system came to be treated with much scepticism by politicians and policy-makers alike. The declining confidence in the welfare ethic as the impact of the wartime Beveridge Report receded may be linked to the more general climate of growing scepticism about reliance on the rehabilitative ideal and perhaps a general loss of faith in the ability of criminal justice and social welfare professionals to prevent and control delinquency. It must also be set against a series of moral panics around issues of 'law and order' (street crime, mugging, race riots) and the sanctity of the family—all contributing to a more coercive approach. These developments were paralleled by the emergence in the 1970s of a vocal feminist movement following similar developments in the United States. In fostering the establishment of women's groups, incest survivors' groups, and women's refuges, this movement effectively drew attention to the extent of abuse and violence within the home.[42]

It is against this background that concern about the physical and psychological impact of child abuse on victims themselves developed. The identification of the so-called 'battered baby syndrome' by the paediatrician Henry Kempe and his co-workers in the 1960s provided clear medical evidence of the extent of non-accidental injury to children.[43] A series of highly publicized cases of physical abuse of children was also crucial in transforming this problem into a matter that demanded radical changes in social policy.[44] Perhaps the most important of these was the Maria Colwell case, in which 8-year-old Maria was brutally murdered by her parents. The case led to considerable publicity and an official inquiry in 1974, which in turn generated enormous public concern about the failure of social services to prevent physical abuse. In the years following the Colwell inquiry, numerous reports resulted from similar public inquiries into allegations of child abuse (for example, those on the death of Paul Brown, Darryn Clarke, Jasmine Beckford, Kimberley Carlile). In these inquiries social workers were criticized for trying to support and work with the family, rather

---

[42] R. E. Dobash and R. Dobash, *Violence against Wives* (New York, 1979); E. A. Stanko, *Intimate Intrusions: Women's Experience of Male Violence* (London, 1985); D. Russell, *The Secret Trauma: Incest in the Lives of Girls and Women* (New York, 1986); J. Hanmer and M. Maynard (eds.), *Women, Violence and Social Control* (London, 1987); L. Kelly, *Surviving Sexual Violence* (Oxford, 1988).

[43] Dingwall *et al.*, *The Protection of Children*, 33.

[44] Violence Against Children Study Group, *Taking Child Abuse Seriously*, 8.

than invoking their statutory powers to remove the children from situations of risk.[45]

Government circulars on child abuse during the 1970s and 1980s emphasized that in responding to allegations of child abuse, the primary concern of those involved should be to protect the best interests and welfare of the child. Systems for the management of child abuse were developed and this led to changes in the way social services department handled these cases including the introduction of area review committees, multidisciplinary case conferences, and the establishment of local 'child protection registers', on which children thought to be at risk from abuse were recorded. The overall outcome of these inquiries was to place the burden of responsibility on social and welfare professionals and, in doing so, to direct them into a far more interventionist role. Prosecution of the offender was now more readily considered if thought to be in the best interests of the child.

Considerable attention has been focused upon the ways in which agencies intervene once a case of child abuse has come to light or is suspected. A number of agencies may be involved, either in identifying possible cases of abuse or in dealing with known cases. The 'core' agencies responsible for action and decision-making are normally local authority social services departments, the police, and the NSPCC. Legal powers to protect children are vested in these agencies, who are authorized to institute care proceedings through the juvenile court. Any of them is empowered to obtain a place of safety order on a child where there is 'reasonable cause' to believe that one or more of the criteria for bringing care proceedings are met, for example 'exposure to moral danger'. The police are involved in cases of child abuse as a consequence of their general responsibility for the protection of life and limb, the prevention and investigation of crime, and the submission of cases for criminal proceedings.

However, the management of child abuse cases is complicated by the number of professions and agencies involved, each with its own 'operational philosophy' and definition of the child's best interests. Abused children are liable to become 'victims' of a system made up of diverse professionals having to make delicate judgements, sometimes based on conflicting evidence. Nowhere was this more evident than in

---

[45] *A Child in Mind: Protection of Children in a Responsible Society* (London, 1987), 278–81, gives details of the central and local government inquiries into child abuse 1973–87.

Cleveland, where in 1987 the vulnerability of the interagency system to breakdown was demonstrated in the full glare of national publicity.

It had for some time been suspected among sections of the 'caring professions' that far greater numbers of children were being abused than those being identified as such. The so-called 'Cleveland Crisis' blew up when, following independent action by key professionals, more than 100 cases of sexual abuse were diagnosed in the five months between March and July 1987—compared with only two cases during the whole of the previous year. Social services obtained place of safety orders to take many of the children into immediate care. The situation was exacerbated by the lack of locally agreed guide-lines for diagnosis—an omission which also explains the low number of cases confirmed in 1986. Conflict, however, arose first because of disagreement over the course of action to be followed, including whether or not to initiate criminal proceedings against alleged abusers. These differences, mainly between the 'caring agencies' and the police, were not resolved by an interagency working party set up in April 1987 by the County Council. The most explosive element in the situation was a major difference of medical opinion about the reliability of techniques for determining whether sexual abuse had occurred—in particular the test of reflex anal dilatation. The arguments continued to rage throughout a series of distressing court cases in which parents sought the return of their children. Joining together under the umbrella of 'Parents Against Injustice' (PAIN) and with the backing of local MPs, Cleveland parents gained massive publicity for the plight of their families. The crisis not only placed great strains upon a system unprepared for dealing with such a flood of cases, but fundamental differences in professional perceptions of abuse became a focus of considerable public disquiet.

The Cleveland affair led to a major inquiry headed by Lord Justice Butler-Sloss.[46] This produced voluminous findings about the inadequacies of existing practice in responding to allegations of abuse and made lengthy recommendations for the improvement of the management and monitoring of abuse cases, interagency co-operation, and the protection of parents' and children's rights. This controversy spurred on the government and professional agencies to produce revised guide-lines on diagnosing and managing abuse cases.[47]

---

[46] *Report of the Inquiry into Child Abuse in Cleveland 1987*, Cm. 412 (London, 1988).
[47] DHSS and Welsh Office, *Working Together: A Guide to the Arrangements for Inter-*

Heightened public and professional anxieties, better training in identification, improved referral procedures to core agencies, the proliferation of helplines and preventive initiatives all seem to point to the conclusion that child abuse is, in the early 1990s, being treated more seriously as a social problem. However, it would be premature to assume that effective action against abuse is now being taken or that the best interests of the children concerned are necessarily being served. Indeed, four years after the Cleveland scandal, new controversy erupted in 1991 about the response to allegations of ritual 'satanic' abuse of children in Nottingham, Rochdale, Orkney, and Kent. Social workers were criticized for allowing an apparent breakdown of working relations with the police to occur, for their failure to follow prescribed procedures, and an over-readiness to take children away from their families. The fact that there was little firm evidence of satanic rituals, black magic, sacrifice of babies, fetuses, or animals, or any other of the bizarre episodes alleged only raised further questions about the appropriateness of making numbers of children wards of court and taking them into local authority care. The policy of 'Pin-Down' whereby children in care were subjected to severe disciplinary actions by social workers in children's homes in Staffordshire and South Wales in 1991 revived this public concern.

All these examples illustrate the difficulties inherent in interpreting the child's best interests in cases of abuse and neglect. Whilst the earlier inquiries into cases of physical abuse of children had led directly to a more interventionist approach by social workers, it was this very approach that attracted most criticism in the aftermath of Cleveland and the later scandals about ritual abuse. The Cleveland Affair and the subsequent controversies thus forced the problem of child sexual abuse into the arena of public debate. The debate focused, however, on the system—on the power and roles of different medical experts and social work professionals, on the dysfunctioning of families, and on the interference of the State in family life—rather than on the child or the development of services to deal with the problem. By contributing to a 'moral panic' about the sanctity of family life, it led both to calls for more State intervention into the private sphere and to equally insistent demands for parents to be free

agency Co-operation for the Protection of Children from Abuse (London, 1988); Department of Education and Science Circular 4/88; Local Authority Circular 10/88.

from State interference.[48] A concerted campaign to assert the rights of parents to be protected against State involvement in family life prompted a public and judicial backlash against the social work profession. This came at a time when the mood of the eighties emphasized a distaste for social engineering or sociological categorizing.

The child abuse crises during the 1970s, 1980s, and 1990s and the way in which they have been handled by social workers have produced much public disquiet. They have served to heighten public awareness of the problem of child abuse. But there have also been wider concerns about the protection of children more generally. Throughout the 1970s and 1980s there has been a vigorous debate conducted amongst academics and policy-makers questioning the relative merits of the welfare philosophy or the 'justice model' as the basis for the legal structure for dealing with juveniles.[49] Although critiques of the social welfare approach have more often been applied to its use for children who offend, there has been mounting criticism throughout the 1980s from politicians, academics, and pressure groups of the child care and control work of social workers.[50] In particular, there has been increasing concern expressed about the growing State intervention into domestic or family life, particularly that of working-class families, one example being the indiscriminate use of place of safety orders and care orders. Emphasis has been laid on the importance of a child himself or herself being heard on any issue which affects him or her directly.[51] Integrally linked with this has been a vocal debate about the role of the juvenile court,[52] including demands for its reform. The DHSS *Review of Child Care Law* in 1985 proposed a number of measures which would move the juvenile court away from the use of adversarial proceedings in civil cases. It suggested that a range of new powers which sought to

[48] N. Frost, 'Official Intervention and Child Protection: The Relationship between State and Family in Contemporary Britain,' in The Violence Against Children Study Group, *Taking Child Abuse Seriously*, 25–40.

[49] S. Humphries, *Hooligans or Rebels?* (Oxford, 1981); S. Asquith, 'Justice, Retribution and Children'; M. D. A. Freeman, 'The Rights of Children who do Wrong', in M. D. A. Freeman, *The Rights and Wrongs of Children* (London, 1983); J. Pratt, 'Corporatism: The Third Model of Juvenile Justice', *British Journal of Criminology*, 29(3) (Summer 1989), 236–54.

[50] H. Parker *et al.*, *Receiving Juvenile Justice* (Oxford, 1981); Harris and Webb, *Welfare, Power and Juvenile Justice*; Dingwall *et al.*, *The Protection of Children*.

[51] M. King, 'Welfare and Justice', in M. King (ed.), *Childhood, Welfare and Justice: A Critical Examination of Children in the Legal and Childcare Systems* (London, 1981).

[52] McCabe and Treitel, *Juvenile Justice in the United Kingdom*; H. Giller, 'Is there a Role for a Juvenile Court?', *Howard Journal*, 25 (1986), 161–71; A Morris, H. Giller, E. Szwed, and H. Geach, *Justice for Children* (London, 1980).

promote consensus between the parties involved should be introduced.[53] Another suggestion made by the National Association for the Care and Resettlement of Offenders (NACRO) was for the abolition of the juvenile court 'steeped in the adversarial, legalistic and punitive traditions of the adult criminal court system' and its replacement with a family court.[54] The Finer Report in 1974 argued strongly for the setting up of a family court as a means of improving the judicial treatment of the family, as did the Cleveland Report in 1988.[55]

As a result of this heightened interest in legal responses to child abuse, a number of improvements in the way in which cases are handled in the juvenile courts were introduced in the 1970s and 1980s. These included such innovations as the legal representation of children and parents and a move towards a civil model of procedure in cases involving child victims. The culmination of these efforts at improving the civil child care system came with the Children Act in 1989, which has been hailed as 'the most comprehensive and far-reaching reform of child law which has come before Parliament in living memory'.[56] This Act drew together existing legislation to produce a more practical and consistent code. It was implemented in the autumn of 1991. It consolidated laws relating to the duties and powers of local authorities concerning children and sought to strike a new balance between family autonomy and the protection of children: to strengthen the rights of parents and children and to limit those of social workers, and to give the courts more control in care cases. These cases are now heard in a new, purely civil forum, the family proceedings court. This took over care proceedings from the juvenile court; the latter became solely a juvenile criminal court, renamed the youth court, thus separating child protection proceedings from juvenile criminal proceedings for the first time. Section 1 of the Children Act put the child's welfare as the court's paramount consideration and demanded that the court have regard to the ascertainable wishes and feelings of the child concerned in civil proceedings. It emphasized the importance of the role of the child advocate or guardian *ad litem* in the court

[53] DHSS, *Review of Child Care Law* (London, 1985); see also J. Williams, 'Family Courts: Justice for the Children?', *Social Work Today*, 10 Nov. 1988, 17–19.

[54] NACRO, *The Future of the Juvenile Court in England and Wales* (London, 1986).

[55] M. Finer, *Report of the Committee on One-Parent Families*, Cmnd. 5629 (London, 1974); *Report of the Inquiry into Child Abuse in Cleveland 1987*, Cm. 412 (London, 1988), para. 16.66.

[56] Children's Legal Centre, 'The Children Act 1989', *Childright*, 66 (May 1990), 7–18.

process. One of the greatest strengths of the legislation is said to be 'its underlying philosophy of partnership between families and the state in the promotion of the child's welfare'.[57] Despite the problems inherent in interpreting the child's best interests, the Children Act endorses the 'welfare' approach in dealing with children in need of protection.

In conclusion, child abuse is regarded as significantly different from other offences. The fact that it occurs primarily within the family has led to the belief that criminal prosecution is not a particularly appropriate response. The development of a separate system for dealing with child abuse which focuses on the welfare of the child rather than on the prosecution of the offender may well obscure the fact that a criminal offence has often been committed. The tendency to marginalize children as victims of crime is reinforced by the use of the term 'abuse' rather than 'assault'. Nevertheless, the fact remains that the problem of child abuse and the plight of its victims has long been recognized. Since the beginning of the twentieth century a separate legal structure for dealing with juveniles who are abused or who offend has existed. Its principles and philosophy were to give primacy to the welfare of the child. Despite the difficulties inherent in the system described in this chapter, the 'welfare and best interests of the child' remain the principles underlying child protection. Child abuse is now recognized as a serious social problem in society; the needs of these children have been acknowledged and are high on the political agenda. Children as victims of other crimes, however, are a different story.

[57] J. Tunnard, 'Countdown to the Children Act', *Magistrate*, 46(10) (Nov. 1990), 186.

2

Children as Victims of Other Crime: The Evidence

In the literature on crime, children and young people are far more likely to be viewed as offenders than victims. It is well known that juvenile offenders contribute significantly to the total volume of recorded crime, but only in the 1990s is it being recognized that young people, especially those of school age, figure disproportionately as victims. Children are prey to the whole range of crimes from petty theft to serious assault. Not only are children direct victims of most crimes; they may also be witnesses to crimes committed against their households, parents, or siblings, and have to live with the consequences of such offences. Over a third of the 400,000 households which experience burglary each year include children. Domestic violence and other serious personal assaults, including rape and even homicide, all too often take place in the presence of children or in circumstances of which the children are aware.[1] In some cases children may be affected by other crimes which have occurred within their neighbourhood—an extreme example of which was the trauma suffered by many children in the wake of the massacre at Hungerford in 1987. Commenting on the lack of attention paid to 'indirect' child victims, Maguire and Corbett reported that in a sample of victims of burglary, robbery, assault, and 'snatch' theft, '70 per cent [of those with

---

[1] For an extensive literature review of domestic violence see L. J. F. Smith, *Domestic Violence: An Overview of the Literature*, Home Office Research Study, No. 107 (London, 1989); also S. Horley, *Love and Pain: A Survival Handbook for Women* (London, 1988); L. V. Davis and B. E. Carlson, 'Observations of Spouse Abuse: What Happens to the Children?', *Journal of Interpersonal Violence*, 2(3) (Sept. 1987), 278–91; R. S. Pynoos and S. Eth, 'Witness to Violence: The Child Interview', *Journal of the American Academy of Child Psychiatry*, 25(3) (1986), 306–19; C. P. Malamquist, 'Children who Witness Parental Murder: Post-Traumatic Aspects', *Journal of the American Academy of Child Psychiatry*, 25(3) (1986), 320–5; R. S. Pynoos and S. Eth, 'The Child Witness to Homicide', *Journal of Social Issues*, 40(2) (1984), 87–108; D. Black and T. Kaplan, 'Father Kills Mother: Issues and Problems Encountered by a Child Psychiatric Team', *British Journal of Psychiatry*, 153 (1988), 624–30.

children] stated that the children had been badly frightened or upset'.[2] This study provided further evidence that most crimes have more than one victim, and that these additional victims are often seriously affected and have needs which are yet to be met.

For children, the status of victim has to be earned in some way in order for them to be recognized as needing a response. The position of children as the dependants of others limits their capacity to acquire this status. Moreover, the validation of victim status usually depends upon the precipitating act being defined as criminal. Yet many types of crime committed against children are not regarded by adults as sufficiently serious to merit any formal response. Routine acts of minor violence such as bullying, chastisement, or assault appear resistant to being defined as criminal when committed against children. To this extent, children are liable to be denied recognition as victims. Still less attention has been paid to the fact that children are often also 'indirect' victims of crimes to which they have been witnesses or bystanders.

The criminal statistics, which provide the most comprehensive picture of recorded crime for England and Wales, provide no information on rates of victimization of children, with the exception of homicide.[3] However, it is possible to build up a profile of crimes committed against children by using other sources. There is an increasing body of information available about the nature of child victimization. This takes two main forms: victimization surveys of children and young people, and literature describing research findings about specific types of crime against children. In addition, we were able to develop a profile of a cohort of child victims who had been affected directly or indirectly by crime, over a specific period of time in the two field-work areas of Oxford and Bedfordshire.

Victimization Surveys

Since its inception in 1972 the US Department of Justice National Crime Survey (NCS) has included questions about offences against

---

[2] Maguire and Corbett, *The Effects of Crime and the Work of Victims Support Schemes* 53.

[3] The most dangerous age of all is under 1 year, with 28 homicide victims per million babies.

children and young persons over the age of 11. Other surveys carried out locally in the United States have also covered this age-group and have shown that teenagers have reported consistently higher rates of victimization than other age-groups and exhibited higher levels of fear of crime. The NCS published in 1986 estimated that from 1982 to 1984 American teenagers (aged 12–19) experienced an average of 1,800,000 violent crimes and 3,700,000 thefts per year—rates about twice as high as those of the adult population.[4] Older teenagers (aged 16–19) suffered higher victimization rates for violent crime (rape, robbery, and assault) than did younger ones (aged 12–15), but rates of theft were similar between these age-groups. The NCS showed that both younger and older teenagers were less likely than adults to be seriously injured by violent crime. This was possibly because teenage victims and offenders were more likely to be known to each other than are adult victims and offenders. However, the differences are not large: 51 per cent of violent crimes committed against adults, 43 per cent of those against older teenagers, and 32 per cent of those against younger teenagers are committed by strangers. In other respects, the characteristics of incidents against the older teenagers closely resembled those against adults. For example, similar proportions of older teenagers and adults were confronted by armed offenders, and the former were almost as likely as adults to sustain serious injuries in the course of an attack. These teenagers rarely reported incidents to the police.

Local studies of child victimization have also been carried out in the United States. Feyerherm and Hindelang carried out a study of school-age children in one American city in 1974.[5] They found that over 70 per cent of boys and over 60 per cent of girls had had 'personal items stolen, destroyed, taken by force, or been threatened, or beaten up'. Children rarely reported crimes against them to the police and even the most common of these crimes, personal theft, was reported in only a third of cases. Eleven per cent of boys and 38 per cent of girls said that they felt unsafe walking in their own neighbourhood after dark, whilst more than 40 per cent believed that they were at risk of being robbed or attacked in their own neighbourhood. In 1977 Hepburn and Monti surveyed the population of a high school in St

[4] *Teenage Victims: A National Crime Survey Report* (Washington, DC, 1986).
[5] W. H. Feyerherm and M. J. Hindelang, 'On the Victimization of Juveniles: Some Preliminary Results', *Journal of Research in Crime and Delinquency*, 11 (1974), 40–9.

Louis using self-administered, anonymous, short questionnaires.[6] Nearly half the children had been victimized during the year: older children, especially boys, were most likely to have been involved. Although older girls indicated higher levels of fear of crime, avoidance strategies by children were most strongly correlated with age and race rather than sex. A further study carried out by Decker *et al.* in 1979[7] investigated the relationship between juvenile victimization and urban structure in twenty-six central cities in the United States based on data drawn from the NCS. Curiously, and contrary to expectation, they found a negative relationship between density of population and juvenile victimization. That is, less densely populated areas had the highest rates of crime against juveniles. They suggested that the increased 'visibility' imposed by high-density living tended to reduce opportunities to commit property crimes in particular, though this thesis requires further examination.

In contrast to the United States, questions relating to children have been conspicuously absent from the *British Crime Survey* carried out in 1982, 1984, and 1988. However, two small studies have been carried out in Sheffield and Edinburgh. These have shown extremely high rates of victimization with only a low proportion of incidents being reported to the police. Mawby carried out a study of 11- to 15-year-olds in two secondary schools in Sheffield in 1975.[8] He found that only 16 per cent of the offences reported to him were probably known also to the police.[9] He also found that in the past year 40 per cent of his sample had had belongings stolen from their person, 32 per cent had articles stolen which they had left unguarded, and 25 per cent had suffered a physical assault. Only 11 per cent had a vehicle stolen but 16 per cent had had goods taken from a vehicle. Just over two-thirds (67 per cent) said that they had been victims of at least one of the crimes included in Mawby's survey. Although he found surprisingly few differences in victimization by social class, Mawby discovered considerable variation by sex: 71 per cent of boys had been victims but

[6] J. R. Hepburn and D. J. Monti, 'Victimization, Fear of Crime and Adaptive Responses among High School Students', in W. H. Parsonage (ed.), *Perspectives on Victimology* (Beverly Hills, Calif., 1979), 121–32.

[7] D. L. Decker *et al.* 'Patterns of Juvenile Victimization and Urban Structure', in Parsonage (ed.), *Perspectives on Victimology*, 88–98.

[8] R. I. Mawby, 'The Victimization of Juveniles: A Comparative Study of Three Areas of Publicly Owned Housing in Sheffield', *Journal of Crime and Delinquency*, 16 (1979), 98–114.

[9] Ibid. 106.

only 62 per cent of girls. Given that he found no appreciable difference in the comparative willingness of boys and girls to report, he postulated that 'girls, who may lead more sheltered lives than boys, were less frequently victimized'.[10]

A study of 1,000 young people aged from 11 to 15 carried out in Edinburgh in 1990 by Anderson *et al.* focused on victimization occurring outside home and school in public places, as well as young people's involvement in crime as offenders and witnesses, and their relations with the police.[11] It found that, over the previous nine months, half the young people surveyed had been victims of an assault, threatening behaviour, or theft from the person. During the same period, 1 in 7 of the 11- and 12-year-old boys had experienced incidents of importuning such as touching or indecent exposure (flashing). These offences decreased as the boys grew older. For girls, however, the figure rose from 17 per cent of 11- and 12-year-olds to 30 per cent of the 14- and 15-year-olds experiencing such behaviour. Only 14 per cent of assaults, 8 per cent of threatening behaviour, and 16 per cent of thefts from the person were reported to the police. Furthermore, less than 1 in 5 (18.5 per cent) of cases of importuning and only 12 per cent of harassment were reported either to the police or to adults in general. The study concluded that children were forced back on their own strategies for dealing with victimization through offering each other mutual support.

Research Findings

In addition to the growing body of information now available about the extent and nature of crime against children, academic research has explored the problems faced by child victims. For example, the problem of bullying became a topic of considerable academic and professional concern amongst educationists in the 1980s. They drew attention to the high levels of violence often involved in bullying and the consequent severity of its effects, both physical and psychological.[12]

---

[10] Ibid. 109.

[11] S. Anderson, R. Kinsey, I. Loader, and C. Smith, 'Cautionary Tales: A Study of Young People and Crime in Edinburgh', Edinburgh, 1990.

[12] See e.g. D. P. Tattum and D. A. Lane (eds.), *Bullying in Schools* (Stoke-on-Trent, 1988); V. E. Besag, *Bullies and Victims in Schools: A Guide to Understanding and Management* (Milton Keynes, 1989); E. Munthe and E. Roland, *Bullying: An International Perspective* (London, 1989); M. O'Moore, *Report of the Conference on Bullying in Schools*

Although bullying is not legally defined as a crime in its own right, many of its component parts (threatening behaviour, assault, and actual bodily harm) are clearly criminal offences which deserve to be recognized as such. The tendency of adults to dismiss bullying as a phase of growing up common to childhood makes it doubly difficult for a child to gain recognition as a victim. Moreover, school subculture imposes a code of silence and shame on the victims of bullying. As a result, it may continue undetected for months or even years until the victim finally breaks down under the pressure. A major international conference was held on the subject of bullying in Stavanger, Norway in 1987. This was the first occasion on which professionals from all over Europe met to discuss the subject.[13] Such events mark the increasing recognition of the need to respond to the problem of bullying, not least by identifying and supporting its victims.

In 1984 a two-year study was conducted by Michele Elliot for Kidscape focusing on 4,000 children.[14] Of these, 68 per cent had been bullied at least once and 38 per cent had been bullied at least twice or had experienced a particularly serious incident. Most seriously, 8 per cent of the students felt it had affected their lives to the point that they had tried suicide, run away, refused to go out or to school, or been chronically ill. In a six-month period after the Kidscape National Conference on Bullying held in 1989 and 1990, Kidscape received over 12,000 letters and 4,000 telephone calls from parents, children, and teachers about the problem of bullying. In 1989 Pete Stephenson and Dave Smith, two educational psychologists working in north-east England, surveyed more than 1,000 Cleveland primary school children. They found that 23 per cent of their sample were involved in serious bullying either as offenders or victims.[15] On the basis of research into the incidence of bullying in Scandinavia which has suggested that 10 per cent of children are bullied, Delwyn Tattum estimated that as many as 870,000 children in England, Scotland, and Wales were made 'unhappy, anxious and fearful' by bullying.[16]

Stavanger 1987, Strasbourg Council for Cultural Co-operation (Strasbourg, 1988); Commission for Racial Equality, *Learning in Terror: A Survey of Racial Harassment in Schools and Colleges* (London, 1988).

[13] O'Moore, *Report of the Conference on Bullying in Schools*.

[14] M. Elliott (ed.), *Bullying: A Practical Guide to Coping for Schools* (London, 1990).

[15] P. Stephenson and D. Smith, 'Bullying in the Junior School', in Tattum and Lane (eds.), *Bullying in Schools*, 47.

[16] D. P. Tattum, 'Violence and Aggression in School', in Tattum and Lane (eds.), *Bullying in Schools*, 10.

Closely linked to bullying, and often synonymous with it, is the problem of racial harassment of the children of ethnic minorities. This too has caused growing concern in recent years. A major report by the Commission for Racial Equality, *Learning in Terror* (1988), revealed that racial harassment in schools and colleges is 'widespread and persistent'. It drew attention to the variety of forms racial harassment may take 'including name-calling and racial insults and abuse, graffiti inside and outside the school premises, and racial violence varying from slapping, punching, jostling, and assault to maiming and even murder'.[17] It has been revealed that, whether harassment occurs inside or outside schools, there is a general failure to identify children who are being victimized in this way. This is exacerbated by the fact that children and their parents do not come forward because they lack confidence in the system. Even when parents do report incidents, they may not be responded to seriously. As a result, children may become virtual prisoners in their own home. One Asian father reported recently that his 9- and 10-year-old children dare not go out because a local gang threatened to beat them up.[18]

As yet there has been little academic research on the extent of racial harassment of school-age children, those few studies there are tending to be small-scale and local.[19] In condemning the lack of nationally recorded figures on the racial harassment of schoolchildren, the Commission for Racial Equality called for 'standardized procedures for reporting and centrally recording incidents of racial harassment so that effective monitoring can take place'.[20] Until such figures are collected it will remain impossible to assess accurately the extent to which children of ethnic minority backgrounds are being victimized in this way, though a problem of some dimensions clearly exists.

Where an offence is committed against a member of a child's family or against their household in general, the child is unlikely to be recognized as a victim in his or her own right. Yet, the child's experience may be such that he or she ought properly to be recognized as an 'indirect victim'.[21] Burglary is the crime which the general

---

[17] *Learning in Terror*, 7.
[18] 'Children Who Cannot Go Out', *Guardian*, 18 Sept. 1989.
[19] For example, the Scottish Ethnic Minority Research Unit in south Glasgow carried out a survey of racial harassment of school-age children in 1986. It found that 25% of its sample had suffered damage to property, 37% had experienced personal racial attacks, and all had been subjected to racial abuse. *Learning in Terror*, 9.
[20] Ibid. 17.
[21] D. S. Riggs and D. G. Kilpatrick, 'Families and Friends: Indirect Victimization

public most fear because of the serious loss and emotional and psychological trauma it inflicts. The effects of such a crime which invades the private family home—often the one safe place for a child—can be traumatic.[22] Perhaps children whose houses have been burgled are the most common 'indirect' victims. But many other serious crimes may take place in the presence of children or in circumstances of which they are aware. A number of inquiries carried out in the United States in the 1980s on children who had been witnesses to extreme sexual or physical violence revealed that these children might exhibit acute stress and suffer long-term adverse effects. Immediate intervention might limit the severity of the post-traumatic stress which is likely to occur in these children, particularly amongst those who were present at the time the offence took place. A recent study carried out by Pynoos and Nader on children aged 5 to 17 years who witnessed sexual assaults on their mothers showed that sexually abused children and children who witness sexual assault share common post-traumatic stress symptoms: disturbances in sexuality, a diminished sense of security and self-esteem, and stress in familial and peer relationships. All the children described their experiences as profoundly frightening.

Recently research in both Britain and America has confirmed that the home is the most frequent setting for serious violence. The Dobashes, for example, in their historical examination of domestic violence, discovered that an analysis of homicides in England and Wales between 1885 and 1905 had shown that over half of all murder victims were women with long-standing relationships with their murderers. Out of a total of 487 murders committed by men, just over a quarter were murders of wives whilst a further quarter were murders of lovers or sweethearts.[23] More recently, studies of homicide conducted by Gibson and Klein between 1957 and 1968 have shown that of all female victims, wives and cohabitants comprised the largest category of victims.[24] Of the 234 women who were murdered in 1989, 48 per cent were killed by their husbands or lovers. Obviously, children who

by Crime', in A. J. Lurigio *et al.* (eds.), *Victims of Crime: Problems, Policies, and Programs* (Newbury Park, Calif., 1990), 120–38.

[22] M. Maguire, *Burglary in a Dwelling: The Offence, the Offender and the Victim* (London, 1982); Maguire and Corbett, *The Effects of Crime and the Work of Victims Support Schemes.*

[23] Dobash and Dobash, *Violence against Wives* (Shepton Mallet, 1980), 15–16.

[24] E. Gibson and S. Klein, *Murder 1957–68*, Home Office Research Study, No. 3 (London, 1969).

witness parental homicide are most likely to suffer major, long-term trauma.[25] Black and Kaplan, in the only British study of such children, state:

The child whose mother is killed by his or her father has to cope with the trauma of violence, the grief associated with the loss of both parents simultaneously, dislocation and insecurity regarding where and with whom they will live, stigma, secrecy, and often massive conflicts of loyalty . . . These children experience both the death of their mother as a victim of what is often an act of horrifying violence, and being the child of a murderer.[26]

In their study of 28 such children of 14 families where the father had killed the mother, they found that all of them experienced extreme stress, which they describe as 'posttraumatic stress disorder (PTSD)', which in some cases was so severe that it inhibited the development of normal mourning. Often the children were the only source of information about the murder and so experienced added distress as they had to describe to others the sequence of events.

Studies of domestic violence in America, although primarily focused on its effects on women, have also begun to reveal its impact on their children.[27] One study estimated that 3.3 million children in the United States witness parental violence annually and that many of them suffer from PTSD.[28] Domestic violence is thought to be one of the most underreported of crimes. Official crime statistics are thus extremely unreliable as a way of calculating the number of such instances and attempting to estimate the number of children who may

[25] Pynoos and Eth, 'Witness to Violence'; Malamquist, 'The Children who Witness Parental Murder'; R. S. Pynoos and K. Nader, 'Psychological First Aid and Treatment Approach to Children Exposed to Community Violence: Research Implications', *Annals of the Institute of Psychiatry*; Pynoos and Eth, 'The Child Witness to Homicide'; R. S. Pynoos and K. Nader, 'Children who Witness the Sexual Assaults of their Mothers', *Journal of the American Academy of Child Psychiatry* 27 (1988), 567–72.

[26] Black and Kaplan, 'Father Kills Mother', 624.

[27] A. Rosenbaum and D. K. O'Leary, 'Children: The Unintended Victims of Marital Violence', *American Journal of Orthopsychiatry*, 51(4) (Oct. 1981), 629–99; J. Pfouts *et al.*, 'Forgotten Victims of Family Violence', *Social Casework*, 27(4) (July 1982), 367–8; M. Elbow, 'Children of Violent Marriages: The Forgotten Victims', *Social Casework* 63(8) (Oct. 1982), 465–8; A. R. Roberts (ed.), *Battered Women and their Families* (New York, 1984); M. Hershorn and A. Rosenbaum, 'Children of Marital Violence: A Closer Look at the Unintended Victims', *American Journal of Orthopsychiatry*, 55(2) (Apr. 1985), 260–6; Davis and Carlson, 'Observations of Spouse Abuse'; R. Grusznski *et al.*, 'Support and Education Groups for Children of Battered Women', *Child Welfare*, 67(5) (Sept.–Oct. 1988), 431–44.

[28] L. Silvern and L. Kaersvang, 'The Traumatized Children of Violent Marriages', *Child Welfare*, 68(4) (July–Aug. 1989), 421–36.

be affected by witnessing and living with such violence. Victim
surveys provide estimates of domestic violence and no more. Moreover, their accuracy is likely to be limited by women's unwillingness
to disclose such details to an interviewer, particularly, as Hough and
Mayhew have pointed out, if the offender is actually present in the
room during the interview.[29] Despite these limitations it has been
estimated that 1 in 8 assaults and crimes of violence involve family,
lovers, or ex-lovers. On the basis of this calculation 200,000 incidents
of domestic assault were uncovered by The 1983 *British Crime Survey*
for England and Wales.[30] Given that more than 1 in 3 households in
Britain contain children, we can estimate that children in nearly
70,000 households suffer indirectly the impact of domestic violence
each year.[31] A disproportionate number of children of abused women
suffer physical, mental, and emotional handicaps, and children with
backgrounds of family violence have a significantly higher incidence
of behaviour problems than comparable groups of children with no
history of family violence.[32]

   Children are also often burdened with trying to stop the violence.
The Dobashes, for example, found that, in their analysis of 'first,
worst and last attacks', almost one-half of the incidents took place in
front of observers, three-fifths of whom were children. 'A majority of
women (59%) reported that the children usually were present during
an assault, and it was not unusual for some children almost always to
observe attacks on their mother.'[33] When their father attacks their
mother children often try to intervene to help their mothers but may
be too weak to do anything other than beg their fathers to stop. Many
feel guilty if they do not come to their mother's aid. Yet they can never
be sure that they are not the next in line for assault.[34] Indeed, research
has shown that in some families where the wife is assaulted by her

---

[29] M. Hough and P. Mayhew, *The British Crime Survey: First Report*; see also
Stanko's criticisms of the British Crime Survey's failure to pick up unreported crimes of
sexual and physical violence against women: E. A. Stanko, 'Hidden Violence against
Women', in Maguire and Pointing (eds.), *Victims of Crime: A New Deal?* (Milton
Keynes, 1988), 40–6.
[30] Smith, *Domestic Violence*, 10.
[31] See Smith, 6–14.
[32] M. D. Pagelow, *Woman Battering: Victims and their Experiences* (Beverly Hills,
Calif., 1981); D. A. Jaffe *et al.*, 'Emotional and Physical Health Problems of Battered
Women', *Canadian Journal of Psychiatry*, 31 (1986), 625–9.
[33] Dobash and Dobash, *Violence against Wives*, 112.
[34] J. Hanmer, 'Women and Policing in Britain', in J. Hanmer *et al.*, *Women,
Policing, and Male Violence: International Perspectives* (London, 1989), 90–124.

husband, the children are also abused. Walker has estimated that a third of wife-abusers also abused their children[35] while other research by Bowker *et al.* has placed a higher figure on this. They estimate that 70 per cent of the children of abused women had been battered by their fathers.[36] Over time witnessing domestic violence may also lead children to believe that violence is a normal, legitimate response to problems. Indeed, research has shown that many men who beat their wives or abuse their children were themselves abused as children.[37] Yet despite the prevalence of domestic violence and its repercussions for the children, there are many obstacles to recognizing that children as well as their mothers have been victimized.

It is therefore clearly evident from a review of the literature that children may be both the direct or indirect victims of a wide range of crimes, often with alarming consequences.

A Profile of Child Victimization in Oxford and Bedfordshire

In order to obtain a profile of child victimization it was necessary to obtain a cohort of child victims. A pilot study carried out in the city of Oxford convinced us that the right approach would be to study the subject of child victimization in depth in two areas, Oxford and Bedfordshire. The ideal method of identifying child victims would have been to carry out a victimization survey in schools. Unfortunately, however, the commencement of the field-work coincided with a period of acute concern about the problem of child sexual abuse sparked off by the 'Cleveland Crisis' in the spring of 1987. Against this climate of heightened awareness and anxiety about child sexual abuse schools were reluctant to allow access for such a survey, for fear that to do so would generate unwarranted parental anxiety. Many teachers were concerned that they lacked the necessary expertise to handle situations which might arise if abuse were revealed. Both teachers and researchers considered it unethical to prompt children to reveal hitherto undisclosed experiences of victimization without having the resources to provide the support which might then have been necessary.

[35] L. E. Walker, *The Battered Woman* (New York, 1979).

[36] L. Bowker *et al.*, 'On the Relationship between Wife Beating and Child Abuse', in K. Yllö and M. Bograd (eds.), *Feminist Perspectives on Wife Abuse* (Newbury Park, Calif., 1989), quoted in A. Morris, 'Interspousal Violence: A Review of Research', in *Cambrian Law Review*, 20 (1989), 7–16.

[37] Morris, 'Interspousal Violence'.

As a result of all these misgivings permissions to carry out victimization surveys in schools were not forthcoming and it was necessary to seek other means of identifying a cohort of child victims from which to draw an interview sample.

The many agencies dealing with children are likely to come into contact with various groups of child victims in the course of their work. Accordingly, personnel in a large number of statutory, professional, and voluntary agencies were contacted and interviewed. All conceded that they dealt with children who had been victims but most only came across specific types of crime. None could furnish a picture of the entire range of crimes against children. Helplines probably deal with the widest range of crimes, but they respond to callers anonymously and so could not provide named data which would allow the researchers to locate victims. Most importantly nearly all agencies, both professional and voluntary, were insistent that their files were confidential.

The only source which provided named data of child victims across the entire range of crime were police records. These records are largely dependent on the victims' willingness to report offences against them and on the police to record such incidents as crimes. In the case of younger children particularly, many crimes are subject to a treble filtering process. First, the child has to disclose that she or he has been victimized to an adult; secondly, the adult has to decide whether or not to report it to the police; and thirdly, the police make the decision whether or not to record the offence. If the adult decides that the incident is not sufficiently serious to warrant reporting, the child will necessarily be denied official recognition as a victim. Mawby and Gill have argued that official data may be said to provide a clearer indication of 'willingness to report' than actual victimization.[38] In the case of children, it is not only their own willingness to report that will determine whether or not they achieve the status of victim, but in many cases the willingness of their parents also. However, Mawby has shown that 'those who have been victims of most types of crime tend to be the ones who reported at least one incident to the police'.[39] To this extent, it may be said that those crimes which are reported and recorded by the police identify at least some of the most salient group of child victims.

---

[38] Mawby and Gill, *Crime Victims: Needs, Services and the Voluntary Sector*, 6.
[39] Mawby, 'The Victimization of Juveniles', 106.

Access was given to all police files and records in the two subdivisions which cover Oxford by the Thames Valley Police in 1987, and for the towns of Luton, Leighton Buzzard, and Biggleswade by Bedfordshire Police Force for 1988. This enabled the researchers to build up a profile of child victims. It revealed 359 cases involving direct child victims recorded on police crime reports in Oxford and 323 in the three study areas in Bedfordshire, of which 223 had occurred in Luton. Obviously, crime reports provide details only of those incidents coming to the attention of the police which they deem sufficiently serious to merit recording as a crime, that is 'a notifiable offence'.[40] Other types of crime which were not 'notifiable' offences, a number of which involved children, were recorded in other ways. For example, during the study periods the police recorded separately 18 incidents of suspicious behaviour in Oxford and 26 in Luton and 26 cases of offences of indecent exposure in Oxford and 31 in Luton involving children.

In Oxford, the single largest category of known offences against children was bicycle theft—making up 57 per cent of all recorded offences. There was a marked, though not entirely surprising, disparity between the two study areas in that bicycle thefts made up only 26 per cent of recorded crime in Bedfordshire. This difference may be due to the well-known fact that bicycles provide a common means of transport in university cities like Oxford and the rate of theft of them generally is high. It is also worth noting that adult victim surveys have shown car thefts to be the most readily reported offence: reporting to the police is essential for insurance purposes and victims also hope that the police may be able to recover their vehicle. It may well be that the same motives inspire children and their parents to report bicycle thefts, and that these are therefore proportionally overrepresented in official crime records. The reporting of bicycle thefts is likely to be highly motivated by financial considerations, as is borne out by the fact that most bicycles recorded as stolen were valued at between £50 and £200 and that very few were recorded as worth less than £50. By far the majority of bicycles were stolen from boys, presumably because offenders are themselves most likely to be boys of the same age with little use for girls' bicycles. If bicycle thefts are included, the proportion of victims who were boys was 70 per cent. When these offences are excluded the disparity between the victimization of boys

---

[40] The many hurdles relating to the reporting and recording of crime that child victims must overcome is discussed at length in Chs. 4 and 5.

TABLE 1. *Total number of direct child victims recorded by the police in Oxford, 1987, and in Bedfordshire, 1988*

Offence	Oxford	Bedfordshire	
		Luton	Leighton Buzzard and Biggleswade
Murder	—	1	
Grievous bodily harm	2	9	3
Actual bodily harm	37	85	29
Robbery	5	15	1
Attempted robbery	1	3	—
Kidnapping	1	4	
Blackmail	—	1	
Rape	1	5	—
Buggery	2	2	—
Indecent assault	44	24	16
Gross indecency	2	1	1
Unlawful sexual intercourse	2	3	6
Burglary	—	3	—
Theft	49	12	11
Cycle theft	210	52	32
Criminal damage	3	3	1
TOTAL (682)	359	223	100

and girls becomes much less marked. Similarly, the fact that 80 per cent of our sample of direct child victims were teenagers (aged 13–16) is in part accounted for by the high proportion of teenagers whose bicycles were stolen.

In Bedfordshire assaults occasioning actual bodily harm (ABH) made up the largest category of recorded crime. There were 114 cases representing over a third of all crimes recorded against children; of these 85 occurred in Luton. ABH made up a much smaller proportion of crimes against children in Oxford, only 23 per cent (37 cases). Whilst the majority of these offences had been committed against teenagers, it is worth noting that there were 11 infants under the age of 5 who were recorded as having been victims of physical assault. More serious assaults, for example grievous bodily harm, were extremely rare—only 12 cases were recorded in Bedfordshire and 2 in Oxford.

The injury caused by assault was nearly always recorded as being merely 'slight'. Only 12 cases in Bedfordshire and 7 in Oxford were described by the police as 'serious'. However, one problem with relying on the police estimation of levels of injury is that there is no indication of how this is assessed, nor can one be sure that the criteria used are consistent amongst different officers. Boys were much more likely to be recorded as victims of physical assault than were girls. Boys made up three-quarters of assault victims recorded in Bedfordshire but rather less—61 per cent—in Oxford. Interestingly, whilst boys were almost invariably attacked by male suspects, girls were assaulted almost equally by male and female offenders.

In both study areas, the next largest single category of offence recorded by the police, accounting for 12 per cent of the victims, was indecent assault: Oxford yielded 44 recorded cases and Bedfordshire 40. In both areas, some cases of indecent assault were relatively minor incidents involving touching, but the majority involved more serious, intimate abuse. Other forms of sexual assault (recorded as rape, buggery, unlawful sexual intercourse with a minor, gross indecency, etc.) together accounted for 18 cases in Bedfordshire and 7 in Oxford. In Bedfordshire over 80 per cent of recorded victims of all forms of sexual crime were girls. In Oxford the numbers were more or less evenly distributed between boys and girls but this may be explained by the large number of cases involving boys which came to light as a result of a single police operation. Victims of sexual crimes were spread evenly across the age range and it is again worth stressing that even very young children were not immune—6 infants under the age of 5 were recorded as being victimized in this way.

Thefts (other than of bicycles) accounted for just over 10 per cent of all recorded crime. These were committed against boys and girls in roughly similar proportions and were mainly of unattended possessions. In addition, in Oxford, a number of thefts from unlocked rooms, were recorded as 'walk-ins', reflecting the number of young people in the city who live or come to stay in boarding or summer schools.

Children were not very likely to be recorded as victims of robbery. In Bedfordshire there were 19 cases, of which 3 were attempts only, and in Oxford only 6 cases, of which 1 was attempted robbery. Other crimes, including criminal damage, burglary, deception, kidnapping, and abduction, were recorded in very few instances.

Having drawn a broad brushstroke picture of the range of recorded crimes against children, it is essential to examine where these crimes which are reported to the police occur. Of all crimes 92 per cent took place somewhere outside the child's own home. It is, of course, probable that a good deal of crime committed within the home, especially where the offender is a member of the household, never reaches a police crime report. Those relatively few cases which were recorded as occurring within the child's home (36 in Bedfordshire and 19 in Oxford) or in someone else's home (26 in Bedfordshire and 12 in Oxford) were, in the main, sexual offences: the girls were proportionally more likely to have been victimized within the home and boys more often victimized in a public place. Recorded physical assaults, robberies, and thefts had generally taken place in public.

In both areas, just over a third of all recorded offences had taken place 'in the street', particularly in shopping areas in the centre of towns where children tend to congregate after school and at weekends. Rather fewer recorded offences, 18 per cent overall, took place in or around schools. However, as noted earlier, this may reflect an under-reporting by schools not wishing to bring in the police in the case of minor offences occurring on their premises. The other main locations in which recorded crimes against children had occurred were in sports, recreational, and community facilities such as ice rinks, swimming pools, playgrounds, and youth clubs. All these figures suggest that very many of the offences against children which are brought to the notice of the police occurred outside the home.

Not surprisingly, in the majority of cases where the victim could identify a suspect they were sufficiently well known for them to be able to be named: in 77 per cent of cases in both areas. In the remainder of cases information about the suspects amounted to very limited descriptions of their sex, age, and appearance. In the case of both male and female victims 9 out of 10 suspects were boys. Most of the instances where females were suspected involved assaults arising from disputes between girls.

Indeed, especially in cases involving assault, a large proportion of suspects were young people, often (so far as the victims could ascertain) the same age or only a little older than themselves. It was notable, given the stereotypical image of the child victimized by an adult, that 47 per cent of known suspects in Oxford and 65 per cent in Bedfordshire were recorded as being under the age of 21. Where the relationship between the suspected offender and the victim was recorded, most known offenders (89 per cent in Oxford and 82 per cent in

Bedfordshire) appeared to be outside the child's household or imme-diate family circle. However, in 18 per cent of recorded cases in Bedfordshire and in 11 per cent in Oxford the suspect was a member of the household and in 13 per cent and 7 per cent respectively they were blood relatives, usually fathers. Neighbours or close family friends were the suspects named in 6 per cent of cases in Bedfordshire and 8 per cent in Oxford in which the relationship of suspect to victim was recorded.[41] It is perhaps not surprising that girls, who were more likely than boys to be victimized in the home, were also more often able to identify the suspected offender.

It is important to consider how crimes became public knowledge. Surveys have shown that the vast majority of crimes become known to the police as a result of reporting by the victim. *The 1988 British Crime Survey* found that 94 per cent of reported offences uncovered had been reported to the police either by victims or on their behalf by family or friends.[42] Establishing precisely who has reported a crime against a child is hampered by the fact that police crime reports tend not to differentiate between offences reported by the aggrieved themselves, or by his or her parent. Or, rather, it appears that offences are commonly recorded as having been reported by the aggrieved whether it was they or their parent who actually did so. In many cases where the aggrieved were patently far too young to have reported to the police in their own right, they were still recorded as having done so.

By far the majority of crimes were recorded as having been reported by the aggrieved or his or her parent (87 per cent in Bedfordshire and 83 per cent in Oxford). In some other cases the person reporting was either unknown or not recorded, and the rest were attributed variously to members of hospital, school, and Social Services staff. The small proportion of cases which had been reported by Social Services staff which reached an official crime report (12 of the 323 cases in Bedford-shire and 7 of the 359 in Oxford) tended to concern children who were already in care or who were known to be at risk and were therefore on the 'At Risk' Register. It may well be that a larger proportion of cases came to light as a result of such intervention but were, as a matter of routine, simply recorded as having been reported by the aggrieved. Only 2 per cent of cases were reported by schoolteachers, which seems somewhat surprising given that 18 per cent of offences against children

---

[41] There were a large number of cases where a suspect had been named but there was no clear indication in the record of the nature of the relationship.

[42] *The 1988 British Crime Survey*, 26.

were recorded as having occurred in or around school. The minor role that teachers seem to play in reporting crime to the police may, in part, be due to children preferring to tell their parents about offences rather than their teachers. It is also possible that teachers who are informed about offences are reluctant to report them to the police. Those whom we interviewed said that their schools tried to investigate and clear up minor offences themselves and to impose their own sanctions without having recourse to the police.

The police themselves seem not to have 'discovered' many crimes against children in the study areas. Those they came across appear to have arisen from admissions by persons against whom other allegations had been made. In Bedfordshire there were very few cases, all of them involving sexual offences against girls. There were a larger number (18) recorded as being the result of 'police enquiries' in Oxford. However, 11 of these came to light as a result of enquiries into a series of offences in a single school. In general, then, it seems that our research confirms the findings of other victim studies: that crimes only reach official records when the victims themselves or their relatives decide, for whatever reason, to report them.[43]

In addition to direct child victims, the researchers also sought to identify children who had not been directly offended against themselves but who were, none the less, potential 'indirect' victims of crimes committed against persons close to them or against the household in which they live. Whilst the police obviously acquire knowledge of only a proportion of direct child victims, those children who are potential 'indirect' victims proved to be even more elusive. The possibility that children may be indirect victims was scarcely recognized by the majority of agencies interviewed. Some voluntary agencies, for example Relate, recognized that children might be indirectly affected by crimes against members of their family. However, no agency could provide data on the number and types of child victim they had seen, nor had they kept any records of child victims who had come to their attention.

---

[43] Mawby and Gill, *Crime Victims*, 6. Our methodology did not allow for examination of the reasons why those who did not report crimes to the police chose not to do so. However, *The 1988 British Crime Survey* did ask victims who had not notified the police to give their reasons: just under half said that the incident was too trivial to report, a further fifth felt that the police would not have been able to do anything about the incident, a tenth said that the offence was not a matter for the police or they dealt with it themselves. Far fewer gave their reason as inconvenience of reporting (2%), dislike of police (1%), or fear of reprisals (1%). *The 1988 British Crime Survey*, 24.

Given this fact, it seemed futile to speculate about the total population of indirect child victims. It was better instead to attempt to identify those children who were known to the authorities. Police crime reports give very little indication of whether there are children in families where a crime has taken place since investigating officers do not as a matter of course record their presence. Children are alluded to only occasionally and without any great consistency, for example if they were in some way involved in the offence or suffered losses in their own right during a burglary. Even then one child might be mentioned but other siblings not. Police records were, therefore, a wholly inadequate means of furnishing a profile of children who may have been affected indirectly by crime.

An ideal method of establishing a profile of children who were potentially indirect victims would have been to conduct a general survey of all adults who were victims over a period of time to find out how many had children who might have been affected by the crime. Since this approach was beyond the resources of the project, the most readily available means of identifying children who were present in households that had suffered crime were the records kept by Victim Support Schemes in Oxford and Bedfordshire. In the field-work areas 141 such families were identified: 39 in 1987 in Oxford and 102 in 1988 in Bedfordshire. Between them, these families had at least 265 children who were potentially indirect victims of crime.

By far the largest category of offence was domestic burglary.[44] In the study areas, actual and attempted burglaries together made up 62 per cent of the cases coming to the attention of Victim Support involving children. One in six burglaries took place whilst children were actually asleep in the house and in a small number of cases it was the child who, waking up first or returning from school before the rest of the family, actually discovered that the offence had taken place. Hardly any children were recorded as being completely unaware of the offence and, of those who were not actually present when the burglary was discovered, most were afterwards informed by their parents of its occurrence and witnessed the damage to their home or loss caused.

In addition to burglary, a further 18 per cent of cases also took place within or immediately outside the family home itself. The remaining 20 per cent of the crimes coming to the attention of Victim Support

[44] For a detailed consideration of the plight of burglary victims generally see Maguire, *Burglary in a Dwelling*, 5.

involving children as indirect victims occurred in other people's homes or in public. Twenty-one per cent of the cases involved physical assault against a parent or sibling, 23 per cent of which were serious enough to be recorded as grievous bodily harm: about 5 per cent of all the offences. The majority of recorded assaults occurred outside the home but a third of them took place within the home, the most frightening of which involved attacks on the mother by her husband or a boyfriend. Significantly, in a fifth of the assault cases the child or children were actually present when the offence took place and were often highly disturbed both by what they saw and by their inability to prevent it.

A small number of the cases (4 per cent) visited by Victim Support involved sexual assaults (recorded as indecent assault, rape, or attempted rape) against sisters or mothers. Although the numbers of such victims were very small, the impact on their entire family was, in every case, extremely grave. In two particularly disturbing cases the children were actually present when the assault took place. And it is, of course, likely that these figures considerably underrepresent the number of families in which a sexual assault has taken place, not least because many victims do not report such crimes to the police, and even those who do report choose to seek help from specialist agencies or their GP rather than a Victim Support Scheme.[45]

Many of the remaining offences appeared to be less serious. However, the official description of an offence may not reveal its true severity. For example, amongst the comparatively 'minor' offences we came across, one case recorded simply as criminal damage was in fact only one incident in a long-running campaign of racial harassment of an Asian family, whose two children were too frightened to go out as a result. Such cases point to the danger of assuming that offences which may appear on record to be relatively trivial will have had no impact on the family concerned.

Thus, it may be concluded from studying a number of different sources of data—victimization surveys, literature on specific forms of child victimization, and records of the police and Victim Support Schemes—that children may be both direct and indirect victims of a very wide range of offences. Very little information is available, however, about the effects of crime on child victims, or about the agencies which are available to help them.

[45] See C. Corbett and K. Hobdell, 'Volunteer-Based Services to Rape Victims: Some Recent Developments', in Maguire and Pointing (eds.), *Victims of Crime*, 47–59.

Method of Inquiry

This study, therefore, aims to fill a vacuum. It sets out to present the experiences of a sample of children (up to age 17) and their families who were involved in cases which came to the attention of the police in Oxford in 1987 and in three towns in Bedfordshire (Luton, Leighton Buzzard, and Biggleswade) in 1988. It describes their experiences, from the commission of the offence and its impact, through their experiences of the criminal justice system, to their views of the response of the social and welfare agencies. It aims to set these experiences in a wider context by examining the policies and practices of agencies both inside and outside the criminal justice system in relation to child victims.

Five linked methods were employed. Broadly speaking they were as follows:

1. A survey of the records relating to 783 direct child victims (i.e. the 682 in Table 1, plus 101 cases of suspicious behaviour and indecent exposure) and 141 cases involving indirect child victims coming to the attention of the police and Victim Support Schemes in the two field-work areas of Oxford and Bedfordshire over the period of a year.

2. Lengthy interviews with 85 direct child victims and their families and with 40 families in which children were identified as indirect victims, and a further 87 replies to questionnaires were received. The sample of children and families contacted was taken from the 924 cases described in 1 above (for a breakdown, see pp. 46–7, fn. 18 below). This information enabled us to assess the impact of the crime, the support children received, the intervention of the criminal justice process, and their reactions to it.

3. Interviews with key personnel from all the agencies in the field-work areas—statutory, professional, and voluntary—who respond to child victims. The purpose of these interviews was to ascertain how many child victims were referred and by whom, what types of crime were involved, and how the various agencies responded to them. We also examined the interrelationship between agencies, in particular their knowledge and use made of Victim Support. Altogether we interviewed over 250 members of these various agencies.[46]

[46] We interviewed 55 employees at various levels of seniority and specialization in the local authority Social Services Departments; 62 police officers representing all

4. Interviews with key personnel and analysis of the records of the Victim Support Schemes in Oxford and Bedfordshire in order to examine their response to the child victims known to them and their relationship with the other agencies in their area. By way of comparison, we carried out similar interviews with Victim Support Scheme personnel in six other selected schemes across the country.

5. An analysis of all cases concerning children which came to the attention of Victim Support Schemes over a period of a month across the country.

This study is not a victim survey but rather it focuses on those children whose victimization came to the attention of the criminal justice system and examines their experiences of that system. The mass of crimes against children which never come to public attention may only be uncovered by the inclusion of questions specifically directed at children in future national and local crime surveys. For the present we must content ourselves with looking at those crimes which have already come to light. The very construction of the child's status as a victim is largely determined by the way in which the police, prosecutors, and the courts respond once an offence has been reported. It is with this official recognition and response that this book is primarily concerned.

ranks; 10 members of the Probation Services; 28 family doctors and health visitors; 50 staff in the education service—head teachers, teachers, school nurses, school counsellors, education welfare officers, and members of the child guidance service and educational psychological service; and 42 organizers and personnel from voluntary groups and helplines ranging through the NSPCC, Relate (formerly Marriage Guidance), Home Start, family centres, women's refuges, Parents Anonymous, the Asian Women's Help Group, Rape Crisis Centres, and a variety of helplines, both national and local, such as Child Line, Incest Crisis Line, and the Leeds Touchline; 9 senior officers in the branch offices of the Crown Prosecution Service serving the field-work areas; 5 barristers who regularly appeared as prosecuting counsel in cases involving children; and 11 court administrators responsible, at various levels, for bringing cases to court.

3

The Impact of Crime on Children

A good deal is now known about the effects of crime on adult victims. In 1984, the British Crime Survey included, for the first time, questions about the impact of crime on the general population.[1] As well as general studies of the effects of victimization,[2] studies of the impact of specific types of crime have also been carried out, for example concerning burglary victims,[3] and victims of violence.[4] These studies have shown the effects of crime on adult victims to be highly complex and variable, and largely unpredictable. None the less researchers have attempted to identify and categorize the main types of effect experienced. Shapland *et al.*, in a study of nearly 300 victims of assault, robbery, and rape, identified eight main groups of effects.[5] These were direct effects of physical injury and financial and property losses, and also effects on home and social life, on work, and on attitudes and feelings. Of these, the most frequently mentioned effects were those involving attitudes and feelings. Indeed most studies broadly agree that psychological distress is the central, dominant reaction of crime victims, though the degree of distress suffered varies greatly according to the severity of the crime and the personal characteristics of the victim. Whilst property offences might be thought less likely to have a profound psychological impact, Maguire found that many victims of burglary suffered considerable distress. The emotional impact of the burglary seemed to be more important to the victims in his sample than the financial loss incurred. Such findings underline the fact that the victims' reactions cannot be predicted by the type of crime alone. The nature and severity of the

[1] Hough and Mayhew, *Taking Account of Crime: Key Findings from the 1984 British Crime Survey.*
[2] Maguire and Corbett, *The Effects of Crime and the Work of Victims Support Schemes.*
[3] M. Maguire, 'The Impact of Burglary upon Victims', *British Journal of Criminology*, 20(3) (1980), 261–75; Maguire, *Burglary in a Dwelling.*
[4] Shapland *et al.*, *Victims in the Criminal Justice System.*
[5] Ibid., ch. 6, pp. 97–116.

offence, the personal characteristics of the victim, prior life stress, and a range of other factors such as family support and assistance from friends or work colleagues will also determine to what extent an individual is affected.

Research on victims has also drawn attention to the persistence of effects. For example, 75 per cent of victims in Shapland's study were still suffering some lingering effects when interviewed.[6] Of the burglary victims interviewed by Maguire, 65 per cent were still suffering some consequences on their lives four to ten weeks after the event: 'the most common persisting effects were a general feeling of unease or insecurity and a tendency to keep thinking about the burglary'.[7] Again, the severity of continuing effects and their tendency to persist has been shown to be broadly related to the seriousness and nature of the offence.

There is now a considerable body of information about the effects on children of crimes which take place within the home. Much attention has been paid to exploring the wide range of abuse to which children may be subjected within the family: physical injury, emotional deprivation, and sexual abuse.[8] Researchers have provided a wealth of data to show that all types of abuse are likely to have profound and enduring effects on children.[9] The child's developmental progress and well-being is liable to be permanently harmed.[10] The damage suffered may take a variety of forms but common indicators include an impaired capacity to enjoy life, low self-esteem, school learning problems, withdrawal, and regressive behaviour.[11] Children who have suffered physical or emotional abuse or neglect can usually be identified by observation of unexplained injuries or poor development. By contrast, the recognition of child sexual abuse usually depends upon the child telling someone. It is very rare that there are

---

[6] Shapland *et al.*, *Victims in the Criminal Justice System* ch. 6, p. 98.

[7] Maguire, *Burglary in a Dwelling*, 126–31.

[8] J. R. Conte, 'The Effects of Sexual Abuse on Children: A Critique and Suggestions for Future Research', *Victimology*, 10 (1985), 110–30; I. Kaufman, 'Child Abuse: Family Victimology', *Victimology*, 10 (1985), 62–71; Finkelhor (ed.), *A Sourcebook on Child Sexual Abuse*, esp. A. Browne and D. Finkelhor, 'Initial and Long-Term Effects: a Review of Research'; C. K. Dorne, *Crimes against Children* (New York, 1989).

[9] Lee (ed.), *Child Abuse: A Reader and Sourcebook*; Parton, *The Politics of Child Abuse*; Violence Against Children Study Group, *Taking Child Abuse Seriously*; Jones *et al.*, *Understanding Child Abuse*; D. P. H. Jones and M. McQuiston, *Interviewing the Sexually Abused Child* (London, 1988).

[10] B. F. Steele, 'Notes on the Lasting Effects of Early Child Abuse throughout the Life Cycle', *Child Abuse and Neglect*, 10 (1986), 283–91.

[11] Finkelhor, *A Sourcebook on Child Sexual Abuse*, 152–63; Caiam and Franchi, *Child Abuse and its Consequences*.

any external physical signs. Children may disclose that they have been sexually abused at many different points in their life and it is probable that many do not tell anyone about their experiences. As a result it is almost impossible to make any certain judgement about the common experience of the sexually abused child.[12]

The label 'sexual abuse' has been used somewhat indiscriminately as an umbrella term which in fact covers a wide range of offences. It is used to describe children who have been victims of incest for many years and also children who have been assaulted by someone outside the family on a single occasion. Yet significant differences have been observed in the effects on children who have been victims of incest and those who have been sexually assaulted. As Jones and McQuiston point out, 'The psychological after-effects of the assault itself are usually only seen in those children who are the victims of a single assault by a stranger.'[13] Here the child shows symptoms of acute anxiety and agitation, and guilt feelings are common. By contrast,

The effects seen during the time that abuse is repeatedly occurring are variable . . . the most-common reactions are non-specific, neurotic disorders or a deterioration of the child's conduct. Thus, children may become more anxious and fearful, be unable to concentrate and attend to their school work as well as they had, and show evidence of sleep and appetite disturbance.[14]

Research has also drawn attention to the impact that continuing abuse may have on later development during adolescence and on future personal and sexual relationships. American research on a sample of adolescent survivors of incest found that they indulged in self-destructive behaviour, such as drug abuse or suicide attempts, in trying to alleviate stress or assert some control over the profound sense of helplessness created by the abuse.[15] Empirical studies on adult women victimized as children show that they are more likely to manifest depression, self-destructive behaviour, anxiety, feelings of isolation and stigma, poor self-esteem, and a tendency towards revictimization. In addition they may experience difficulty in trusting others, sexual maladjustment, and avoidance of, or abstention from, sexual activity.[16]

---

[12] Jones and McQuiston, *Interviewing the Sexually Abused Child*, 3.
[13] Ibid. 5.   [14] Ibid.
[15] F. H. Lindberg and L. J. Distad, 'Survival Responses to Incest: Adolescents in Crisis', *Child Abuse and Neglect*, 9 (1985), 521–6.
[16] A. W. Burgess and L. L. Holstrom, *The Victims of Rape: Institutional Reactions* (Boston, 1978); L. Kelly, 'What's in a Name? Defining Child Sexual Abuse', *Feminist*

Although sexual abuse is the most widely publicized form of child victimization, as shown in Ch. 2 above there is an emerging literature on the effects on a child of being a 'bystander' or witness to a crime within the home. Work carried out in the United States and Britain demonstrates that children who observe serious sexual or violent offences can be as badly affected as those children who are the direct victims of such offences. Bystander victims may both experience acute immediate stress and suffer long-term adverse effects of their experiences. The incidence of post-traumatic stress disorder in children who observe serious crime is well documented.[17]

The Present Study

In order to examine the impact of crime on children we contacted 212 families in Oxford and Bedfordshire in which children had been direct or indirect victims of a wide range of crimes.[18] Of the direct victims, 54 were cases of physical assault involving 12 girls and 42 boys. All had been attacked outside the home, most often in the street, but, in a few cases, in or around school. Most were attacked by other youths either the same age or somewhat younger than themselves. Assaults ranged from unprovoked and apparently motiveless attacks, through street robberies or mugging, to long-running vendettas in cases which were racially motivated; 19 children had been victims of sexual abuse

---

Review, 28 (Spring 1988), 65–73; L. Kelly, *Surviving Sexual Violence* (Oxford, 1988), 188.

[17] Black and Kaplan, 'Father Kills Mother: Issues and Problems Encountered by a Child Psychiatric Team'; Davis and Carlson, 'Observations of Spouse Abuse: What Happens to the Children?'; Pynoos and Eth, 'The Child Witness to Homicide'; Pynoos and Eth, 'Witness to Violence: The Child Interview'; Pynoos and Nader, 'Children who Witness the Sexual Assaults of their Mothers'.

[18] We wrote to the parents of nearly all those children identified by the police or Victim Support Scheme records but received replies from only 42% of cases. We were able to interview only 27% of those to whom we wrote. A number of children, especially in Oxford, were foreign visitors who had subsequently returned home and these we did not attempt to contact. In those cases where a child had been victimized by a member of the family, we did not feel it appropriate to write, given that the offender might well have been the recipient of our letter. The four cases of child abuse included in the interview sample were cases in which the offender was no longer present in the home. In view of the amount of time available, the method adopted for collecting information about children's experiences of cycle theft or of witnessing indecent exposure or suspicious behaviour was by sending a postal questionnaire to the parents asking them or their child to complete it. Over 80 replies were received.

or assault; all 4 cases of sexual abuse involved girls under the age of 12 who had been abused by their fathers, or in one case, stepfather, in the home. The sexual assaults ranged from the relatively minor offence of 'incitement to gross indecency', or in the words of the boys concerned 'a man being rude in the park', to sexual abuse and assaults occurring over several months or even years. With one exception, assaults against younger girls (below 12) all occurred within the home; teenage girls were more likely to have been sexually assaulted outside the home by a stranger. Nineteen children had witnessed an incident of suspicious behaviour and 14 had witnessed indecent exposure or 'flashing'; 66 children were victims of theft, the vast majority having had their cycles stolen.

Of the 40 households in which indirect victims were identified, the majority (27) had been burgled. In 4 cases, the children's mother had been raped: all the offences occurred within the home and in 2 the children were actually present during the assault (both by strangers) and were very badly affected. In 8 cases, a parent had been physically assaulted: the offences ranged from relatively minor scuffles to serious fights and one particularly unpleasant stabbing. Finally, in one case mentioned earlier, which was recorded as criminal damage, an Asian family were the victims of long-running racial harassment.

Assessing the Immediate Impact of the Crime

How best to establish the immediate impact of crime on children is obviously problematic. Whilst a psychologist may be best placed to assess scientifically measurable effects of crime, children and their families are arguably in a better position to talk of their experiences of crime.[19] Subjecting children to long, structured interviews would have produced neat, comparable data. However, in pilot studies it was found that weighty interview schedules tended to intimidate children into silence; younger children became tired or lost interest long before the end; whilst multiple-response questions proved to be too suggestive—clearly putting words into children's mouths. Highly structured schedules were all but impossible to impose as children quickly strayed from the order of questioning laid down. Allowing

[19] In view of the obvious difficulties, both practical and ethical, of interviewing children and their parents about events which may have been deeply disturbing, we took advice from a number of specialists in child development and psychiatry. They gave us much valuable advice about how to go about the task.

children and their parents to talk at random about their experience would have yielded rich but necessarily highly variable and subjective results. By way of compromise a semi-structured interview schedule was drawn up to maximize the collection of consistent data but, within the constraints that objective imposed, to allow children to tell their own story.

Assessing the immediate impact of crime is most easily and accurately done as soon as possible after the incident itself. In practice, acquiring information about the very existence of child victims is largely dependent on crimes against them being reported to and recorded by the police. Gaining access to children is itself mediated by parents, who, even where they agree for their child to be interviewed, may for practical or emotional reasons find difficulty in keeping appointments. Since many parents were naturally apprehensive about the danger of reviving unpleasant or even traumatic memories, interviews were held at their behest at varying times after the crime. Given these unavoidable delays there is obviously a problem of recall. A victim's assessment of his or her initial reaction to the crime is likely to be col-oured by subsequent events which may mitigate or, indeed, aggravate their perception of their original experience.

A further problem, rarely addressed by those writing on the experiences of victims, is just how representative those who agree to be interviewed are of victims in general. Are they likely to constitute a cross-section of all victims, or are they liable to be more or, indeed, less affected than the norm? Those who are most severely traumatized may feel unable to talk about their experiences to outsiders. In the case of younger children in particular, parents may refuse on their behalf on the basis of their own perceptions of the child's emotional state. Of course parental perceptions may well be very different from the child's own feelings. Of those who replied to the request for an interview, one-third declined to participate outright, although there is no way of knowing whether it was the child or parent who made this decision.

Of those who agreed to be interviewed, just under a third of parents stipulated that the interview take place when the children were not present, again presumably because they feared resurrecting unhappy memories or exacerbating a continuing trauma. In the case of children who had been sexually assaulted for example, parents of younger girls were especially anxious not to reawaken memories of the offence and so parents were generally interviewed without the child being present. However, in all the cases involving older girls and boys who had been sexually assaulted it was possible to talk to parents and children together.[20] In 13 of the cases where children had been physically assaulted the parents were interviewed alone but in 30 families parents and children were seen together and in the remaining 11 it was possible to talk to the child alone.

Assessing the Longer-Term Impact of the Crime

The best method of assessing the longer-term impact of crime on children would have been to follow up the initial visit with subsequent interviews, in every case, at uniform, regular intervals (for example, 2, 6, and 12 months after the crime). However, the desirability of doing this was outweighed by two considerations—one practical and the other ethical. Firstly, given the delays experienced in getting to know of the existence of the child victim (outlined in the previous chapter), it was often more than six months before the first interview was carried out. Even then it was not possible to specify the exact time for an interview. Gaining access was entirely reliant on parental co-operation and so interviews had to be arranged at their convenience. As a result, it was not possible to interview all children at the same interval after the crime. Secondly, and more important, interviewing children repeatedly over time raised worries about the further harm that this might inflict. Whilst concerns about carrying out even a single interview were largely allayed by advice taken from medical and psychiatric experts, these same experts warned that repeated interviews might have a serious negative impact on the child victims.

It should also be noted that at the time of this research grave concern was being expressed about the deleterious effects on children of being repeatedly reinterviewed by the police and social workers.[21] Since professionals were being urged to cut down on the number of interviews they carried out, it would have seemed somewhat anomalous to have undermined their efforts in the interests of research.

Thus, in reading what follows it is important to bear in mind that children's and their parents' definition of 'longer-term' depended entirely on when the interview was carried out. In some cases this was just a few months after the incident and in others it was 12 months or

---

[20] The parents of one 14-year-old girl agreed to let her talk to us alone.
[21] DHSS and Welsh Office, *Working Together: A Guide to Arrangements for Inter-agency Co-operation for the Protection of Children from Abuse* (London, 1988).

more. However, in just over three-quarters of cases the interview took place between 3 and 12 months after the crime.

The readiness with which parents allowed us to talk to their children, often about painful or embarrassing issues, and the fact that the children themselves were prepared to go over their feelings about the crime in some detail, was vital in obtaining a clear picture of their experiences. Far from being damaging, many of our interviews with children seemed to have a quasi-therapeutic effect. Many youngsters appeared glad to be the subject of the researchers' attention and may even have enjoyed increased self-esteem as a result of being 'given a voice' in this way.

It is obviously difficult to assess to what degree the effects of victimization which were reported could be attributed to the impact of the crime and to what degree they were the result of other factors, such as a long-standing emotional disturbance which the crime merely exacerbated. The impact of the crime may have been compounded by the effects of other major traumas, such as serious illness, the death of a relative, or other family crisis. In attempting to assess the impact of crime it is not possible, therefore, to be certain that any apparent change reported in the child's behaviour was really 'caused' by the crime itself. What follows is what children or their parents *said* they experienced as a result of the crime.

This chapter will being by looking at the most tangible effects— those caused by physical injury—before going on to examine the emotional impact of crime on children in its immediate aftermath and then to describe the lasting effects. An extraordinary range of experiences and feelings came to light. What emerges is a disturbing picture of emotional distress suffered by nearly all the children in the study in the immediate aftermath of the crime. In all only 8 per cent were not upset in any way at all by what had happened to them. Nearly two-thirds were 'upset' or 'very upset' and well over half spoke of more specific reactions such as shock, fear, and anger. Two-thirds of the children experienced lingering and lasting effects.

Children's Experiences of the Immediate Aftermath of the Crime

In many cases identifying the immediate impact is complicated by the fact that the crime itself consists not of one single event but of a series of occurrences over weeks, months, or even years. In the case of sexual abuse taking place over a long period of time, for example, one cannot readily distinguish between immediate and longer-term effects. This is most problematic in the case of young girls who do not disclose that they have been sexually abused until months or even years later. Where a crime had been going on for several years parental accounts of 'immediate impact' may refer only to those characteristics identified on discovery or disclosure of the crime. The child's feelings on the first occurrence of the abuse may be buried irretrievably or only recalled in the light of subsequent events. For the mass of other crimes which are more discretely located in time, however, such problems do not arise.

The Physical Impact

The most evident effect of crime is obviously that of physical injury. Assessing the extent of injuries, the pain suffered, and the degree of disruption to normal life are important prerequisites to understanding the emotional impact of crimes involving physical violence. Physical assaults by other children are all too readily dismissed as part of the rough and tumble of childhood, so that only the most serious assaults by other youngsters are conceptualized as crimes. Vulnerable children may be subjected to violence in the form of bullying, yet never attain the official status of victim. Children may fear reporting assaults lest there be further reprisals by the offender or his friends, whilst adults may overlook attacks or simply fail to differentiate between rough play and criminal assault. Only when assaults result in quite serious injury or are carried out by an offender much older than the child are they likely to be responded to as criminal. In a different vein older boys, even when seriously injured, often seem reluctant to admit that they are victims or are unwilling to be seen to 'tell' on their assailants for fear of losing status amongst their peers.

Given these obstacles to reporting all but the most serious of physical assaults as crimes, it is perhaps not surprising that a third of children who had been physically assaulted said that the worst thing about the offence was the pain of the assault itself or its subsequent physical effects. A number of those interviewed had received extremely serious injuries: one 16-year-old girl badly beaten up in an alley by a boy she vaguely knew was, according to her mother,

very shocked and had a headache for days. She had an eye infection for 2 weeks afterwards. Her face was swollen and bruised and she had finger-marks round her neck. She went to the doctor for a couple of weeks about the eye infection and her periods stopped.

The temporary loss of menstruation in this case clearly indicates the seriousness of the bodily trauma suffered. Some assaults were so serious as to require hospital treatment, as in the case of this girl who

had bruising to her head and neck, strained neck muscles, and grazes on her lower back. She ran home and collapsed on the doorstep in tears, where her mother found her. Her vision was blurry so Ms B took her to casualty immediately. When she got there she was sick, so she was kept in overnight for observation in case of head injury . . . She was off school and wore a neck brace for a week, and had headaches for longer.

Probably the most serious injuries had been inflicted on teenage boys, often as result of fights or assaults induced by alcohol. One of the boys interviewed had suffered an extremely violent attack at a party, where 'a glass was thrust into the side of my head requiring twelve stitches, I was knocked to the ground and kicked in the head and ribs and taken to the hospital unconscious'; another was 'knocked out for at least two hours after it happened'; and another 'had to have five stitches and they thought his nose was broken because the swelling was so bad. He had footmarks on his stomach.' Clearly these more serious injuries not only had a major immediate impact on the child's life but often caused continuing problems in the longer term.

However, the severity of physical injury was not the sole determinant of the child's reaction. Many boys tended to be more reticent in admitting that their physical injuries had in anyway upset them. Some who had been quite badly injured even insisted that 'it didn't affect me really' or that 'I was glad I wasn't worse hurt.' Such reactions may be partly explained as a determined attempt to preserve their sense of 'macho' pride. Indeed, a few youths interviewed claimed that they were so used to fighting that they were scarcely surprised to have been hit themselves. One 16-year-old boy who was badly cut insisted that he was 'a bit shook up but I could live through it when I got to hospital and they stitched me up [his face was badly scarred]. I didn't feel particularly brilliant after it happened . . . It could have been worse.' Another boy, similarly badly hurt, was unconscious for several hours. The next day his face was extremely swollen. Despite being in pain his main impulse was to go and find the offender and, in his own words, 'pull his head off'. Rather than fear for his own physical safety, he was clearly more concerned that his reputation would be damaged by his failure to look after himself. Another boy, when asked what he felt about his attacker, admitted 'I felt like I could 'it 'im'. For children used to fighting, the loss of peer group esteem, or simply the loss of self-esteem, could be at least as great a burden as any physical injuries caused. One girl regretted involving the police because she felt that she should have stood up for herself and because she feared that 'people think I'm a grasser'. In the same vein, one teenage boy who had been badly beaten up said the worst thing was 'that the bloke who had done it was the same size as me and that I had been too drunk to fight back—I was worried what people would think'.

In general, girls tended to be more willing to express their feelings about their physical injuries. One admitted that she had 'sat for hours with my mother just talking about the offence and trying to work out why it happened to me'. Another girl who had been punched repeatedly in the face on the way home from a disco admitted that she felt very distressed at first. As she was starting college the following Monday, this was a time when her appearance seemed particularly important. She was extremely distressed, therefore, to discover that her face would be permanently scarred. She felt that the worst thing about the assault was that 'she has marked me for life and got away with it'. For girls in particular the costs of physical injury are often exacerbated by the growing sense of physical self which accompanies the onset of teenage. Bruising or scarring, even if only temporary, seemed to be particularly damaging to the fragile self-image of the adolescent girl.

The variety of reactions in the cases described above highlight the danger of assuming that the physical severity of an assault is the main or only factor in determining its impact. Rather, the seriousness of the injury is liable to be mediated by a variety of factors relating to the circumstances of the offence, the character and experiences of the child concerned, and, indeed, their age and sex.

The Psychological Impact

Psychological distress is clearly the predominant reaction of all victims to crime. In children this sense of distress can be intensified by lack of understanding about the nature and meaning of the offence. They may be confused about what actually occurred, why it happened, and even, as in the case of indecent exposure, what it meant. For younger children especially this may be the first occasion on which they have encountered a particular form of behaviour or actions which may, as a consequence, appear deeply shocking to them.

The importance of factors such as the anticipation and comprehension of crime in determining its emotional impact was borne out in the case of physical assaults on younger children. Many children who had experienced less serious injuries suffered shock apparently 'out of proportion' to the gravity of the assault. One was 'sick with the shock', another 'howling his head off and quite hysterical', and many reported being 'trembly', 'shaken up', unable to sleep, or otherwise in shock. The levels of shock suffered appear to be related as much to the child's prior life experience as to the injury itself—quite simply those unused to physical violence were more likely to react badly than those for whom fighting or assaults were more or less a common experience. Other incidents which may seem less serious to adults such as petty property offences could also cause profound shock. Children who experienced theft of a cycle, for example, were often very distressed by the loss.

Shock may also be generated by the very nature of the circumstances in which the offence occurred. One boy who was mugged when walking along during the day reported that although he was not actually hurt 'I felt quite shocked as it had happened in broad daylight and there had been a lot of people around and no one had helped me . . . after the offence I started to sleep-walk at night. My mum got no sleep at all as I was also having very bad nightmares and shouting in my sleep.' Here the child's sense of shock arose primarily from the fact that the assault took place in an environment which he perceived to be safe and was greatly exacerbated by the failure of passers-by to protect or help him. Children necessarily depend heavily on adults for their well-being; where the very presence of adults fails to prevent a crime or adults around fail to respond to stop a crime as it occurs, children are likely to be deeply shaken.

Indirect child victims were by no means immune from shock, especially if they were unfortunate enough to be present during, or at the discovery of, a crime. For example, in the case of burglary, children were often deeply upset to walk in on the disruption and chaos that was once their home. The 5-year-old who had been immediately behind his father when he had walked into the house initially was very upset about what had happened. He was obsessed with the 'nasty man who took the video' for weeks. His father said:

When we discovered the burglary we had all come into the house together. The children saw one of the bread knives in the middle of the floor. R, the eldest, was very upset. He overheard the police saying that the burglar could have used it on us if we were in when he came.

One teenage girl returned home one day whilst her parents were on holiday to discover their home had been burgled. She recalled that 'when I first found out I was all hysterical and crying—in a state I could hardly tell the policemen on the phone what had happened.' Perhaps the most poignant description of the overwhelming sense of shock suffered by children whose homes had been burgled was given by a little girl who recalled 'I sat on the stairs and cried and cried. The burglars had completely taken my room apart.'

For children who witnessed crimes being committed against their parents or siblings at first hand the impact was almost invariably traumatic. Children who were onlookers to sexual or physical assaults on members of their family were particularly badly affected. Although we were only able to interview four families in which the children's mother had been sexually assaulted or raped, the effects were so disturbing in every case as to justify describing them in some detail. In three of these cases the mother had been raped and in the other she was the victim of an attempted rape.[22] All the offences took place within the home and in two the children were actually present during the assault (both by strangers) and were very badly shocked. In one of these cases the assailant had abandoned his attempted rape after hearing the victim's baby cry upstairs. Her 7-year-old son witnessed the assault when he awoke in the middle of it. But he was too terrified to move as the man pointed at him and threatened his mother 'one word out of you and I'll kill him'. In cases such as this, the shock of seeing or finding the parent badly hurt seems to have been compounded by the child's basic lack of understanding of the sexual nature of the assault. In cases of physical assault against parents or siblings, the meaning of the event may not be so obscure to the child but the visible impact of the injuries sustained is no less severe. The man returned a few weeks later and attacked her again with a knife. The 7-year-old boy

came down and found me covered in blood—I had fainted and was on the floor. He set off a police alarm linked to the station which I had been given

---

[22] Although the children were present during two of our interviews, in all four cases it was the mother who did the talking.

after the first attack, and he let the police in as I was still unconscious. He was screaming his head off when the police came . . . Finding me bleeding was the worst thing for him . . .

Interviews were held with eight other families in which a physical assault had been carried out against a parent. Half had occurred inside and half outside the home. They ranged from relatively minor scuffles to serious fights and one particularly nasty stabbing. The sight of parents bruised or bleeding clearly had a powerful visual impact. For young children, especially, the shock of seeing parents badly hurt seems to have been exacerbated by the fact that the assault rudely shattered a belief that their parents were in some sense invulnerable. Largely reliant on parents for their own physical safety, children are shocked to find that their parents are apparently unable even to protect themselves. One father who was punched in the face after a minor car accident recalled that 'my daughter [4 years old] was really upset and in shock for some three weeks afterwards. She saw me covered in blood and was very afraid of the stitch marks on my nose . . . She now says don't come back covered in blood every time I go out.'

Where children were physically present at, or immediately after, an assault on their parent the sense of shock was even more profound. In one case, in which a woman's ex-husband returned to stab her present partner, her two young daughters who were upstairs in bed at the time came rushing down. Their mother said: 'they were half awake and heard me screaming—B [aged 7] thought her mum was being murdered. This was exacerbated by the fact that they saw that I'd been cut and was bleeding.' In cases like this, children may not have the knowledge or ability to assess the severity of an injury and tend to assume the worst. Given that assaulted parents are likely to be in shock themselves, they may not be able to reassure their children that they are not in fact bleeding to death. Even relatively minor assaults on parents tended to leave child onlookers severely traumatized. Several parents commented that their children had been concerned primarily because they were themselves visibly distressed. Where the parents were not themselves badly affected, or where they managed to conceal their reaction, the impact on children tended to be lessened.

After the initial shock of impact, the most common feeling expressed by victims was a general sense of psychological distress ranging in its seriousness from mild upset to severe trauma. Clearly a major problem in deciding what a child means when they speak of being 'upset' or 'very upset' lies in deciphering what these terms mean in each instance. A child who is 'very upset' about the loss of a fishing rod is unlikely to be talking of the same order of psychological distress as the child who has been raped. This said, as we have seen in relation to physical injury, one should be wary of making any too ready assumptions about the degree to which a child will be traumatized by a given type of crime. Moreover, children's perceptions of the relative seriousness of offences may well not tally with adult notions of the scale of criminal acts.

Sexual offences, whether single assaults by strangers or continuing abuse by a member of the child's family, probably provoked the worst traumas: the emotional response of 26 per cent indicated that they had been severely disturbed. For example, one 14-year-old who was sexually assaulted by a neighbour whilst baby-sitting said: 'I felt very low and cried a lot . . . I still feel awful but I'm trying to forget it. I still have trouble sleeping—nightmares.' Yet even apparently less serious occurrences such as incidents of 'suspicious behaviour' could also provoke quite serious trauma. The following quotes give some flavour of the range of reactions: 'I was very shaky and upset and I kept on hearing his voice. I was crying because I was very upset'; and 'very upset'; 'a bit bothered'; 'very tearful'; 'fear and slight panic'. Similarly, all but three of the children who witnessed indecent exposures, were to some degree upset by their experience. Their reactions ranged from 'very distressed', through 'shocked'; 'very panicky'; 'weepy'; to 'a bit shaky' and 'embarrassed'. Although many children who witnessed indecent exposures quickly got over the incident, a few were more seriously disturbed: one girl was, according to her parents, 'very distressed indeed—she kept thinking he was in her bedroom at night and kept telling him to get out'.

Indirect child victims were also prone to emotional distress, for example nearly three-quarters of children in houses which had been burgled were said to have been 'upset' or 'very upset'. In only four cases (18 per cent) were the children said to have suffered no after-effects at all. The other two were described as having been merely 'curious' or 'excited' by the event. In several of these families, children were said to be concerned only about the material loss, particularly of the family television or video. In these cases parents maintained that the replacement of the lost items quickly allowed children to forget all about the crime.

In general, younger children were less able to verbalize their feelings and inevitably tended to 'act out' what older children were better able to put into words. Responding to younger children often relies therefore on parents being able to decipher the meaning of their behaviour. In a number of cases of sexual assault or abuse, parents had only discovered the crime as a result of observing changes in the child's personality or behaviour. For example, one mother of a young girl who had been assaulted by her father only discovered the abuse after seeking help for her daughter's highly disturbed behaviour: 'To start with she was aggressive towards me and really naughty. She wouldn't sit on the toilet or pull her knickers down. She still doesn't take her knickers off now at night. She bit, scratched and kicked me and scratched the baby. She wouldn't even go to the toilet without screaming.' Other behavioural changes which seemed to be related to the psychological trauma of victimization included continual lapses into silence, becoming withdrawn, crying, panic attacks, clinging to their mother, and even violence towards others. It is, of course, likely that less overt signs of disturbance are often overlooked or misinterpreted by parents with the result that the crime that causes them never comes to light.

Younger indirect child victims, like direct victims, were often unable to express their feelings coherently and exhibited varying degrees of disturbed behaviour. Very young children were often unable to grasp quite what had happened, yet were affected by the disruption caused, for example by the coming and going of police. One mother whose home had been burgled commented that her '5-year-old boy was very excited about the police car and the fingerprint men. It took a while for him to realize that what it meant was that someone had been in our house when he was asleep. When he realized this he started to sleep badly and come into my room at night and want to get into bed.' Where parents had been physically or sexually assaulted, young children were liable to become very 'clingy'. The impact (whether the shock of seeing a parent assaulted or resulting anxieties about both their parent's and their own safety) often revealed itself as highly disturbed behaviour. For example, in the case described above where the father returned home to stab the mother's present boyfriend and also to wound her, the two daughters were profoundly disturbed: 'A had nightmares in which I was being murdered; also started sleep-walking. B became extremely naughty.' It was interviews such as this that underlined how seriously violence within the home can affect children. To explore this further, mothers and their children in women's refuges in Oxford and Bedfordshire were interviewed about the effect violence had had upon their lives. Many of the women said that their primary reason for deciding to leave home was the effect domestic violence was having on their children. In several cases women had lived with such violence for years and only decided to leave home when their children began to show signs of disturbance or their partner turned violent towards the children. As one woman put it 'every woman who comes into a refuge is doing it for the children's sake and not her own'.

The disruption caused by leaving home, generally in haste, and, for the children, amid some confusion, generated feelings of anxiety and insecurity which they often directed against their mothers—'If you can leave their dad, you can leave them.' Children arriving at refuges with their mothers, often in the middle of the night with few or no possessions, were commonly very distressed. They suffered from nightmares, bed-wetting, and a sense of being quite literally 'dispossessed' of all that was familiar to them. There were a considerable number of cases where the children had to take on adult responsibilities. They might become embroiled in seeking to avert or to stop violence. Where their mother was badly hurt they often had to tend to injuries, call out a doctor, or even, in extreme cases, an ambulance. Older children found themselves acting *in loco parentis* for younger brothers and sisters. One teenager looking back on her experiences remembered that 'when I was at home I was often too frightened to go to school as I wanted to stay at home to make sure that my mother was OK'. A mother recalled that 'my children used to try to stop their father attacking me. One time my younger child [a girl then aged 6] phoned the police, who said they couldn't do anything about it anyway.'

Children saw the break-up of the home as the major cost of domestic violence. Some said that they chose not to intervene because they felt loyalties to both parents which they were not prepared to betray. Their father may have been assaulting their mother, but he was still their father and they feared the consequences for him if they sought outside help. One girl said: 'I am old enough to call the police but it would be calling the police on my own dad—you are piggy in the middle. You have loyalty to both.' Where the father had subsequently gone to prison, the children lamented the loss of someone they still loved. One mother commented that she had received 'a lot of stick from my eldest child, who blames me for the break-up of the marriage. All my children have very strong loyalties to their father.' Over and above the traumas inflicted by other types of crime, domestic violence involved children in recurrent dilemmas about how they should react and imposed responsibilities way beyond their years.

In addition to the broad sense of distress or emotional disturbance spoken of or exhibited by many children, a number mentioned more specific feelings. Fear was an important response mentioned by a third of those interviewed. It was a particularly important factor for children who had been physically assaulted, many of whom were often more affected by fear of the offender than by the injury itself. Thirty-seven per cent of physical assault victims said they felt fearful in the first few days after the attack. The most common reason was the fear of recurrence or of retribution for involving the police.[23] One boy said: 'I was very worried that if he found out I'd said anything he'd come and get me.' Fear of this sort could have horrifying consequences as in the case of one boy whose mother related that he

was cycling along one night in the dark through the village when he was set upon by three boys he knew. One held his arms behind his back and pinned him on the fence while the others daubed his face with paint in the form of National Front slogans. One boy had a knife, which he threatened him with. They said that if he told his father they would put him in intensive care. He returned home and tried to remove the paint himself, he used petrol and burnt his face quite badly . . . he is a very nervous boy but was hysterical when this attack happened to him.

Terrified of the repercussions of disclosure this young boy brought terrible injury on himself in his panic-stricken attempt to obliterate the evidence of the assault.

Fear was by no means confined to young or nervous children. One 16-year-old boy was badly assaulted by two adults known to be part of the 'local mafia'. Normally confident and outgoing, this teenager was terrified both because of the reputation of his attackers and by the fact that his father, with whom he lived alone, was on holiday in America, leaving him by himself in the house. He was by his own admission 'very frightened about what would happen next because I found out that the two men were involved with a family known locally to be

[23] During the course of our interviews we were told of one serious incident of mugging and of a number of lesser assaults which the victims had not reported to the police 'for fear of repercussions'.

dangerous. I didn't go out for weeks. I had no one to "back me up" because my friends were too frightened to be involved. I was worried to death.' These were undoubtedly extreme cases in which children were literally terrified for their safety, but other children also admitted feeling reluctant to go outside, to return to school, to go into town, or to be left alone for fear of being confronted by the offender. To give just a few examples, children said that 'the worst thing about being assaulted was the prospect that it can happen again'; 'it made me feel very unsafe and vulnerable'; and 'my social life has really shut down and I've lost really good friends because they won't stick up for me'.

Feelings of fear were not confined to victims of physical assault but were also voiced by children who had suffered other crimes. Many children who had been sexually assaulted were nervous of a future encounter with their assailant. Some went to great lengths to avoid the offender's home or other location where he might be found. Many young girls in particular were extremely fearful of their attacker: one 'wanted to sleep with me [her mother] and was afraid that he would return to the house'; another 'was terrified that she'd be taken back to the offender's mum's house where the incident happened'. A teenager assaulted by a boy she knew was terrified when the day following the attack he took a gang of boys up to her school and 'caused a fracas by throwing a brick through the window and threatening to kill C'. In another case the children of a man accused of sexually assaulting a teenage girl knocked her off her cycle and kicked her teeth in. She was afraid to go to school for some considerable time. Amongst those who had witnessed incidents of indecent exposure or suspicious behaviour many commented that whilst they were not especially upset by the incident itself they were fearful of what it might have led to. As one mother put it, 'it only hit my daughter after this person had passed and he stopped his bike and waved his bottom at us. She got very panicky because she thought he was coming back. Her voice was a bit broken and she clung to me in fear, not for the exposure but that he was going to get her'.

The mother of another boy who witnessed an incident of suspicious behaviour commented that 'he was rather shaken up and was afraid to go out anywhere on his own'; whilst one girl was worried 'about going past the place where it happened'. Their very physical vulnerability and sense of powerlessness means that incidents which may seem relatively trivial to adults can appear profoundly threatening to children.

Half the indirect child victims also suffered feelings of fear or insecurity in the immediate aftermath of the offence. In most cases the child's fears for his or her own safety were compounded by anxieties about the safety of their parents. Often the two sets of fears were intricately linked, even indistinguishable from one another. Children of women who had been raped or sexually assaulted displayed clear signs of fear. One mother said of her son: 'he is OK during the day but is very insecure at bed time. He gets up a lot—four or five times—and comes into my bed.' This sense of insecurity was confirmed by another mother whose children witnessed her being raped at knife-point in their home: 'immediately afterwards they were quite agitated, very insecure, wanted to know where I was going if I went out, how long I would be . . . when I was coming back'. In both cases the children were really too young to understand what they had seen. However, they correctly perceived it as an extreme threat to their mother and reacted by becoming both more dependent on and more protective of her.

Physical assault against a parent also caused profound anxiety in many cases and most were fearful that the offence might happen again. For example, one boy whose father was a publican who had been assaulted whilst trying to break up a fight was 'concerned that there would be repercussions and that the men would come back'. For children who had been living in homes where violence was often a daily occurrence, such anxieties were liable to form the basis of the child's whole outlook on life. Women in the refuges visited were very aware of the impact on their children of living in a situation where violence was always possible. One said: 'one of my daughters won't talk about it. They are both very scared of going home and wary of all men. They don't like to see people drinking. They associate it with violence. Bruises heal but not the mental torture of never knowing who's coming through the door and in what state'. Continual fear and anticipation of the next onslaught was held by mothers and children to be the worst aspect of domestic violence. For many the profound anxiety and insecurity it caused became an overbearing burden.

Fear, then, is a common response to victimization in children. It can take a variety of forms ranging from nervousness about going to specific places to a more generalized, pervading, and often debilitating sense of terror.

Crime-Specific Reactions

Other aspects of the immediate impact of crime tend to be related specifically to certain types of crime. In the case of sexual assault or abuse, for example, even quite young children expressed feelings of violation. Older girls seemed better able to verbalize a sense of intrusion or contamination, whilst younger children spoke more vaguely of feeling 'dirty' or 'ashamed'. Perhaps contrary to expectation these children often displayed a strong sense of private space and recognized that the offender had invaded this. One 14-year-old girl reflected on the feelings of contamination and consequent isolation she had experienced: 'I felt scared. I wanted to tell somebody but I couldn't. I thought he might do it to someone else. I felt dirty. It had happened to me, not to my friends, and I felt everyone would know.' In fact, disclosure or discovery of the offence often allowed these children to express their feelings for the first time and was a great relief from the burden of secrecy. In a curious way public disclosure allowed the child to regain control and, by publicly shaming the offender, to offset to some degree their sense of violation.

By far the most common crime of which children are potentially indirect victims is household burglary.[24] Although their parents are formally recorded as the victims by the police, and recognized as such by support agencies, children are often just as much victims themselves. They may have suffered losses which, though quantitatively smaller, are of a similar relative value, and they almost always share in the loss of goods common to the family. They may also be party to the shock of discovery, to seeing their home disrupted or vandalized, to the feeling of invasion, to the loss of a sense of security, and to coping with the influx of police, fingerprint, insurance, and repair men who follow. Many children felt that their home was no longer a safe and inviolable place. When asked what was the worst thing about the burglary, this sense of invasion was by far the most common reaction, affecting boys just as much as girls. Many of the children became anxious and a few were badly affected. Some children became fearful of coming home alone, of being left in the house, or of sleeping by themselves. One pair of twins

---

[24] For the impact of burglary on adult victims see Maguire, *Burglary in a Dwelling*, 122–42.

would not come into the house on their own. They would not go upstairs on their own . . . They slept together in one room in a double bed for about a week after it happened.

Two small girls

wouldn't go upstairs unaccompanied . . . They were worried about going to bed and kept looking under their beds . . . the boys were more macho about it.

In another family

the children were very tearful, very upset . . . they were too frightened to sleep in their own bedrooms that night so slept with a parent each. E was very worried as it was her bedroom which had been got into and she was frightened they would come again the same way.

Many girls suffered an additional sense of violation that was not mentioned by boys. One girl said of 'her' burglars that she didn't like them taking the sheets off her bed as they might have 'had dirty hands and been unhygienic' and another 'also felt very "dirty" because they had been through all her belongings. She wouldn't sleep in her room until it had been completely spring-cleaned.' Although it was not explicitly stated, nor perhaps consciously felt, the fact that the burglars were assumed to be male may have added to the sense of invasion and contamination in these cases. Many of the immediate reactions of indirect child victims were, then, very much akin to those of children who are recognized as direct victims of crime. Indeed, in many cases, it is questionable whether children in households which are burgled should properly be called 'indirect' victims, but rather should not be recognized as victims in their own right.

The impact of other property offences on children also raised specific emotional responses peculiar to this type of crime. Children were, understandably, particularly dismayed if the loss was of an expensive item such as a bicycle. Those who had saved up to buy bicycles themselves were most distraught. One said that he 'felt really upset and disappointed as I'd been saving a long time for the bike—I felt I'd lost the one thing I've worked all my life for and I burst into tears'; another that he was 'bitter because some people can get things so easily and I had to save up such a long time to get it'; and a third noted that 'I had saved up £150 to buy it. I was very cross and annoyed at the theft.' Younger children tended to be less aware of the financial value of their loss than older ones but they were no less upset. One noted 'I was very unhappy', another that 'I was very angry I felt like beating the wall', and another that 'I cried because it was only a few months old. I had it for my birthday.'

Whilst adults often tend to dismiss bicycle theft as a relatively minor offence, for many children it represented the loss of probably their most valuable possession and, more importantly still, their major means of mobility. Consequently annoyance and anger were common sentiments, expressed by just over a third, ranging from feeling 'angry and let down', 'totally upset and annoyed', to one child who admitted 'this might sound silly but I felt like killing someone'. Only a few children were not the least bit perturbed by their loss, generally because the bike was in poor condition.

Many of those children who had reported the theft of cycles or other relatively expensive items were primarily concerned about parental reactions: 'R panicked when he discovered it had been stolen as it was a very expensive item. He was very worried about telling his father'; another said 'I felt really hurt, especially since my mum couldn't really afford to buy me it.' Many feared parental anger: 'I thought my dad would kill me.' In such cases the personal sense of loss was greatly exacerbated by the fear of having to admit the loss and trepidation of parental recriminations. Many older children, with a keener sense of the financial value of the lost item, also experienced feelings of guilt for their self-perceived carelessness in 'allowing' the theft to occur, even in cases where it was not clear that they were at fault.

Children Unaffected by the Crime

Obviously not all child victims suffer psychological distress. However, of the sample barely 8 per cent specifically said that they were not upset by the crime. The numbers of children who were left wholly unscathed by their experience of victimization would appear to be very small indeed. In only 4 cases of physical assault and 2 of sexual assault was it claimed that the child had not been upset at all by the assault. Significantly, some parents refused to allow their children to be interviewed on the grounds that they had not been at all upset and that to raise the subject of the crime would be to invest it with an importance it did not have in the child's mind. Where, as a result, children were not present and parents were interviewed alone, it was not possible to test this. It may well be that in many cases their perception was entirely accurate. However, in a number of cases of quite serious crime parents seemed intent on denying that their child suffered any distress.

It is notable that this tendency to play down the impact of the crime was most marked in those families where the son had been sexually assaulted. One mother of a boy who suffered the relatively minor trauma of being the victim of incitement to gross indecency felt certain that 'he was unaffected. He probably can't remember what happened . . . He would adjust to anything.' Less plausibly, parents of boys who suffered quite serious assaults, and in one case buggery, insisted: 'he took it in his stride, I don't think he realized what had happened to him.' Similarly, another mother of an indecent assault victim said that she didn't think her son was badly affected: 'he seems to want to forget all about it'. Whether boys are indeed likely to be less traumatized by sexual assaults or abuse than girls or whether their parents for some reason assume this to be the case remains unclear. Even where it was possible to interview the boys themselves, they were not very forthcoming about how they felt. Just how far they were disturbed by the crime became more readily apparent when we went on to investigate the effects in the longer term.

Thus, very few children or their families escaped the experience of victimization without being affected. The vast majority suffered some degree of immediate psychological impact. Recovery was undoubtedly most rapid in the case of property crimes against children where even the initial impact was often slight and easily forgotten. Where the goods stolen or damaged had been replaced, most children readily recovered. However, it would clearly be wrong to assume, as adults all too easily do, that all children are 'naturally resilient', or have short memories, or readily put unpleasant experiences behind them. It should be stressed that two-thirds of the children in the sample suffered some form of longer-term effect.

Longer-Term Experiences

Persisting Physical Effects

Where victims suffer serious injuries physical problems may continue for many months or even become a source of disability, recurrent illness, or permanent scarring. Where such problems persisted it was obviously far harder for the child to recover his or her psychological well-being. As Shapland *et al.* have pointed out, a significant factor in exacerbating the impact of physical injury over time is 'the unexpected persistence of physical effects after the injuries had healed'.[25] One 16-year-old boy who had actually been knocked unconscious by his assailant was suffering severe physical problems when he and his parents were interviewed a month later. His mother said 'S is not the same child—he gets terrible headaches and complains of vision problems. He was a lively child before but now he's always day-dreaming.' The mother of another teenage boy who had been badly beaten up at school spoke of physical effects three months later: 'he still has headaches and the side of his face sometimes aches. He has trouble sleeping when this happens. The scar where the stitches were is still visible and he has a large black circle under that eye.' Quite apart from the pain and discomfort caused by such long-term injuries, physical scars often caused considerable distress. In part they represented a continuing reminder of the suffering endured. As mentioned above, for girls particularly, facial scarring could have a dramatic effect on self-confidence.

Persisting Emotional Effects

Emotional upset was the most persistent effect for the majority of the children in the sample. For many, fear, most commonly of meeting the offender, continued to dog their lives in the longer term. Of the children who had been physically assaulted, 46 per cent remained fearful several months after the attack, either of meeting their attacker or of unknown potential assailants. A number of these children said that they were afraid to go out alone or that they avoided going to places they knew the offender to frequent: 'I try to keep out of the way of him.' For some, the fear was more generalized. One girl, nine months after she was attacked, said: 'I am a lot more wary of people now because you never know what they're going to do.' This feeling can result in marked changes to children's normal behaviour and severe restrictions to their social life. Note, for example, the following comments about children interviewed three or four months after having been assaulted: 'He does not go out in the evening any more . . . He still thinks about it a lot. He very rarely goes out on his own—just

---

[25] Shapland *et al.*, *Victims in the Criminal Justice System*, 101.

outside the house—or one of us [his parents] accompany him. He goes to school and returns in the company of friends so that he is not alone'; and one girl 'has lived in fear of someone waiting for her outside school'. Most, however, only avoided those places or times of day they deemed to be high-risk. For example, one teenage boy who had had a beer glass smashed in his face said, a month later: 'I'm a bit more cautious now . . . I don't go out on my own if I can help it. I don't walk the streets at night like I used to before.'

Fear of the offender was also a significant factor affecting the lives of children who had been sexually assaulted. The relationship of power over the child that allowed the abuser to act in the first place often continued to cause children anxiety for a long time afterwards. Such fear was particularly apparent where the abuser was a family member or neighbour who they might well continue to meet. Nearly two-thirds of the victims of sexual abuse or assault interviewed became afraid of going out or of being left at home alone and went to great lengths to avoid places where the offence occurred or where they might meet the offender. If the offender received a prison sentence such fears were likely to be greatly alleviated, at least until such time as he got out. But release from prison could resurrect feelings of fear and distress. In one case, in which a family friend had repeatedly committed buggery with two young brothers, the boys made a good recovery until the offender came out of prison, at which point one of the boys started having nightmares and headaches. His mother, speaking eight months after the disclosure, said 'he went to pieces. We thought he was doing well till then. To go to school he had to pass the offender's sister's house and he was terrified to do this. He himself suggested he change schools.' Only by major reorganization of the child's life to minimize the risk of contact with the offender could this sense of terror be allayed.

In addition to outright fear, many children felt generally more wary as a result of their experience. For example, several of those who had been victims of theft said that they had learned bitter lessons from the experience. One boy who had his personal stereo stolen at school said that 'I feel that the experience will make me a lot more careful and selective about the sort of people I keep company with. I sort of trusted people whereas I wouldn't do so much now.' Another boy who had some expensive fishing equipment stolen seemed to be even more wary and embittered and had resorted to measures that might lead him into trouble

When I am down the same place fishing now it's like you have to be alert the whole time . . . if you're tired you can't sleep and feel uncomfortable. The event has made me much more wary of strangers and I am a lot more careful when I goes fishing now. In fact I always takes a mallet or brick with me in case I am attacked to defend myself with it.

This kind of continuing fear was not confined to direct child victims. It also affected many who were anxious about their parents' well-being or safety. This was most marked in cases of physical or sexual violence, particularly if the child had witnessed the assault itself. For example, although one 12-year-old boy who had been forced to watch his mother being raped at knife-point seemed to have largely recovered ten months on, his mother told us that he remained nervous: 'He talked about it for a long time afterwards, I feel he is over it now but wonder if it will affect him in later life. He still won't leave me unless he knows he is going somewhere secure.' Her two other children, who had not witnessed the rape, also showed signs of continuing insecurity and took to sleeping in their mother's bed.

Physical assaults could also have a long-term impact on the offspring or siblings of those who had been attacked. In 25 per cent of physical assaults on parents the children reported continuing concern about their parents' safety. One 10-year-old expressed anxiety about his parents having to appear as witnesses in court and the possibility of repercussions. This was exacerbated by the family's lack of under-standing of the criminal justice process. His mother recalled

The court case reawakened fear in my son when it came up seven months later. He knew that Daddy was going to court as it was reported in the local paper. He wanted the man to go to prison and be punished. But he was worried that his father would be sent to prison too. If his father was late home any time he kept asking if he'd gone to prison.

Whilst she hoped that she and her husband had succeeded in conceal-ing their nerves, it seems highly likely that the child had picked up on his parents' tension as the trial approached.

It is important to remember that children are liable to be affected not only by crimes against their parents but also by those against other family members. The attempted rape of a girl D (aged 12) by a boy who was roughly the same age as her elder brother K (aged 15) had serious ramifications for K in the longer term. The mother's comments about K provide a good example of how deep an impact indirect victimization may have

For a long time K tailed his sister everywhere. He has become very possessive of her and very protective in quite an aggressive way. For example, he tells her she can't go out and this leads to rows. It has also affected K's relations with his own friends as he has been forced to realize that boys can do such things and thinks that kids should be protected from them. When one of his friends began pestering D and asked her out, K got very angry. Also, whilst a lot of his friends are beginning to experiment with sex, K is very against it and feels one should know the person really well first.

Whilst children in situations such as this are unlikely to be recognized in any formal sense as victims (and would probably be overlooked by support agencies) it is clear that they may be deeply affected by offences against their siblings.

Where the offence is directed against the household as a whole rather than a specific individual, as in the case of burglary, the experiences of children in the longer term were very mixed. In half of the cases where the children had been aware of the burglary the impact lasted no more than a few days or weeks and in many cases was largely forgotten as soon as possessions such as the television had been replaced. In the other half of the families the children were said to have retained some degree of nervousness or fear by the time of the interview, but only in a fifth of the cases did this disrupt their normal behaviour in any serious way. For example, one 11-year-old girl said that she had never liked the dark but used to go off to bed by herself. After the burglary she did not want to go downstairs (the bedrooms were downstairs) at night by herself. Three months later she still would not go downstairs at night alone. A more extreme example was given by the mother of a teenage girl:

N and I arrived home almost immediately after her father had discovered the burglary. N saw everything in a mess. Until we moved house she was afraid to go anywhere in the house on her own, even the lavatory. We reassured her . . . but here fear remained until we moved and was one of the reasons for moving.

A 4-year-old whose parents were interviewed nine months after the crime seemed to be even more seriously affected:

F still talks about it now. He said he would put a bread knife through the burglar if he caught him. This worried us as he was not like this before. He has also been having nightmares. He keeps asking all the time if the burglars are coming back.

And a 3-year-old, was very seriously traumatized by the event. His parents said: 'He was very upset. He just wouldn't stop screaming and crying for ages. He was very good before the burglary took place and was a "happy normal child". He has now really changed. He is very afraid to be left alone in the room and follows his mother everywhere.'

Perhaps the most profound psychological damage shown by child victims took the form of enduring changes in behaviour or personality. Half of the 19 children interviewed who had been sexually abused or assaulted continued to show signs of disturbance. Children who had been abused over a period of time were the most likely to remain seriously disturbed. Several months after the incident or incidents had ceased such children were still suffering from difficulty in sleeping and nightmares, were prone to emotional outbursts, or were generally aggressive. Some expressed vehement hatred of the offender whilst others were psychologically scarred in a more general way—as one girl put it, 'I am wary of any man now.' Individual cases illustrate the character and depth of such effects. One girl who had been sexually assaulted by a family friend over a three-year period (between the ages of 7 and 10) underwent profound changes in character and nearly a year later her mother observed:

She does not speak to us and is very sullen and quiet as if she blames us for what has happened. She bullies her brother as if she blames him too . . . her feelings are very bitter—she has a lot of hate for the offender. She has no friends at school. We feel this is because she is sullen and snappy to other children. She is very depressed and recently has been unable to sleep until about 2 a.m. She used to be a very cheerful girl.

It was possible, of course, for children to overcome such difficulties, particularly with professional help. For example, one young girl who had been abused by her father was referred to the Park Hospital for Children in Oxford and attended for psychiatric support fortnightly. Within three months (six visits) her mother was able to report: 'The bed-wetting and nightmares stopped as soon as she told her social worker at the Park [Hospital] . . . She used to be very sexual—she still is but it's calmed down a lot now. She still complains about stomach pains and is still aggressive towards me [her mother] but to no one else now.' Once provided with an outlet for her feelings and the support of skilled counsellors, the child had apparently begun to recover.

In a number of cases, the disclosure of the offence and the publicity it attracted had lingering effects. For example a girl abused by her father for two years finally confided in her aunt. However, when the affair became public both she and her younger brother suffered further and were still very disturbed some six months later. According to her mother

The children at school all know and have made her life hell by saying 'your dad's a dirty old man and should be in prison'. The children are both very angry and say they haven't got a father. P [the little girl] is only just now calming down. She still gets very angry with anyone around. She has kicked and punched me.

It would be very dangerous to assume that all children are badly affected by disclosure or publicity. Indeed, we came across several for whom the end to secrecy was a relief. One 15-year-old girl had been repeatedly abused by her stepfather, who told her that if she told anyone they would both go to prison. Despite these threats she eventually disclosed the facts to her mother, with the result that the offender was sentenced to three years' imprisonment. Interviewed just four days after the Crown Court decision (five months after the last offence), the girl said 'I now want to put the experience behind me and I've started to stop wanting to talk about it. I feel relieved about everything really.' The burden of secrecy inflicted on a child by sexual abuse induces feelings of shame and guilt which can be partly dispelled by disclosure. The public condemnation of the offender via the sentence of the court can play an important part in ridding the child of any enduring sense that they were in some sense culpable.[26]

Indeed, guilt can be an enduring, highly damaging effect of victimization. In the case of sexual abuse by a member of the family, or sexual assault, disclosure is liable to entail considerable distress and severe disruption. In one family, in particular, the sense of guilt appeared to be profound and enduring. The youngest daughter (of three children), C, disclosed that she had been sexually abused by her father over a period of time. The mother, interviewed alone nine months after her daughter's disclosure, said that 'We all seem to blame each other for what has happened for different reasons: I blame the girls for breaking up my marriage; the girls blame me for letting it happen; the other two [children] blame C for telling.' In such a case the damage to family relations may be irrevocable and the child is likely to bear the permanent blame for having broken up her family and possibly also for having sent a close relative to prison.

---

[26] Z. Adler, 'Prosecuting Child Sexual Abuse', in Maguire and Pointing (eds.), *Victims of Crime: A New Deal?*, 140.

Conclusion

It is apparent that very few children and their families escaped the experience of victimization unaffected. Over 90 per cent of the child victims in the sample were to some degree distressed in the immediate aftermath of the crime. Persisting effects were mainly confined to children who had suffered physical or sexual assault, or abuse, or whose parents had been severely assaulted. However, many children who were victims of other, less intrusive crimes, such as theft, were also quite often upset in the immediate aftermath. A significant minority of children whose homes had been burgled were also deeply and lastingly affected. Where parents themselves were visibly distressed, their children's reactions were exacerbated. Conversely, where parents were not badly affected or managed to conceal their reactions, the impact on children tended to be lessened. Where an offence is committed against a member of the child's household or against another family member, the child is unlikely to be recognized as a victim in his or her own right. However, their experience may be such that they ought properly to be recognized as victims'. Indeed, very few so-called indirect victims emerged from their experience wholly unscathed.

4

Police Policies and Practices

Children's experiences as victims are impossible to isolate from everything that happens as a direct consequence of the crime. The effects may be heightened or diminished by the response of those with whom they come into contact in its aftermath—the criminal justice system and the social and welfare agencies. Throughout the 1980s the position of victims in the criminal justice system was the subject of much debate. There was a growing recognition that the legal response could make a significant contribution to the overall impact of the crime on the victim. Helping victims of crime became one of the major platforms of criminal justice policy. In February 1990 the Thatcher government published a *Victim's Charter*[1] in which it expressed an avowed commitment to recognize the rights of victims and respond to their needs.

This and the following two chapters will describe the policies and practices of the criminal justice system in so far as they relate to child victims. They will provide a snapshot of the working of these policies in Oxford and Bedfordshire and will describe the experiences of the child victims in the study sample. In the penultimate chapter we will describe the provision of support to child victims and their families.

The Police and Victims

The police are the gatekeepers to the criminal justice system: they are responsible for the detection and investigation of crime. As such they play a key role in the lives of victims. Indeed, the success or failure of the victim's recourse to the criminal law depends upon their response. Although, since the advent of the Crown Prosecution Service in 1986, they are not now responsible for prosecuting the offender, they

[1] Home Office, *Victim's Charter: A Statement of the Needs and Rights of Victims of Crime.*

remain the most visible agency to the victim throughout the criminal justice process. The police are the body which he or she will contact first and which will provide the victim's main point of contact with the criminal justice system.

The major role which victims themselves play in the success or failure of the criminal process was recognized in the 1980s.[2] The majority of offences which come to the attention of the police are reported by the victim or those acting on his or her behalf; very few are discovered by the police.[3] Not only are the police dependent upon victims to report crime, they are also dependent upon them for co-operation throughout the investigative process. Victims, in turn, expect a sympathetic and helpful response from the police and to be provided with information about the progress of their cases and about services which may be available for them such as compensation and Victim Support. When this is not forthcoming their satisfaction with the police response declines.[4] The stress which victims may suffer when required to appear as witnesses in court has been highlighted during the latter part of the 1980s in the report *The Victim in Court*.[5] This emphasized the anxieties experienced by victims, not only about their appearance in court, but also during the period leading up to the trial. Lack of information about the progress of the case and any delay in bringing the case to court may be causes of much apprehension whether or not the victim is eventually required to appear as a witness. The report stressed the need to improve procedures and to modify court buildings to take account of the interests of victims and also the necessity of providing information and support to victims both before and during the trial.

Home Office Circulars to the police have thus emphasized the importance of keeping victims informed about the progress of the investigation; about compensation, whether from the courts or

[2] Hough and Mayhew, *The British Crime Survey: First Report*; Hough and Mayhew, *Taking Account of Crime*; Mayhew *et al.*, *The 1988 British Crime Survey*; Jones *et al.*, *The Islington Crime Survey*.

[3] S. McCabe and F. Sutcliffe, *Defining Crime: a study of police decisions* (Oxford, 1978); G. Chambers and A. Millar, *Investigating Sexual Assault*, Scottish Office Central Research Unit (Edinburgh, 1983); Shapland *et al.*, *Victims in the Criminal Justice System*.

[4] Shapland *et al.*, *Victims in the Criminal Justice System*; T. Newburn and S. Merry, *Keeping in Touch: Police–Victim Communication in Two Areas*, Home Office Research Study, No. 116 (London, 1990).

[5] National Association of Victims Support Schemes, *The Victim in Court: Report of a Working Party* (London, 1988).

the Criminal Injuries Compensation Board; about the existence of Victim Support and providing advice to witnesses attending court.[6] Leaflets which explain procedures to victims—such as 'Victims of Crime' and 'Witnesses in Court'—have been drawn up by the Home Office, and advice about compensation is contained in the leaflet 'Victims of Crimes of Violence: A Guide to the Criminal Injuries Compensation Scheme'. The police have been told to provide all such victims with this information. As has been shown in Chapter One, children are referred to only very briefly in the *Victim's Charter* and not at all in the Home Office Circulars about victims or in the report *The Victim in Court*. Where young persons are alleged to have offended or when children are deemed to be in need of protection from abuse or neglect, the legal process gives special recognition to their vulnerability. Until 1991 the juvenile court, with its more sensitive and informal approach, heard both cases involving juvenile offenders and those involving civil child protection proceedings. Since the implementation of the 1989 Children Act on 1 October 1991, civil matters concerning children are heard in a renamed Family Proceedings Court; the juvenile court deals with criminal proceedings only. The priority of both courts is the welfare of the child. In contrast, children who become victims or witnesses to crime are thrust into an adult system that traditionally does not distinguish between children and adults.

National Policies towards Child Victims

Although policies relating to adult victims also have implications for children, at present the only area of national policy relating specifically to children is that which concerns the investigation of sexual abuse or assault. Such allegations are likely to become known to the police through other agencies, particularly local authority Social Services Departments. Physical abuse can usually be identified by clearly visible injuries. Sexual abuse on the other hand is rarely identifiable by physical examination alone. The child's account of what happened is, therefore, crucial to the establishment of the case.[7] For this reason, the child concerned is likely to be interviewed by social workers to establish the facts before the police are involved.

---

[6] Home Office Circulars 20/88, 7/89.
[7] Jones and McQuiston, *Interviewing the Sexually Abused Child*, v.

The procedures will then be repeated by the police. This duplication of interviewing and possible medical examination of the child has caused concern, not least because research has revealed considerable evidence about the secondary victimization which the child is likely to experience as a result. In order to lessen the stress to the child in such situations, the police have been encouraged to undertake investigation jointly with social workers.[8] The pioneer in this innovation was the London Borough of Bexleyheath, which set up a pilot project involving both the police and the local authority social services department. The training of police officers and social workers together was intended to facilitate the integration of operational philosophies and to lay the foundations for joint interviewing by the police and social workers.[9] The main priority of the joint management of child sexual abuse cases was agreed to be the welfare of the child victim and other siblings. Criminal justice considerations, such as arrest and prosecution of the alleged abuser, were to be secondary.

The basic aims of the project were as follows:

1. to enhance co-ordination and co-operation between social services and police via joint investigation;
2. to increase awareness of both child sexual abuse and the different professional roles of each agency;
3. to reduce repeat interviews and/or medical examinations of children;
4. to use new techniques of investigation in order to facilitate both disclosures and decision-making; and
5. to provide protection for children and services to their family.[10]

Following the implementation of the 'Bexley' project the joint management and investigation of child sexual abuse cases was endorsed by senior police officers and Social Services managers and efforts made to implement it in many of the police forces and Social Services Departments in England and Wales in order to reduce trauma to child victims.[11] However, the Cleveland affair in 1987–8, served to illustrate

[8] Home Office Circular 52/88.

[9] Metropolitan Police and Bexley Social Services, *Child Sexual Abuse: Joint Investigative Programme: Final Report* (London, 1987); S. Holdaway, 'Police and Social Work Relations: Problems and Possibilities', *British Journal of Social Work*, 16 (1986); B. Cornick, 'Proceeding Together', *Community Care*, 17 Mar. 1988.

[10] See Metropolitan Police and Bexley Social Services, *Child Sexual Abuse*, 6.

[11] Metropolitan Police and Bexley Social Services, *Child Sexual Abuse*. For a critical analysis of the Bexley experiment see L. Kelly and L. Regan, 'Flawed Protection', *Social Work Today*, 19 Apr. 1990, 3–5; K. Byrne and N. Patrick 'Bexley Bounces

that all was not well. It arose because of the lack of proper understanding by the main agencies of each other's functions in relation to child sexual abuse; poor communication between the agencies; and differences in views at middle-management level which affected the views of those working with families.[12] The Report by Lord Justice Butler-Sloss on the Cleveland Crisis drew attention to the widespread nature of abuse and raised fundamental questions about the management by doctors, social workers, and the police of cases involving allegations of sexual abuse or assault. The Report criticized medical practitioners for the fact that the police and social workers were excluded from important decisions about children and families. The police were specifically criticized for their refusal to co-operate with other agencies in a multi-agency approach.[13] It also emphasized that the welfare of the child should be the prime consideration where allegations of sexual abuse or assault were made. It urged the importance of avoiding repeated interviews with or repeated medical examinations of the child for the purposes of gaining evidence. It emphasized the need for agencies to co-operate and to acknowledge that no one agency has sole responsibility in the assessment of child sexual abuse. The Report also recommended the setting up of specialist assessment teams, composed of a social worker, an experienced medical practitioner, and a police officer, to undertake a full multidisciplinary assessment of particular cases.[14]

After the publication of the Cleveland Report, new guide-lines on interagency work in the field of child abuse were produced. These were contained in the policy document *Working Together*,[15] which also endorsed the joint police–social work approach to investigation of child sexual abuse. Joint training by police and social workers to facilitate this approach was recommended. As a result, it is now widely recognized that all agencies should respond more sensitively to children involved in allegations of sexual abuse. There is an extensive literature on the investigation and diagnosis of child sexual abuse and how this should be carried out. Child-centred, treatment-orientated ways of responding to disclosures of child abuse are now advocated

Back', *Social Work Today*, 24 May 1990; S. Conroy *et al.*, *Investigating Child Sexual Abuse: The Study of a Joint Initiative* (London, 1990).

[12] *Report of the Inquiry into Child Abuse in Cleveland 1987*, 243.
[13] Ibid. 98–100.   [14] Ibid. 245–9.
[15] DHSS and Welsh Office, *Working Together: A Guide to Arrangements for Inter-agency Co-operation for the Protection of Children from Abuse* (London, 1988).

by clinical child care practitioners.[16] Interviews and insensitively performed medical examinations with child victims which are seen to be carried out solely for the needs of the agency concerned rather than the child should be avoided at all costs.[17]

In all the forces in England and Wales the police have developed special procedures for responding to and investigating allegations of child abuse and sexual assault. They have been advised in a national circular:

The concern of all agencies involved in the prevention of child abuse is the protection of the victim and others who may be at risk, and the need to provide for their welfare. The key to effective action is a close working relationship between the agencies concerned, particularly the police, local authority social services, the NSPCC and health authorities. . . . The investigation of allegations of the sexual abuse of children by a member of the family can raise sensitive issues. Family relationships may make it more difficult for the investigators in gathering evidence to establish what has happened and in deciding whether the public interest requires the bringing of a prosecution. It is also necessary to ensure that effective arrangements are made for the protection, support and care of the child in situations where this may not be adequately provided by the family. . . . In all these areas, decision making can be improved through consultation between the agencies involved in the case.[18]

A Case-Study of Policies and Practices relating to Child Victims

However, a number of areas of police policy and practice have implications for child victims: the recording of crime, dealing with children at risk, and the provision of services for victims. In Oxford and Bedfordshire the only area of policy relating specifically to child victims is that which deals with the investigation of child sexual abuse.

[16] Jones and McQuiston, *Interviewing the Sexually Abused Child*; E. Vizard *et al.*, 'Interviewing Sexually Abused Children', *Adoption and Fostering*, 11(1) (1987), 20–5; Conroy *et al.*, *Investigating Child Sexual Abuse*, 14–30.
[17] Jones and McQuiston, *Interviewing the Sexually Abused Child*; Interview with Dr D. Glaser, 'Detached Amid the Clamour', *Social Work Today*, 30 June 1988, 18–19.
[18] Home Office to Chief Officers of Police, 12 Jan. 1988; see also Home Office, *Report of the Advisory Group on Video Evidence* (London, 1989). On the police response to adult victims of sexual assault, see Chambers and Millar, *Investigating Sexual Assault*, 129 ff.

The Specialist Response to Child Sexual Abuse

The Thames Valley and Bedfordshire police forces have introduced specialist units to respond to both female victims of sexual assault and children who are victims of sexual abuse and assault or serious physical assault. The idea for these specialist units can be traced back to 1983 when a documentary television programme showing a male detective in the Thames Valley police interviewing a rape victim in a particularly unsympathetic manner brought the plight of victims of sexual assault to the forefront of public debate and caused considerable public disquiet. A Home Office Circular followed which offered advice to Chief Officers on the handling of investigations of rape and the treatment of victims of sexual assault.[19]

There was an immediate commitment on the part of senior police management to improve procedures. In 1983 Thames Valley Police established permanent Women's Specialist Units in each of its seven divisions. The division which includes Oxford City has four officers out of a total allocation of 30 for Thames Valley as a whole. These units consist of specially trained women Police Constables, detached from all other duties, and on call for twenty-four hours a day. They are responsible to a Detective Inspector for the initial investigation of allegations of rape and child abuse. In the Bedfordshire police force the Community Involvement Co-ordination Unit, established in its present form in 1985, handles cases of child abuse. Allegations of child abuse are investigated by Victims' Liaison Officers (VLOs), whose posts were set up in August 1988. Alongside their routine police duties, these officers are on call to provide special assistance to victims.[20] Their objective is 'to obtain evidence and information from the victim in such a way as to cause as little trauma to the victim as possible, and to ensure that the victim obtains help and assistance with understanding of procedures from other agencies'.[21] This commitment is continued throughout the investigation and court process, with follow-up referrals if necessary after the court appearance. In addition, specialist officers have been advised to ensure that, if a child victim needs to be medically examined, this is done as soon as possible

[19] Home Office Circulars 25/83 and 69/86. For a detailed account of the response to rape victims see L. J. F. Smith, *Concerns about Rape*, Home Office Research Study, No. 106 (London, 1989).

[20] There are four sections in each police division on 8-hour shifts, with at least one VLO in each section.

[21] Bedfordshire Police Force, Job Description for Victim Liaison Officers (1988).

after the allegation is made and is carried out with care and sensitivity by a police surgeon and/or a paediatrician who is trained in forensic examination.[22]

Joint interviews by police and social workers of child victims involved in allegations of sexual abuse or assault were introduced in Oxford in 1987 and in Bedfordshire in 1988.[23] The main policy objectives of this joint investigation were to provide assistance in the criminal investigation of the alleged perpetrator and to create the basis for further help and support to the child and family. To further this aim several police–social worker joint training courses have been held. Specially equipped suites for interviewing and examining victims of rape and child abuse and sexual assault have been opened in both areas.

But commendable though these specialized procedures are, they are not without their own internal problems. The purpose of the joint interview is to provide support for the child and to prevent the child from having to repeat his or her story. But there was a fundamental difference between the perceptions of the police officers and those of the social workers about their respective roles when conducting a joint interview. The police expressed the traditional view that their primary concern was to obtain evidence which could lead to the prosecution of the offender, whereas the social workers felt that their role was to provide support for the child and to gather information so that they would be in a position to make an informed decision on what action to take in the best interests of the child and family. Specialist police officers said that they always informed social workers of the need to ask evidentially sound questions. In fact, the majority of police officers said that they felt that the joint interview only went well from their point of view if the social worker involved did not say anything at all. Yet, the social workers expressed a great deal of anxiety about the emphasis placed by the police on the need for evidentially sound questions to be asked. They felt this had the potential to act against the best interests of the child and were unsure, in these circumstances, what their role in the joint interview should be. They were unable, therefore, to participate fully; control over the

---

[22] Home Office Circular 52/88.
[23] Thames Valley Police and Oxfordshire Social Services, 'Joint Statement regarding the Investigation of Child Sexual Abuse' (Oxford, Dec. 1987); Bedfordshire Police 'Report of Force Working Party – Rape and Child Abuse' (Bedford, 1988).

character and pace of the interview seemed to remain in the hands of the police.

Preparation for the interview was felt by both agencies to be essential. As one specialist police officer in Bedfordshire put it, 'the kid doesn't stand a chance if we haven't got our act together'. While all the police and social workers said that they would obtain as much information as possible about the child victim and his or her family before the interview, in Oxford emphasis was laid on the necessity for allegations to be dealt with speedily. As a result, all the interviews were carried out within an hour of the report of the allegation being received, leaving little time for any preparation.

One of the main reasons for carrying out the joint interview was that the child would have to tell his or her story once only. However, both social workers and police said that usually there was more than one interview with a child victim. Social workers often had not been able to obtain the information which they required at the joint interview and had, therefore, to go back to reinterview the child. Some detective officers distrusted the interview techniques of the specialist officers, and did not, therefore, consider it inappropriate to reinterview the child if they felt it necessary.

As seen above the specialist police officers have a number of other duties in this connection: to decide whether a medical examination of a child who alleges abuse is required; to arrange for the examination to be carried out if it is deemed necessary; to accompany the child to the examination; and to collect any forensic specimens. Chief Officers of Police have been advised to ensure that certain guide-lines are followed. These examinations, when conducted, must be carried out in a sensitive manner by a police surgeon and, if available, by a paediatrician with forensic training. They should take place immediately after the investigator's interview and the victim and the parents should be given a choice of a male or female police surgeon to conduct the examination. The doctor carrying out the examination of the child should ask the consent of the child, or a parent, or guardian when a child is not old enough to understand, and the number of medical examinations should be kept at a minimum to reduce stress on the child. Consequently, wherever possible, the forensic medical examination should be carried out at the same time that the victim is examined by a doctor who is considering the need for medical treatment.

In both field-work areas, police surgeons (who are also general practitioners) have been appointed and employed by the respective Police Authorities to examine cases of injury and abuse which come to the notice of the police. In Bedfordshire there were a number of paediatricians who have been used in conjunction with the police surgeons to examine child victims, but in Oxford there were no paediatricians available whom the police could use in this way. The choice of a male or female police surgeon was, however, available in Oxford whereas none of the female doctors in Bedfordshire was a designated police surgeon, and could not therefore be used by the police in this capacity. Although all the police surgeons in Oxford had taken part in in-service police surgeon training courses and the majority of them had attended the annual course on the examination of children, in Bedfordshire none of the police surgeons had taken part in any training in the examination of children since their appointment. A subcommittee of the Bedfordshire Force Working Party on Rape and Child Abuse was in the process of reviewing the situation with regard to the employment and training of police surgeons.

Several basic differences existed between the views of the specialist police officers and police surgeons about how the medical examination of the child should best be conducted. The specialist police officers all felt that the interview suites provided for the examination of children were the best venues. On the other hand, the majority of police surgeons said that they carried out their examinations in their own surgeries or, in the case of paediatricians, the hospital treatment room, even though the latter agreed that this was not ideal for the child. The police surgeons in Oxford said that they conformed with the wishes of the police officer to carry out a forensic examination of the child without questioning the child about what had happened. In Bedfordshire, none of the police surgeons would agree to this, thus provoking a long-running dispute with the police. In neither Oxford nor Bedfordshire did the police surgeons or paediatricians routinely inform the child's own GP about the examination.

After the initial investigation had been completed, a case conference was called and a 'plan' for the long-term help of the child and family was usually formulated. In both field-work areas social workers were always appointed to co-ordinate the implementation and review of this plan. But those interviewed were unanimous that there was very little support available for the child and its family in the period after all the evidence had been collected. All agreed that it was urgently needed. There were very few agencies to which child victims of sexual abuse or assault could be referred for support. The police and social services refer children who are under the age of 13 in Oxford to the Park Hospital for Children and in Bedfordshire to Great Ormond Street Hospital. In both areas there were a number of groups run by social workers for girls who had been sexually abused or assaulted. But all these agencies were over-subscribed and it was widely recognized that there was a need for greater provision. Although the police in Bedfordshire did provide a booklet for victims of sexual assault containing a list of agencies to which they can turn for help, the police officers interviewed recognized that the agencies listed were much more appropriate for older teenage and adult victims than for children. All the specialist police officers said that they were called upon to provide a supportive role where these children were concerned, a role which none of them felt qualified to fulfil. As one officer put it: 'At the end of the day, I'm there to get evidence. I'm not there as a therapist. I cannot devote eight hours a day to these things.'

The Victim Support Schemes in both Oxford and Bedfordshire offered a service to the families of children who had suffered abuse and the Women's Specialist Police Unit in Oxford said that they regularly referred such cases. But in Bedfordshire, the majority of the VLOs interviewed were unaware that Victim Support were able to provide support for mothers in the case of child abuse and for the families of child victims of sexual assault. Those few officers who were aware of this service were those who had personal contact with the Victim Support co-ordinators in their areas. They had made considerable use of Victim Support in this capacity.

All those interviewed agreed that, in order for the police officers and social workers involved in the joint interviewing of abused children to give maximum support to child victims, they themselves needed to have access to supervision and support in this very stressful work. But although this was available for the social workers involved, there was no such provision for the specialist police officers in either of the field-work areas. The lack of support was said to be a particular problem in Bedfordshire, where the officers are not part of a specialist unit and also have to carry out routine police duties alongside their specialist duties. After six VLOs resigned, the Bedfordshire force recruited Relate counsellors to help police officers involved in working with sexual abuse or sexual assault. This practice has been followed in a number of other police forces throughout England and Wales in 1990.[24]

Thus, although the introduction of joint investigation in cases of child sexual abuse and the philosophy which underlies it—that of reducing the stress to the child—is, in principle, a move in the right direction, in practice a number of problems have arisen in implementing the scheme. These stem, in the main, from the fact that each of the two agencies involved placed emphasis on its own objectives rather than the child victim's needs for security and therapy. The findings relating to the experience in Oxford and Bedfordshire are consistent with those findings relating to the experience of joint police–social work investigation in other parts of the country[25] and also in relation to interagency working in other areas in which the police are involved, such as crime prevention, juvenile crime, and drug abuse.[26] However, research has been carried out on joint investigation, and attempts are being made to improve interagency procedures both locally and nationally.[27] In addition there are further indications that the interviewing of sexually abused children will become more 'child-centred'. The Criminal Justice Act 1991 contains provisions for videotaping an early interview with a child, and a code of practice for conducting such interviews with child witnesses is being drawn up by the Home Office.[28]

In marked contrast to these detailed policies and procedures which have been developed specifically to deal with children who have been abused, there are no guide-lines in existence for how the police should respond to children who are victims of other crimes.

[24] For example, Dyfed–Powys Police Authority recruited Relate counsellors to treat police officers suffering from stress after six officers resigned in 1990 from stress-related illness.

[25] S. Holdaway, 'Police and Social Work Relations'; H. Blagg and P. Stubbs, 'A Child Centered Practice? Multi-agency Approaches to Child Sexual Abuse', *Practice* 2(1), 1987, 12–19.

[26] D. Smith, 'The Limits of Inter-agency Co-operation', *Crime U.K. 1988* (Newbury, 1988) pp. 55–60.

[27] Conroy *et al.*, *Investigating Child Sexual Abuse*.

[28] The code of practice will refer to (1) the conduct of the interviews (e.g. techniques), (2) the videotaping of the interviews (including what should be available on the monitor to observers of the video recording, and the location of such interviews), and (3) the admonition given to the witness (i.e. what the child should be told about telling the truth).

Recording the Crime

Police policy on the recording of crime can have implications for victims, and child victims are no exception. A crime report transforms an event or incident which was the subject of a complaint to the police into a crime requiring investigation. If a crime report is not completed, it can affect the victim's eligibility for referral to Victim Support or for compensation from the courts or the Criminal Injuries Compensation Board (CICB). CICB requires that, to be eligible for compensation, all cases concerning adult victims must have been reported to the police. In the case of a child, a more sympathetic attitude is taken. The 'appropriate authority' to whom the offence must be reported may be a headteacher or the child's parents, but their failure to inform the police would not make the child ineligible for compensation. However, the Board 'must be satisfied on the balance of probabilities that the events alleged actually took place and this will be much easier if the police have been informed on the child's behalf and been given the opportunity to investigate and prosecute'.[29] It is well known that not all crimes reported to the police are recorded by them and cases involving child victims were no exception to the rule. In both the Thames Valley and Bedfordshire police forces official policy is that a crime report will be completed as soon as possible for every crime made known to the police. In practice, the process by which matters are 'crimed' is not so straightforward. Although detailed statistical instructions are issued to all police forces by the Home Office, many decisions are taken locally about recording, classification, and counting of crimes. Local practices relating to the recording of offences against children (particularly child abuse) indicate that criminal statistics are likely to be unreliable as indicators of level of offences committed or even reported.

The police exercise a great deal of discretion over whether to record a crime or not. Once a crime is reported to the police, the crime is assessed by an officer to discover whether it is a notifiable offence.[30]

---

[29] Criminal Injuries Compensation Board, *Twenty-Sixth Annual Report*, Cm 1365 (1990), p. 43.

[30] The term 'notifiable offence' covers those offences for which, if any suspect were apprehended (although this does not apply to a juvenile), proceeded against at court, and found to have a case to answer, he would have to be tried by a jury; it also covers those offences for which a defendant could—prior to July 1978—be tried by magistrates in accordance with s. 19 of the Magistrates Courts Act 1952.

Even if it is found to be a notifiable offence there is no guarantee that the police officer will complete a crime report. For example, an officer must investigate whether there is an actual complaint by an injured party. In the early stages of child abuse cases, there is often no complainant; therefore an investigation has to be conducted first. In this situation, a Thames Valley police Superintendent explained that an incident would not be 'crimed' until a full investigation had been made. Officers in both field-work areas indicated that in child abuse cases crime reports were generally filled in only where there was tangible injury. Cases of neglect, even where the child's consequent failure to thrive was extreme, almost never ended up on a crime report. Lacking any concrete guide-lines in this area, police officers appeared to assume that such cases would be diverted out of the criminal justice system to be dealt with instead by civil care proceedings.

Even where a crime report is completed initially, police policy may permit a crime report to be written off as 'no crime' at the discretion of a senior CID officer. This arises if following investigation of an allegation it is found: that the circumstances do not amount to a criminal offence; that, on legal advice, there is considered to be insufficient evidence of a crime; that property was wrongly believed to have been stolen; that allegations are unfounded or withdrawn; or that the value in offences of criminal damage is found to be under £20. In Bedfordshire, the Force Working Party on Rape and Child Abuse, which reported in 1987, noted a tendency by investigating officers to 'no crime' offences because of lack of evidence or corroboration, and recommended that this practice cease.

There are a number of offences which, even where reported to the police, are not defined as crimes by them and are not recorded on a crime report. In the field-work areas these included incidents involving criminal damage under £20, and incidents of suspicious behaviour and offences of indecent exposure, which are recorded on separate forms rather than official crime reports. Many of these involve children. Children who are indirect victims of crime also tend to be overlooked by the police in that they do not uniformly record the presence of children in households where crimes, for example burglary or domestic violence, occur.

Children 'At Risk'

In Oxford and Bedfordshire, in common with all areas of England and Wales, there are special procedures for dealing with children who come to police attention and are deemed by them to be 'at risk'. The names of these children are recorded on a juvenile report whose primary purpose is to communicate information about such cases to the social services departments (although in urgent cases the telephone is sometimes used instead). A survey of such cases in Luton in 1988 showed that they covered such incidents as abduction, child abuse, actual bodily harm (ABH), grievous bodily harm (GBH), drunk in charge of a child, sexual assault, rape, buggery, and domestic violence. However, the identification of children at risk rested in the end on the discretion and judgement of individual officers. There were no guidelines for what kinds of situation warranted the identification of a child as being at risk. The information recorded on the juvenile report was often vague and imprecise. For example, the reasons given might be recorded simply as 'concern for welfare and safety', without any indication of what had given rise to this concern. Indeed, there were enormous variations in the extent to which these forms were used. In one field-work area they were extensively used, whereas, in the other, attempts to cut down police paperwork resulted in fewer of these records being completed. The majority of police officers in this area seemed unaware of their duty to alert social services to the existence of these children. In neither field-work area was there any mechanism for cross-checking the names of families involved in such cases. The inherent danger in this practice is that different officers may be called out repeatedly to the same home without any individual officer becoming alerted to the possibility that a child is at risk.

In relation to domestic violence, the government has made several attempts to encourage the police to take measures to protect vulnerable members of the household, particularly children. Under section 25 of the Police and Criminal Evidence Act 1984 the police are empowered to make an arrest to protect a child or other vulnerable person. A Home Office Circular in 1990 called for radical changes in the police response to domestic violence modelled on the best of existing practice: 'police called to the scene of family violence will in future be expected to . . . make the safety of the victim and children their first priority. If necessary they will escort them to shelters or to examination suites staffed by specially trained police women.'[31] Their first priority is to protect the victim and any children from further attack. It is to be hoped that the police are now following these policy guide-lines and providing support for children in situations of domestic violence and other 'at risk' situations.

Services for Victims: The Criminal Injuries Compensation Scheme

Financial aid in the form of compensation from the courts and the Criminal Injuries Compensation Board, is available for child victims.[32] Compensation in family violence cases became payable for incidents occurring since October 1979. Child victims of violence (whether committed within or outside the family) may be entitled to compensation for their injuries under the scheme, whether or not there has been a prosecution or conviction. This applies to cases where there may be no physical injury but emotional trauma as in cases of sexual assault. Awards of compensation cannot be made for injuries assessed at less than a specified figure (currently £750), but substantial sums are awarded for more serious injury.[33] There is a three-year limitation period on making a claim after the incident, but this may be waived at the Board's discretion, particularly in claims relating to child victims.[34]

The police play a key role with regard to a victim's access to compensation and in providing information about its availability. Home Office Circular 20/88 reinforces the advice contained in previous circulars that victims of violent crime should be made aware of the existence of the CICB and of the possibility of compensation from the criminal courts. The circular states: 'it remains important that police officers, who in the vast majority of cases are the first to come into contact with victims of violent crime, should bring the Scheme to the victim's attention.'[35] In fact, research on adult victims has shown that the police do not routinely inform victims about the availability of compensation either from the criminal courts or from the CICB.[36]

---

[31] See 'Guide for Police on Home Violence', *Guardian*, 1 Aug. 1990. Leading article, 'Violence in the Family', *Independent*, 1 Aug. 1990.

[32] D. Miers, 'The Criminal Justice Act: The Compensation Provisions', *Criminal Law Review* (1989), 32–42.   [33] Prior to 1990 the minimum was £550.

[34] CICB, *Twenty-sixth Annual Report* (1990), 40.

[35] Home Office Circular 20/88.

[36] Shapland *et al.*, *Victims in the Criminal Justice System*; Newburn and Merry, *Keeping in Touch*.

This finding was borne out in our research on child victims. The interviews conducted with the police in Oxford and Bedfordshire revealed that very few of them were even aware of the availability of compensation for children. Some mistakenly believed that compensation was not available for sexual abuse within the family, or that the offender had to have been prosecuted successfully before an application could be made.

Services for Victims: The Police and Victim Support

There are well-established Victim Support Schemes which can offer support services to child victims in both Oxford and Bedfordshire. As with all Victim Support Schemes (see Chapter 7), these two areas are heavily dependent upon the police for their referrals. A policy of automatic referral of all crime (apart from sexual abuse and assault) had been agreed between the police authorities and Victim Support Schemes and 99 per cent of the referrals to both schemes came from the police. The co-operation of the police is therefore essential. In both Oxford and Bedfordshire senior police officers of the rank of Superintendent or Chief Inspector were responsible for maintaining contact with Victim Support. Referral of children to Victim Support was carried out by civilian referral officers using crime reports in all police stations. In theory police officers who deal with victims are well placed to inform them about the availability of this service. Yet across the ranks the majority of police officers were unaware that child victims were included in their force's policy of automatic referral to Victim Support. When told, many were ambivalent about this. Indeed, the majority thought that Victim Support was not a suitable organization to provide assistance for child victims. As will be seen in Chapter 7, the result was that very few child victims in the fieldwork areas were referred by the police to Victim Support.

Conclusion

Victims depend upon the police to respond sympathetically and to provide them with information about the progress of their case and about the availability of compensation and support. In turn, the police are dependent upon victims to report crimes to them and to co-operate during the investigative process. The police have been advised to take account of the needs of victims. Yet little mention is made in official Home Office Circulars of the special needs of child victims. It is hardly surprising that it is in the area of child sexual abuse alone that the police have developed special policies, nationally and locally, for responding to these allegations. Here, despite initial difficulties, progress is being made in providing a sympathetic, supportive approach for such children.

Other police policies also have implications for child victims, ranging from the recording of crime to providing information about support and compensation. Given that child victims are easily over-looked, it is all the more important that the police should be made aware of the implications of failing to record crimes against them. As a vital source of information about Criminal Injuries Compensation and Support, police awareness of children's eligibility for these services should be raised.

5

Policing: The Experiences of Child Victims

We turn now from policies of the police to examine how the children in our sample viewed their experiences from the moment the crime was reported.

Reporting and Recording the Crime

Victims or persons acting on their behalf are far more important in bringing crime to the notice of the police than investigation by the police themselves. Cases which involve child victims are no exception to this rule. Of the 212 cases involved in the study sample, only one was discovered by the police themselves. In just 12 per cent (32) of the cases (mostly thefts of cycles) the children said that they reported the incident themselves. Of the rest, the vast majority were reported to the police by the child's parents, but a handful were reported by other adults—10 by schoolteachers, 1 by a social worker, and 4 by the child's doctor.

The reliance of children on adults to report crimes on their behalf creates something of a barrier to such events coming to the attention of the police. This is well illustrated in our research. In many cases children and their families did not turn immediately to the police but first sought help from other agencies. Assistance from their GP or the hospital casualty department was sought by half the 73 children who were victims of sexual or physical assault. In only 4 of these cases did GPs suggest that children or their parents report to the police. In 33 cases the parents involved the child's school. In 10 of these cases the school reported the crime to the police. But in the other cases they appeared to do nothing themselves and in none of them did the school refer the victim, or even suggest referral, to another agency. Indeed, child victims and their families were generally less than satisfied with the response they received. The majority did not feel that the school took them seriously. In 2 cases of sexual assault which were disclosed in school, the school did nothing initially, and did not inform the parents or any other agency. None of the cases of physical assault which were reported in school were followed up by the school authorities. In 3 cases, the schools positively discouraged parents from reporting to the police. The school usually concentrated on dealing with the offender in cases of assault but victims felt that they were expected to set aside what had happened and simply recover from their experience on their own.

In one particularly grave case of bullying, which resulted in an assault, the head said he could do nothing, even though the parents counted 32 bruises on their child's body and their doctor wrote to the school saying that it was the most serious case of bullying she had ever seen. In 2 cases of serious assaults on boys which had occurred in school the offenders were suspended for a week or so, and the victims told that they would be moved to other classes. In neither case was this done: the parents felt 'we were fobbed off by the school'. In another case of a teenage girl who was beaten up by a schoolmate, her mother took her immediately to casualty whilst the father went to see her headmaster to say that he wanted the police involved. The head tried to dissuade him by saying that it was purely a school issue; but when the father made it clear that he was going to report, the head was obliged to agree. In another instance of racial assault at school the headmaster advised the mother to 'go home and discuss it with my husband as to whether we wanted to report it to the police'. Similarly, where victims had reported cases of theft they felt that these were not taken seriously or acted upon adequately by the school. In one instance the mother had to press the school to report to the police. Even when they did so the loss was reported as lost property rather than theft. The reluctance of schools to respond to offences as crime left many children feeling distinctly aggrieved.

The difficulty for children in obtaining any help at all where there are no visible injuries as a result of the crime is well illustrated in cases of sexual abuse and sexual assault. Whilst fear of parental anger inhibited a considerable number of children from disclosing crimes such as physical assaults or thefts by outsiders, the greatest reluctance to reveal a crime undoubtedly arises in sexual crimes, particularly abuse which takes place within the family. Very young children may not even understand that what has happened to them is wrong or may not possess the vocabulary to seek help. In one case where a 3-year-old girl had been abused by her father, her mother only discovered this after she had taken her daughter to the hospital since she was complaining of persistent stomach ache. Here the paediatrician examined her and she was interviewed by a social worker, to whom she eventually disclosed the abuse. In another case of an 11-year-old girl indecently assaulted by a man who worked for her parents, the mother said 'she was crying and ran to her bedroom, I went up to talk to her and it took a lot of getting out of her what had happened'. The majority of the 19 children who were direct victims of sexual abuse or sexual assault had been threatened of the dire consequences which would occur if they told anyone. In the most extreme case, the father of a 9-year-old girl told her that if she told anyone he would kill the entire family.

In another example, that of a teenage girl who had been sexually assaulted by the son of a family friend, she was reluctant to tell her parents. At first she told her doctor, who said that she had 'asked for it' and should go away and forget about it. She then revealed the offence to her aunt, who told the parents herself. The parents, unsure of what to do, telephoned Childline, who advised them to report it to Social Services, which they then did. A social worker came to the house and persuaded them to report it to the police. In another instance, the child told her teacher that she had been sexually assaulted by the family's next-door neighbour. The teacher failed to tell the head teacher for a week and the head then left it for three weeks. She then told the vicar, who in turn told her to consider the matter for a couple of weeks before telling anyone else. Eventually the head summoned the parents to the school to tell them. The parents did not believe their daughter and it was a further two weeks before the police were finally informed. Such instances provide graphic substantiation of research findings that adults are often highly reluctant to believe children when they allege that they have been sexually assaulted.

Thus, child victims are heavily dependent upon others to report offences against them to the police. Indeed, a much lower percentage of children than adults reported the offence to the police themselves. Shapland found that some 35 to 41 per cent of cases involving adult victims were reported to the police by the victim himself or herself and Newburn found that 64 per cent of victims contacted the police themselves,[1] whereas we have seen that for children the figure was only 12 per cent.

The vast majority of the children we spoke to considered themselves to be victims of crime. They felt that by involving the police they could get something done about the offence. In the majority of cases, however, it was the parents who assumed primary responsibility for deciding to involve the police, largely because they wanted to see justice done. Strikingly, the views of the child are all too often lost amid adult wrangling about whether the police should be involved. Whilst most children were positively keen to see the police involved, some were further traumatized by this prospect. For example, one girl who had been indecently assaulted phoned Childline for advice. They told her to tell someone she trusted. She confided in her boyfriend's mother, who felt obliged to inform her father. The girl was very distressed and 'begged her father not to report it to the police', despite her pleading he went ahead and did so. Children had a variety of motives for not wanting to involve the police. Some, as we have seen in Chapter 3, feared retaliation; others were simply afraid of being labelled a 'grasser'. One teenage girl who had been assaulted said 'the worst thing about the offence was the teasing I got at school for going to the police'. Another teenage boy who had also been assaulted recognized one of his assailants and was afraid 'of having to point a finger at her at school'. This is not to argue that children are necessarily best placed to make the decision to report for themselves. It is well known that victims may not be in a fit psychological state to make decisions in the aftermath of the crime; they may even be physically incapable of doing so. It must be concluded that, although parents may discuss the decision to report to the police with the child, adult views about the appropriate response tend to override the child's wishes. Often the final decision lay with the parents alone. British Crime Surveys have shown that victims often do not report offences to the police because they feel they are too trivial. Child victims may not come to the attention of the police because the adults acting on their behalf may take a similar view.[2]

As we have seen, not all offences which are reported to the police are recorded by them as crimes. The offences in the study sample (see

---

[1] Shapland *et al.*, *Victims in the Criminal Justice System*, 17; Newburn and Merry, *Keeping in Touch: Police–Victim Communication in Two Areas*, 5.

[2] Hough and Mayhew, *Taking Account of Crime: Key Findings from the 1984 British Crime Survey*, 19–21; Mayhew *et al.*, *The 1988 British Crime Survey*, 24.

Chapter 3) were no exception. In over a third of the 212 cases (33 direct and 40 indirect), the names of the children concerned were not recorded on a crime report. These children were thus neither officially recognized nor responded to as victims of crime. As shown above, police policy in Oxford and Bedfordshire dictates that offences of indecent exposure and incidents of suspicious behaviour are not entered into a crime report but are recorded separately at the police station. Thus the 33 children in the study sample who witnessed these were not officially recognized as victims even though all of them felt that these incidents were crimes. Also the children involved in the 40 cases in the study sample as indirect victims were not personally identified as victims on the crime report. These were completed in the name of their parent or parents as the sole 'injured party'. In all cases where children's names did not appear on a crime report, victims and their parents were unaware of this or of its importance in respect of eligibility for compensation or referral to Victim Support.

To sum up, the police are heavily dependent upon cases involving child victims being reported to them by children or their relatives. However, this study shows that even where children feel themselves to be victims of crime, a series of obstacles make it particularly difficult for them to be brought to the attention of the police. Even when they are, there is no guarantee that they will be officially recorded by the police as victims. This may well affect their eligibility for support and compensation.

Initial Contact between the Police and Child Victims

When any offence comes to the attention of the police, they are concerned to discover exactly what has happened and the nature of the victim's complaint. During their first meeting with any victim, the police necessarily seek to obtain information from the victim and to tell him or her formally of the types of enquiry they propose to make.[3] In the field-work areas the police did not differentiate between their approaches to adult and to child victims (except in the case of the specialist approach to sexual abuse or sexual assault described above in Chapter 4). As with adult victims, because of pressure on their time, they are usually unable to revisit the child victim unless they

---

[3] Shapland *et al.*, *Victims in the Criminal Justice System*, ch. 2; Newburn and Merry, *Keeping in Touch*.

need to obtain further information. Despite this, the majority of the police we interviewed felt that it was important that child victims and their families should be provided with information about the progress and outcome of the case. All of them said that they would provide victims with their names and telephone numbers in case they wanted to make further contact. For their part, the child victims and their families in the study sample said that when they reported an offence to the police they expected the police to respond sympathetically, to take details of what had happened, to do something about their complaint, and to keep them informed about the progress of the case and its outcome.

In the vast majority of cases, the police were quick to respond to telephone calls from parents about crimes which involved child victims. They usually arrived at the home of the victim within two hours or else asked the parent to bring the victim to the police station as soon as possible. In over half the cases, the initial meeting with the police took place in the child's home; a quarter of the child victims and their parents met the police initially at the police station. In three cases of physical assault they were called to see the child at the hospital but in each instance they only carried out a brief interview here, with the remainder of their inquiry concluded at the child's home at a later stage. In the remaining cases—all of them thefts—parents contacted the police and provided details of the offence over the telephone. In no case did the officers take the victim to the special interview suite available.

During this initial contact the police usually took a statement from the victim and gave the child and his or her parents details of how the investigation would proceed. In all cases where the child was the direct victim (except in three where the child was under the age of 3) the police spoke directly to the children themselves. But in none of the 40 cases which involved children as indirect victims did the police either talk to the children or ask after them.

In cases of sexual abuse or sexual or physical assault, where the victim was the main prosecution witness, forensic evidence of the injuries sustained, gained by medical examination or photographs, could supplement the child's statement. Of the 53 children who were victims of physical assault, 12 had photographs of their injuries taken. The majority of these were arranged by the police but a quarter by the parents themselves. Thirty-one of the children were medically examined as a result of the crime. Half of these examinations were arranged by the parents or the victims and half by the police. Where the police did not suggest that photographs be taken, many parents of children who were victims of physical assault were angry that this had not been suggested since the injuries were so severe.

In nearly 90 per cent of cases, the initial contact between child victims and the police was completed in one interview. In only 3 of the 22 cases of sexual abuse or sexual assault did a joint interview with a police officer and a social worker take place, although the majority of these children were interviewed by specially trained police officers. The length of the initial contact between the police and child victims varied between a short 5-minute telephone conversation in which the parent of a child who had had his cycle stolen described the offence to the police, and a similarly short time ranging between 5 and 30 minutes for all the other victims of theft and burglary, to the lengthy interviews experienced by all the children who were victims of physical and sexual assault. All the children who had been physically assaulted were interviewed for between 1 and 4 hours. In cases of sexual abuse or assault, the victim is the chief witness and there may be no evidence other than the child's word. The police were particularly vigilant in interviewing these children. One 3-year-old girl was interviewed 5 times in a 3-week period. All the child victims of sexual abuse or sexual assault were interviewed for between 2 and 5 hours on the first occasion; over half of them were interviewed at length on subsequent occasions. All these victims and their families found these long-drawn-out procedures extremely stressful and tiring. In only a fifth of the cases—all the sexual abuse and sexual assault cases and a handful of instances of physical assault and theft—did the police provide the child and family with their names and telephone numbers for further contact. These were the only cases in which the children and their parents been told that they should telephone the police if they had any further information to offer or wished to be informed about the progress of the case by the police.

Views of the Initial Police Response

Whether child victims and their families were satisfied with the way in which the police responded was heavily influenced by their perceptions of the attitude of the police officer or officers who first dealt with them. It was also shaped by police practices such as the speed with which they came to deal with the complaint and their handling of the investigative process. Child victims and their families had almost identical expectations of the police as adult victims. However, whereas surveys of adult victims have shown high levels of satisfaction with the initial police response (the 1988 British Crime Survey, for example, found that over 80 per cent of adult victims were satisfied with the police response[4]) a much lower proportion—two thirds—of children and their families were satisfied with the way in which the police responded to them initially. It is perhaps not surprising that those children and their parents who were most enthusiastic about the police response were those victims of sexual abuse or sexual assault who were dealt with by specialist police officers.

In half the cases of sexual abuse or assault, children and parents expressed satisfaction about the demeanour of the police themselves (usually policewomen, sometimes operating in collaboration with social workers). All the parents and children interviewed jointly by police and social workers were unanimous in their praise of way in which they worked together. One mother of a 3-year-old girl said 'the WPC could not have been nicer. She believed K. The social worker at the interview put her at her ease as she already knew her. I don't think K would have gone into the room with the WPC on her own but with the social worker there, she was perfectly happy.' Another mother of a teenage girl who had been assaulted by a family friend said 'the WPC was very good and tactful. She did not press N when N found it difficult to talk but let her talk about something else until she felt like coming back to the subject.' And yet another teenage girl, who had been sexually assaulted by a neighbour, said 'the WPC was better than the psychotherapist I saw'. The mother of a teenage girl who had been indecently assaulted by a boy she knew said 'two uniformed officers came within five minutes. On hearing what had happened they telephoned for a WPC. The WPC was wonderful and very supportive. A was worried that no one would believe her but the WPC assured her that the police did believe her.' Another mother of an 8-year-old girl, who had been sexually assaulted by her parents' gardener, said 'M cried when she saw the WPC but the WPC put her at her ease by telling her not to worry. The WPC got a lot more out of her than I

---

[4] Mayhew *et al.*, *The 1988 British Crime Survey*, 26–8. In addition, the studies carried out by Shapland *et al.* (*Victims in the Criminal Justice System*, 176) and Newburn and Merry (*Keeping in Touch*, 13) showed that the great majority of adult victims were satisfied with the initial police response.

did. I think this was because she was more detached.' The mother of a 9-year-old boy who had been a victim of indecent assault said 'the interview and statement-taking were extremely well done and carefully done. They didn't rush it.' In all these cases victims and their families were clearly highly appreciative of the sensitivity of the officers concerned.

The majority of child victims of other crimes and their families expressed general satisfaction with the way in which the police responded initially. The parents of two boys who had been physically assaulted by some unknown youths said of the police 'they did the job well. They were very supportive to the boys and they understood we were upset.' Another father of a boy who had been physically assaulted said 'I felt the police handled the situation well and the officer concerned was very careful about details.' Another said 'they handled the situation well and put M at his ease'. Again, it was the ability of the police to tailor their response to the needs of the child which was most appreciated. Whilst parents who had been victimized themselves or whose homes had been burgled were generally satisfied, few of them seemed to think that the police should have paid any attention to their children. These children often felt overlooked or disregarded by the police.

However, in over a third of the cases—mostly involving sexual abuse or assault, physical assault, or theft—dissatisfaction was expressed by children and parents. There were two major sources of this discontent: first, police attitudes towards child victims, and secondly, the procedures followed. Where the police were slow to respond to the victim's complaint or gave no impression of urgency, children and their parents felt that to the police the offence was 'just run-of-the-mill' and of little concern and this caused distress. An important factor which many children found stressful was the time taken for the police to respond and spent waiting in the police station. One child, a teenage boy, said 'the police were very nice but we were at the station for two hours while the police decided whether the case was a common assault or an ABH'. In a case in which a teenage girl had had her head banged against a wall by another girl at school, the parents were 'disgusted . . . although two uniformed officers came out, they didn't take notes and didn't take their hands out of their pockets. We were told it would be followed up by a local officer, but this took eight days to arrange. The police seemed totally unconcerned about our daughter.' In the case of a girl who had been badly attacked and had her nose broken by another girl in a youth club, both she and her mother forwarded complaints. The girl said

when we went to the police station the man at the desk said there was no one there to see us as there was a football match on and all the police were there. He said a policeman would come round to see us but he didn't come for another week and only then after we telephoned the station. When the PC came he was quite good but you could see he was overworked. He said there was a lot of crime around. He made us feel that what had happened was just something he had to deal with every day. Although it was serious for us we felt it wasn't for the police.

As noted earlier, many of these parents were angry that the police did not take photographs of their children's injuries or suggest they take them for a medical examination. One hypothesis could be that the police tend to see juveniles as potential offenders; as problems for the criminal justice system. They are, therefore, less sympathetic towards them than they are to adult victims of assault.

A handful of those interviewed were initially questioned by the police in hospital. Although they all felt the police were sympathetic in themselves, the majority pointed out that they were feeling unwell at the time the statement was taken. One boy who had been wounded in the head said 'the police came to interview me in casualty an hour after the offence. They did half the interview and then I had to go to be stitched. They did the other half when I felt a bit groggy.' In another case of assault the police called an ambulance and, while waiting for it to come, asked the boy if he would make a statement. He said 'I was shocked at this suggestion and in the end they let me go to the police station the next day with my mum.'

In well over half the instances of suspicious behaviour and indecent exposure, neither of which are recorded as crimes, children and their families also complained of police attitudes towards them. Several parents criticized the police for being 'abrupt' or 'offhand and disinterested [sic]', whilst one mother commented 'I felt that they should have talked to the children and I was annoyed they didn't take down any details'. In these cases, as in those of physical assault discussed above, the fact that the police did not seem to take the children seriously as victims was a major source of complaint.

Above all child victims wanted their accusations to be believed. In fact, the majority of children involved in offences of violence—sexual abuse or assault or physical assault—said that they felt that the police did not believe their account. This was particularly likely in cases of sexual assault where there were no external signs and the child was the only witness. To give some examples: in a case of sexual assault, that of an 11-year-old boy who was assaulted by a baby-sitter, two male CID officers took the mother and her son round to the police station. The son was interviewed, in the presence of his mother, for six hours by a WPC in 'a small, stinky, smelly room'. During this time two CID officers came in; 'they said that they did not think P was telling the truth and that he could have no food or drink until he did so'. The mother said 'my son went through hell'. One teenage girl who was assaulted when baby-sitting said the policewoman 'asked me if I had led him on. I said it was out of the question as he's a grown man with three kids.' In another case of a teenage girl who had been abused by her father over a long period, the mother reported the WPC as saying that she was going over the statement carefully 'to see if S was telling the truth'.

Interviews lasting between four or five hours were felt to be too tiring for the children involved. One teenage girl said 'although they made me feel better, they asked me the same questions again and again'. Another commented: 'The hardest thing was having to tell all the intimate details, which I had to repeat over and over again.' In four cases further interviews were held. The mother of a teenager girl who had been sexually assaulted by a neighbour, and who had been interviewed at length by a WPC and a social worker and then by a CID officer the following day, said 'we felt very shell-shocked and in a way we felt we had been taken over. T wished she'd never said anything about it to anyone.' Indeed, all those children who were interviewed on more than one occasion felt that the police had returned to ask the same questions again to see if they were telling the truth and this caused distress. No other explanation was offered by the police themselves.

Where children who were victims of sexual abuse or assault were required by the police to undergo a medical examination for forensic purposes, this could also be a traumatic experience. The mother of a teenage girl described the medical examination as 'one of the worst parts of the whole incident'. Her daughter had been examined in 'a surgery that was cold and bare . . . B was very upset because she had not started her periods yet. The doctor said in front of her that her hymen was broken but that he could not say whether she had had intercourse.' When the researchers interviewed the family of an

8-year-old boy who had been sexually assaulted, the child himself clearly remembered the medical examination with fear. His mother said 'the doctor asked him what had happened. Only his anus was examined and this caused him considerable pain.' The examination had taken place at night, they had not returned home until 1 a.m., and the boy and his brother could not sleep. The trauma for two siblings who were medically examined on the same occasion was graphically described by their mother: 'I stayed outside but heard A screaming, so I rushed in. It was awful. I asked the doctor to stop taking swabs as A was so upset. H cried a little when he was examined. They were both very hyped up after this.' Whether there was anything that could have been done to lessen the stress of these examinations it is difficult to know.

As Shapland *et al.* have pointed out in relation to adult victims of sexual assault, most find medical examination 'unpleasant and humiliating, but necessary if the victim wanted the case to proceed'.[5] It may well be that children require even more careful explanation by the police of the reasons for medical investigation in order to understand why they are being subjected to what may, if unexplained, seem to them to be an unwarranted further ordeal. It is also worth noting that the reactions of adult victims to medical examination have been found to depend largely on the attitude of the doctor carrying it out. The need for a friendly and supportive approach to medical examination and treatment must be all the greater in relation to children.

In the majority of cases of sexual abuse or assault or physical assault, further distress was caused by the police. When explaining to the victim that the case could go to court and that they might have to appear as a witness, they implied that the victim would have difficulty in convincing the court if the offender denied it. The mother of a girl who had been badly injured after being pushed to the ground and kicked and punched by another girl complained 'the police try to put you off. They said "do you know you will have to go to court?" When I said I was willing, they said "But will your daughter be willing to go?" ' In another case, of a teenage girl sexually assaulted by a family friend, her mother said 'The police seemed to believe T but said that if the family wanted to withdraw the accusations then the police would go no further.' In yet another case, the victim, a teenager who had been sexually assaulted, was told by the police 'We believe you but it is

---

[5] Shapland *et al.*, *Victims in the Criminal Justice System*, 103.

just your word against his so it won't be a very good case.' In another case of a teenage girl who had been sexually assaulted by an employee of her parents the WPC said that they could press charges but 'the way the law stood if an adult denied it he could get away with it and they [the police] couldn't get him'.

In a number of cases, the children decided there and then that they did not wish to appear in court as a witness. One teenager who had been sexually assaulted by a boy she knew said 'I panicked. I did not really want to have to repeat what K had said to me in front of other people and decided I didn't want to appear in court.' In another similar case, when her daughter was asked whether she would testify in court if needed, the mother said 'Forget it. He can go free. The details are too harrowing and intimate.' In five cases of sexual abuse or sexual assault where the police failed to elicit an admission from the accused, the police decided to discontinue the case. All this contributed to children feeling distressed in that, even if the police believed them, no one else would and for that reason nothing could be done about the offence.

Child victims and their families experienced particular anger and distress in those cases where the police seemed reluctant to do anything about the victim's complaint. In the case of a teenage boy who had been seriously assaulted by another boy—the culmination of a long spate of bullying—the father said 'the police came to the school, but were not going to do anything, as there were no marks. The next day I phoned the police as there were visible bruises. I felt frustrated as they did not take it seriously.' The general impression of parents whose teenage children had been physically assaulted was summed up by the father of another victim, who said 'the police seem to think that where there are youngsters involved, it doesn't matter because they've asked for it'.

Distress at the thought that the police were not going to do anything about the complaint was not confined to victims of assault. Over three-quarters of the 65 children who were victims of theft reported that the police were far from positive in their response. A girl who had had her jacket stolen said 'They said they could not get it back.' Children who had their cycles stolen made comments like: 'They didn't seem very hopeful'; 'I was disappointed, but understand that the police have more important thing to do than look for stolen cycles'; 'They said there was no chance of finding it'; 'They were not very interested and said there was no hope of recovery'. Adults tend to trivialize offences such as theft. However, these are often children's first experiences of victimization. If children are not taken seriously on the first occasion that they report an offence to the police, their attitude to the police may be permanently affected.

Thus, although nearly two-thirds of children and their parents were satisfied with the way in which the police responded to them initially, over a third found the experience stressful and were critical of police procedures. There is a need for a much more sympathetic initial response by the police to all children who are victims of crime. It may be concluded that police procedures involving child victims need to be modified to suit children, not, as at present, operated essentially for the convenience of the police themselves.

Longer-Term Contact between the Police and Child Victims

Once a victim has reported an offence to the police and provided them with basic information concerning the crime, the police are responsible for determining subsequent action, pursuing the investigation, and preparing the case. The decision to prosecute a case is now taken by the Crown Prosecution Service. However, if the police decide, for whatever reason, not to proceed or to caution the offender, then the case will go no further. The police have been advised by the Home Office that 'victims welcome information about progress in the enquiries made into the offence against them, and in any resulting prosecution'.[6] But research has shown that keeping victims informed about the case and its outcome is not a priority for the police. Moreover, since the introduction of the CPS, they often do not have access to information about prosecution decisions and court dates, which further impedes communication.

Perhaps not surprisingly, the majority of children and families in the study sample expected the police to keep them informed about the developments in their case and its outcome. In the case of victims of burglary or theft, they all appreciated that it would be difficult for the police to find the offenders. But even if the offender was not caught the majority wanted to know the outcome of the police enquiries. This was very important to them. Research on adult victims has shown that satisfaction with the police declined markedly as a case progressed

[6] Home Office Circular 20/88.

because information about progress and outcome was not generally provided.[7] Similarly, this study found that well over three-quarters of child victims and their families were not satisfied with the way in which the police handled their cases in the longer term. Significantly, these levels of dissatisfaction were markedly higher than those revealed by the 1988 British Crime Survey, where just over a half of adult victims felt that not enough was being done to keep them informed about the progress of the investigation.[8]

Only a handful of victims had been told about the distinction between the role of the police and the Crown Prosecution Service and therefore were unaware that the police may no longer have access to information about the prosecution decision and case outcome. At the time of our interviews, which took place at least a month after each offence and in most cases six months after it, the majority (three-quarters) had received no further information nor had any further contact with the police. In all the cases of sexual abuse or assault, the police had been diligent in keeping victims and their families informed about the progress of their cases. But victims of other crimes had experienced difficulties in obtaining such details. In the small number of cases where the police contacted the victims it was to obtain more information, to warn them that they would be needed as a witness in court, or to tell them the outcome of the case. The way in which this was done frequently caused stress. For example, in a number of cases of assault the only further contact the victims had with the police was when the police asked them to drop the charges against the offender, presumably because they felt they did not have enough evidence.

When child victims were required to appear in court as witnesses, they usually heard nothing from the police until they received a letter addressed to the child personally informing of the date on which he or she was required to attend. In all cases where children received such letters the lack of any explanation of court procedures or information about giving testimony caused added worry for both children and parents. Yet even in the only case where the police actually informed the victim personally about the court hearing date, much distress was still caused. The mother of a teenager who had been assaulted said

---

[7] See Newburn and Merry, *Keeping in Touch*; Mayhew *et al.*, *The 1988 British Crime Survey*; D. Crisp, *The Police and the Public*, Home Office Research and Statistical Department Bulletin, No. 29 (London, 1990).

[8] Mayhew *et al.*, *The 1988 British Crime Survey*.

After the initial report I heard nothing until two uniformed officers came to the house at 8 a.m. on Saturday morning before we were up. They said D was expected at court the following Wednesday. No one explained anything at all about the court. My son was very worried about the prospect of going to court and reluctant to go.

When victims were informed of the outcome of the case, it was usually by a letter which contained bare details of the sentence but no further explanation. One mother said 'We very much wanted to be more involved. We got the letter to say that M.B. had been cautioned. We never got to see this happen. We wanted to see justice done and feel he's just walked away with it. The police should have come back to tell us why it didn't go to court.' The mother of a boy who had been assaulted by some classmates at school was angry when she heard they had been cautioned. She said 'I would have liked to have seen it go to court as it was a vicious attack and they could do it to someone else.'[9] Thus, although the police did communicate with these children and their parents, the way in which they did so was liable to cause more distress.

The majority of child victims and their families received no further communication from the police. Victims of physical assault and their parents were particularly angry and frustrated where they did not feel the police were doing anything about the offence, or where they seemed to be failing to do anything to catch or prosecute the offenders. In the case of an apparently racial assault by a half-Chinese teenager on an Asian boy, the first contact the latter had with the police after the initial report was some months later, when he was told that the police understood that he did not want to prefer charges. He denied saying this and felt bitter. His father alleged that the police in Luton believed that Asians have a reputation for sorting things out for themselves. He said 'When I think that the police did not do anything I go mad, particularly as the boy was seen in school with a knife the day after he attacked A.' He felt that if his son had been the offender 'the police would certainly have taken him away. The only protection we have is from our families.' Such instances illustrate the danger of the police

---

[9] The police have been advised, regarding the use of the caution, that the interests of the aggrieved party are a most important factor in deciding between prosecution and caution. But they did not consult child victims or their parents on this matter. For a fuller discussion of the procedures being adopted see C. Wilkinson and R. Evans, 'Police Cautioning of Juveniles: The Impact of Home Office Circular 14/1985', *Criminal Law Review* (1990), 165–76.

assuming that ethnic minority groups will always be responsible for distributing their own forms of justice.

In another instance, the parents of a teenage boy said that after taking the statement the policeman did not come back to see them even though he had promised he would. They felt bitter and said that they felt that 'the police are not responsive to crime in this community'. The father of another teenager who had been assaulted said

we have heard nothing from the police. We would like to know if it's going to court. I felt if it had been me that had been hit on the head they'd have taken me seriously. They didn't with X because he was a kid. If I'd got the service from a shop that we got from the police I'd have taken my business elsewhere, but we've only got the police to go to.

The mother of a teenage girl who was badly beaten up by some other girls was distressed that she had had so little information from the police. She would have liked to have been kept informed about the case and to have gone to court to hear the plea. She still did not know what this had been when we interviewed the family. She was most dissatisfied about the sentence, which she had read about in the newspaper. She believed that a conditional discharge was 'a let-off' and wished someone had explained what sort of sentence this was. Another parent, who read about their case in the local paper, said 'we were reasonably happy with the outcome, but we still don't know what the offender was charged with or whether he went to Crown Court or magistrates court'. In another case of one boy who had been badly beaten up by another, the parents learnt that the offender had admitted the offence but then heard nothing more from the police. They assumed that the offender had been cautioned; they felt that justice had not been done and said that they were sorely tempted 'to take matters into our own hands and punish him ourselves'. Indeed, in a considerable number of cases which involved children who had been assaulted and where the parents had heard nothing from the police, they concluded that the police had done nothing. It is perhaps not surprising that they were tempted to take the law into their own hands.

In a handful of cases where the police failed to provide information, the onus fell on the victims and their families themselves. In several cases, including all the physical assaults, the parents contacted the police to ask about the progress of the case but all of them found it difficult to obtain information. In a few, where the parents feared the police were taking no action, they became so concerned that they actively involved themselves in finding out information about the offenders to enable the police to pursue the investigation. In one case, the parents placed an advertisement with a £75 reward for information about the offenders in the local paper. The mother said 'We gave the police the information obtained from this and since then they have been very good about keeping us informed.' When she heard nothing more from the police, another mother said 'I felt powerless to do anything to protect my daughter.' She even went so far as to obtain the offender's address from the electoral roll and wondered whether she should go round to the offender's house to reprimand her. She eventually sought advice from her solicitor. In another case a father obtained information about the offender from someone with contacts in the 'criminal fraternity'. The reasons why these parents were prompted to seek information themselves were summed up by a mother whose teenage daughter had been badly hurt in an assault: 'The police gave no impression of urgency. I wanted something done immediately to keep the offender away from L in the future. It is important to teach children to stand up for their rights and to promote justice at all costs.'

In a fifth of cases parents obtained information about their case from other sources such as Victim Support, the local newspapers, friends, the offender's probation officer, the offender, work colleagues, or the court itself. In a handful of cases, Victim Support provided information for victims about the progress of the case, about court dates, and eventually the result of the court hearing. Children and parents found this very helpful. However, when information was forthcoming from other sources, this could cause distress. One teenager who had been assaulted received information about the outcome of the case when confronted with his attacker who said 'I have had the last laugh on you. I was taken to the police station and given a caution and let off.' This was the first the victim or his family had heard since they reported the offence.

It is clear, therefore, that both child victims and their families expected the police to inform them about the progress and outcome of their cases. In the vast majority of cases this information was not forthcoming, and a considerable number of victims and their parents were caused added distress. The police themselves observed that victims had unrealistic expectations of their ability to provide these details and that they had had difficulty in obtaining information about prosecution themselves since the introduction of the CPS. However, in very few cases were victims informed that the police would not be providing them with any further information, nor was the difference between the role of the police and the CPS explained to them.

Provision of Information on Support Services

As noted in Chapter 4, the police are an important source of information about the services available to help victims, such as financial help in the form of compensation, either from the courts or from the Criminal Injuries Compensation Board, and Victim Support and other agencies that can provide assistance. Although the police have been advised by the Home Office to provide victims with information about compensation, the majority of the officers interviewed were very unsure about the eligibility of child victims. It is perhaps not surprising that only two of the children in the sample were told about the CICB by the police, although three others were told about it by friends and four by Victim Support. None of the children had received an award from the Criminal Injuries Compensation Scheme. This may have been because applications take a considerable time to be processed and most of our interviews took place within six months of the offence.

None of the children or their parents in the sample were informed about the possibility that the court might order them to be compensated by the offender. Although a number of parents of physical assault victims thought that the court did not have adequate information about the injuries suffered by their child. In fact, three children, all victims of physical assault, did receive court-ordered compensation, greatly to their surprise.[10] In each case they received a cheque through the post from the court with no explanation attached. One said 'I received £15 but I did not know where it came from'; another was 'pleased' to receive £25. In the third case the family were alarmed when they received '£50 damages' since they had not been aware that the case had gone to court. Subsequently, the offender had threatened

[10] Findings in a recent research study showed that compensation orders from the courts to adult victims tended to be made more often in cases in which there is material loss than in cases in which there is personal injury. T. Newburn, *The Use and Enforcement of Compensation Orders in Magistrates Courts*, Home Office Research Study, No. 102 (London, 1988).

'to get us again as he had paid his price'. None of the families where children had been indirectly affected by a physical or sexual assault on a parent had been told that their child might be eligible for a criminal injuries award if their shock or psychological disturbance could be shown to be directly attributable to the crime.

There are well-established Victim Support Schemes which can offer support services to child victims in Oxford and Bedfordshire. In each area, there was an agreed policy that the police should refer automatically all crimes involving children to Victim Support, though with a number of exceptions, in particular, cases of child abuse and sexual assault. In this latter instance, official policy in Oxford and Bedfordshire required the police to refer such children and their families to Social Services. The police referred 79 of the 212 cases in the study sample to Victim Support. These included all the 40 cases in the sample involving indirect child victims. This is not surprising as it reflects the way in which the sample was obtained from Victim Support records; but 39 of the remaining 172 cases involving direct child victims were referred to Victim Support. Thus, only a fifth of the direct child victims were referred to them. In addition, the police referred 10 children who had been sexually abused or assaulted to Social Services and one teenager, the victim of sexual assault, to Rape Crisis.

The majority of child victims and their families were unaware of the availability of compensation and support and were therefore heavily dependent upon the police to provide information about them. In 1989 the CICB attempted to heighten awareness about its policy of payment of compensation to victims of child abuse and also to speed up the handling of claims. It is to be hoped that this will alert more victims to their rights to compensation and encourage claims which may provide resources for future treatment or to alleviate the effects of crime in other ways.[11] Victim Support Schemes can provide valuable help to victims in their recovery from crime: a fuller discussion of their role is provided below. Suffice it to say here that their close links with the police and the criminal justice system make them admirably suited to help and support victims in the aftermath of crime. At present police policies and practices tend to hinder child victims' access to such assistance. The police, therefore, need to be made more

---

[11] R. White, 'Child Abuse and Compensation', *New Law Journal*, 139(6437) (22 Dec. 1989), 1758–9.

fully aware of the availability of these services for child victims, and of the importance of providing information about them.

Conclusion

Within the criminal justice system, children are dependent upon others taking their victimization seriously, defining the precipitating act as criminal, and bringing it to the attention of the police. When children entered the criminal justice system most were satisfied with the way in which the police responded initially. However, even at the outset a significant minority were dissatisfied with the way in which they were treated by the police. All were children who were victims of physical or sexual assault. In the longer term levels of satisfaction declined markedly. The majority of child victims and their families were not kept informed about the progress of their case or its outcome, nor were they provided with information about compensation and Victim Support or other support services for child victims. Thus, the child victims and their families in the study sample found their contact with the police far from satisfactory. Indeed, the majority found the overall experience added to their stress.

Once children enter the criminal justice system the only policies which exist specially for them pertain only to abused children. The police themselves were generally very sensitive in their approach in cases involving allegations of child abuse. However, policies on the interviewing of children and their medical examination caused considerable stress in a number of cases. These could be improved. Although a specialist response has been developed in respect of children involved in allegations of child abuse, no such response has been worked out for children who are victims of other crimes. There is no special treatment for other child victims and the general approach of the police to these children and their families caused added distress in the many instances, particularly in their failure to provide information about progress in the case. The greatest problems were experienced in relation to the provision of information in the latter stages of the case and about the outcome. Yet very few victims or their parents made enquiries for themselves. A final source of concern is that the police are ill informed about the availability of compensation and Victim Support for child victims, and it is clearly an area in which the police should receive more systematic training in order to ensure that child victims are not denied what help is rightfully theirs.

There is a need to implement fully existing policies for abused children and to adapt this approach for children who are victims of all crime. Given that considerable stress was caused to victims by the lack of information about the progress of their case, police policy-makers should follow up the suggestion offered by Newburn and Merry:

To institute a reliable system by which victims could be reasonably assured of up-to-date information.[12]

Such a measure would meet the needs of child victims and their families without imposing burdens that would act to the detriment of the investigative process.

[12] See Newburn and Merry, *Keeping in Touch*, 5–7, for discussion of when and why people report crimes to the police.

6

The Child Victim, The Prosecution Process, and the Court

Interest in the impact of criminal proceedings upon child victims has focused almost entirely on the prosecution of cases of child sexual abuse and, in particular, on the traumatic effects of court appearance for child witnesses.[1] There has been considerable debate amongst professionals about the desirability of prosecution in cases where a child is abused by a member of their family.[2] In such cases, the overriding factor to be considered is that the child's best interests are served. Without stringent safeguards prosecution may risk further victimizing the abused child. The Criminal Law Revision Committee (1984) took the view that the intervention of the criminal justice system should be limited as far as possible in cases of abuse within the family.[3] By implication, it suggested that all but the most serious cases should be dealt with by a caution alone, so that rehabilitative work with the family could begin as rapidly as possible. The policy document *Working Together* emphasizes that 'There are competing public interests in the handling of criminal offences and child protection. It may be possible for a case to be handled so that the interests of the child prevail over the public interest in dealing with an abuser and the

---

[1] G. S. Goodman and D. P. H. Jones, 'The Emotional Effects of Criminal Court Testimony on Child Sexual Assault Victims: A Preliminary Report', in G. Davies and J. Drinkwater (eds.), *The Child Witness: Do the Courts Abuse Children?* (Leicester, 1988); D. Glaser and J. R. Spencer, 'Sentencing, Children's Evidence and Children's Trauma', *Criminal Law Review* (1990), 371–82; J. R. Spencer and R. H. Flin, *The Evidence of Children: The Law and the Psychology* (London, 1990), ch. 12; S. Lloyd-Bostock, *Law in Practice* (London, 1988), 84 ff.

[2] L. Blom-Cooper, 'Criminal Law that Leaves Children at Risk', *Independent*, 7 Aug. 1989; J. Temkin, 'Child Sexual Abuse and Criminal Justice: 1', *New Law Journal*, 140(6447) (16 Mar. 1990), 352–5.

[3] Criminal Law Revision Committe, *Fifteenth Report: Sexual Offences*, (London, 1984). Cmnd. 9213.

prosecution not proceeded with.'[4] Civil child protection proceedings (which require a lower standard of proof than criminal proceedings) may be instituted in the juvenile court to protect the child. Indeed, a welfare approach, emphasizing understanding rather than blame, has been seen by many as a more productive and humane response to the problem of child abuse.

At the same time, powerful arguments in favour of prosecution have also been voiced.[5] These arguments are well articulated by Adler:

First, it validates their experience by making it clear that the perpetrator's behaviour is unacceptable . . . Secondly, successful prosecution can help relieve the guilt which many children suffer as a result of acts for which they are not responsible, and in which they were only involved because of their vulnerability. Finally, it may help to break the cycle of abuse whereby abused children have a significantly higher likelihood than others of becoming abusing parents.[6]

One of the most important factors in restoring the abused child's subsequent mental health is to compel the abuser to assume responsibility for what he has done. This can most effectively be achieved by publicly endorsing the truth of the child's account, by emphasizing that the child is not in any sense culpable, and by squarely placing the burden of guilt on the offender. More generally, it is increasingly accepted that the jurisdiction of the criminal law should not stop at the door of the family home. Temkin has argued that 'increased awareness of the extent of violence in the home has resulted in the acceptance in many quarters of the need for greater rather than less intervention in the family domain'.[7]

If the need for prosecution in a child abuse case is accepted, it is always fraught with difficulties. In most cases of child sexual abuse there is little evidence for what happened apart from the word of the victim or of other child witnesses. When such a case comes to light the majority of the alleged abusers deny the abuse. In the face of denial by the offender, the probability of a successful prosecution diminishes

---

[4] DHSS and Welsh Office, *Working Together: A Guide to the Arrangements for Inter-agency Co-operation for the Protection of Children from Abuse* (London, 1988), 35.

[5] For an overview of these see Temkin, 'Child Sexual Abuse and Criminal Justice: 1'.

[6] Adler, 'Prosecuting Child Sexual Abuse: A Challenge to the Status Quo', in Maguire and Pointing (eds.), *Victims of Crime: A New Deal?*, 140.

[7] 'Child Sexual Abuse and Criminal Justice: 1', 352; see also Smith, *Domestic Violence: An Overview of the Literature*.

significantly. For the most part, therefore, only those who admit the offence are prosecuted. Most cases result in civil child protection procedures in the juvenile court or High Court.

A major reason that so few offences involving child sexual abuse result in prosecution is that the court system places barriers in the way of successful prosecution of such cases. Doubts about the reliability of child witnesses led to restrictions being placed on their eligibility to testify in court. Even when children were able to give evidence, child witnesses were not treated differently from adults during cross-examination and, as a result, defence counsel could easily undermine their testimony. Criminal lawyers have pointed out that prosecution procedures and rules of evidence in the criminal court not only fail to recognize the vulnerability of children or to afford them adequate protection, they also inhibit the presentation of their case.[8] John Spencer has summed up the difficulties faced by children: First, there is anxiety caused by waiting, often for months, to hear how the defendant will ultimately plead and whether or not the child will have to give evidence. Secondly, if the case is contested and the child is called, the rules of evidence 'currently require the child to retell the story, live, on the day of the trial and the process is likely to be a painful one'.[9] The minutely detailed examination of their story may be extremely harrowing. Cross-examination will inevitably entail direct or indirect accusations that the child is telling lies. The child who cannot comprehend the requirement that their testimony be tested in this way may believe that 'the adult world . . . has now rejected their story and turned against them'.[10] This impression is liable to be exacerbated by the fact that many adults tend to consider that children's testimony is inherently unreliable and, accordingly, treat them as liars.[11] Indeed, even where children were able to give evidence, competency and corroboration requirements meant that it was virtually impossible to gain a conviction on their evidence alone. Finally, as John Spencer points out, 'the child may suffer deep distress when the outcome of the prosecution is that the abuser goes to prison'.[12] The abused child may already have been made to feel guilty

---

[8] Adler, 'Prosecuting Child Sexual Abuse', 143.
[9] Glaser and Spencer, 'Sentencing, Children's Evidence and Children's Trauma', 374.   [10] Ibid.
[11] Lloyd-Bostock, *Law in Practice*, 83; 'Prosecuting Child Abuse', *Prosecutors' Perspective*, 2(1) (Jan. 1988).
[12] Glaser and Spencer, 'Sentencing, Children's Evidence and Children's Trauma', 374.

for their part in the abuse and this feeling of guilt may be exacerbated if the offender is then imprisoned. Where the offender is a relative, the child may suffer even further remorse for having broken up their family and feel responsible for the distress of mother and siblings when the father is taken away.

A report on the way in which the courts treat victims, *The Victim in Court*,[13] emphasized the anxieties suffered by victims, not only about their appearance in court, but also during the period leading up to the trial. Lack of information about the progress of the case and any delay in bringing it to court may be causes of much apprehension, whether or not the victim is eventually required to appear as a witness. The report stressed the need to improve procedures and to modify court buildings to take account of the needs of victims. No mention was made in the report of the needs of child victims. However, two major inquiries in 1989 and 1990 were charged to look into how the courts treat abused children: the Advisory Group on Video Evidence and the Scottish Law Commission *Report on the Evidence of Children and Other Potentially Vulnerable Witnesses*.[14] The reports produced by these bodies have drawn attention to the particular needs of abused children and made a number of recommendations for how these may be met by the courts. In addition, psychological research has cast doubt on the belief that children are more highly suggestible and less able to differentiate fantasy from reality than adults.[15] As a result, attempts have been made to facilitate prosecution by changes in the law of evidence and, by the introduction of a number of innovative court procedures, to lessen the stress caused to child witnesses. The enactment of legislation has assisted this process. The Criminal Justice Act of 1988 abolished the requirement that the unsworn evidence of a young child be corroborated before it could be used to support a conviction and contains provisions for the setting up of a video link to make it easier for abused children to give evidence. The Criminal Justice Act of 1991 abolishes the presumption that children are incompetent witnesses; allows a video recording of an early investigative interview with a child victim or witness of a violent or sexual

---

[13] National Association of Victims Support Schemes, *The Victim in Court: Report of a Working Party* (London, 1988).

[14] Home Office, *Report of the Advisory Group on Video Evidence* (London, 1989); Scottish Law Commission, *Report on the Evidence of Children and Other Potentially Vulnerable Witnesses*, Scottish Law Commission Study, No. 125 (Edinburgh, 1990).

[15] G. S. Goodman (ed.), 'The Child Witness', *Journal of Social Issues*, 40(2) (1984), 1–194.

offence to be played to the jury as the child's main evidence; precludes the accused from cross-examining in person his alleged victim or a witness to the commission of the alleged offence; gives the DPP power to by-pass magistrates' courts commital proceedings in cases of sexual or violent offences involving a child witness/victim; and imposes a clear duty on the courts to avoid unnecessary delay.

These changes suggest that the government now accepts the findings of research carried out, mainly in the United States, that the experience of appearing in court is likely to be traumatic for children who are victims or bystander witnesses, whatever the crime.[16]

This chapter will examine the policies and practices relating to child victims in the prosecution and court process. Using the field-work areas as examples, it will explore how far the needs of child victims are taken into consideration in making the decision to prosecute, and how cases involving child witnesses of all crimes are dealt with in the lead-up to the trial. Finally, it will examine the procedures adopted at court.

The Child Victim and the Decision to Prosecute

Responsibility for prosecution now rests with the Crown Prosecution Service (CPS), which was established throughout England and Wales in 1986. After the police have investigated a crime and charged a suspect it is for the CPS to decide whether to prosecute and then to conduct the prosecution. Separating investigation and accusation on the one hand from an objective review of cases and the dispassionate presentation of evidence before a court on the other has been seen as an important way of improving the quality of justice.

The CPS remain dependent upon the police to put forward cases to be considered for prosecution. If the police decide not to proceed or to caution the offender, the case will not be reviewed by the CPS, however strong the evidence may be.

---

[16] R. Flin and R. Bull, 'Child Witnesses in Scottish Criminal Proceedings', in J. R. Spencer *et al.*, (eds.), *Children's Evidence in Legal Proceedings: An International Perspective* (Cambridge, 1990). This survey of 1,000 children cited as witnesses in Scotland found that the majority were bystanders; C. P. Malamquist, 'Children who Witness Parental Murder: Post Traumatic Aspects', *Journal of the American Academy of Child Psychiatry*, 25(3) (1986), 320–5. R. S. Pynoos and S. Eth, 'The Child Witness to Homicide', *Journal of Social Issues*, 40(2) (1984), 87–108.

An example of this is the police role in case conferences. Initiatives being taken in joint investigation of child abuse cases by police and social workers are now being extended (albeit informally and cautiously) into the area of decision-making about prosecution. Often the case conference may have information which is relevant to the prosecution. However, there is no formal avenue of communication between the social workers or the case conference and the CPS: they must rely on the police representative at the case conference to pass on relevant information. Although the police are supposed to act as intermediaries between the Social Services Department and the CPS, social workers sometimes felt that important information about the child had not reached appropriate prosecution personnel. Even when information is received by the CPS, they are not bound to take account of it.

In the Thames Valley, both the Oxfordshire and Berkshire policy statements on the investigation of child sexual abuse accept that joint planning requires 'joint decision-making' by the police and social workers. This means that the views of social workers are now being taken increasingly into account by the police in decisions affecting prosecution. At the case conference at which the CPS was not represented, it was common in both the field-work areas for the police and social workers to reach a view on whether it was in the interests of the child to send the case forward to the CPS for prosecution. However, the final decision was still always left to the police. In child abuse cases, the police have been advised by the Home Office:

When a case of child abuse has been investigated and it is established there is sufficient evidence to justify prosecution, the police should consider whether there is an acceptable alternative to prosecution in the interests of the child and family, such as a caution. In reaching this decision, the police will wish to take full account of the views of other agencies concerned with the case, in particular the social services department, on how a prosecution might affect the victim and others in the family.[17]

In practice, the police would not normally go against the recommendation of the case conference on prosecution. If the decision is made not to proceed or to caution the offender, then this is not reviewed by the CPS.

However, if the case conference decides that the case should go forward for prosecution, local prosecutors said that even if the police

[17] Home Office Circular 52/88, para. 25.

decision was taken in conjunction with social workers this would not affect the CPS's assessment of the case since their role is as an independent prosecuting body. In Bedfordshire, the CPS were apparently unaware, and when informed were unhappy to learn, that a child-centred approach was being used by case conferences to reach conclusive decisions about sending cases to the CPS for prosecution. One prosecutor summed up his misgivings in the following way:

It is difficult to proceed when running against the professional agencies. Any comments, if notified, will be taken into consideration on the public interest ground: such comments cannot override the sufficiency of evidence test. The case conference is child-centred and the decision to prosecute is offender-centred. The purpose of the police presence at the case conference is not to consult about the possibility of prosecution.

In deciding whether to prosecute, the police and CPS might consider care proceedings, in which a lower standard of proof is required. Bedfordshire prosecutors mentioned two cases. In one a care order was made and the child was returned home before the criminal case came to court. The views of social workers were rejected as the CPS decided that it was in the public interest to prosecute. The defendant pleaded guilty and was given a three-year conditional discharge. The CPS was satisfied with the result. In another case, involving physical assault, the CPS discontinued the prosecution in concurrence with the social workers' opinion that, since the defendant had admitted the offence, the 'situation was solved by a care order'. However, in certain areas of child abuse—particularly emotional abuse and non-organic failure to thrive—the police and CPS may defer to action by the Social Services because of often intractable problems of gaining evidence.

Cases received by the Crown Prosecution Service fall into two categories: those received pre-charge for advice and those received post-charge. Although the police retain the right to charge, in practice they will not proceed against CPS advice. The Crown Prosecutor now reviews the evidence and circumstances of each case and decides whether that case should go to court.

Cases involving child victims are assigned to lawyers in the CPS in the normal case allocation process. Staff are likely to cover different courts by rota, therefore a single case may be handled by several lawyers as it progresses. With minor exceptions there has been no specialization in staff. Indeed, the CPS wishes to avoid the development of specialisms in order to maintain the widest use of any prosecutor. The CPS offices in Thames Valley and Bedfordshire do not, therefore, provide specialist training for their staff in dealing with cases involving children. The *Code for Crown Prosecutors* contains only two brief references to child witnesses (although it contains two lengthy sections about juvenile defendants, with specific reference to their welfare).[18] The Crown Prosecutor's manuals on policy, practice, and procedure are confidential and it is therefore not possible to know what, if any, references they contain to child victims.

CPS policy requires that the decision to prosecute should only be made if there is a 'realistic prospect of conviction', (that is, that there is enough evidence to make a conviction more likely than an acquittal), and, if this test is passed, where the prosecution is in the public interest. Both these issues raise special concerns in cases involving child victims. The CPS must make decisions which would benefit from personal knowledge of the child and its circumstances. However, unlike the Procurator Fiscal in Scotland, the prosecutor never sees the child before court and must make judgements based solely on information contained in the police file. In both Thames Valley and Bedfordshire the police felt diffident about contacting the CPS. Verbal communication about witnesses was extremely rare. Thus, when a prosecutor assesses the 'realistic prospect of conviction' he has to do so without personal knowledge of the parties and has only the written materials in the file to assist his review.

CPS policy on how to interpret 'a realistic prospect of conviction' in cases involving child victims is the same as that for adults. They distinguish between children who were bystander witnesses and those who were themselves direct victims. In the latter situation, they would consider to what extent the evidence relied on the child's testimony alone, and to what extent there was other evidence. The child's value as a witness depends largely on his or her age and understanding. The prosecutor must consider if the child is of sufficient intelligence, emotionally capable of testifying, and willing to do so. In cases reliant on the testimony of a child witness, the value of the evidence, and thus 'a realistic prospect of conviction', may turn on the child's credibility.

Prosecutors are completely dependent on the police file, not only to provide information about the offence and the defendant, but

[18] Director of Public Prosecutions, *Code for Crown Prosecutors*, repr. in *Law Society Gazette*, 83(28) (23 July 1986), 2308–13.

also about the victim's capabilities as a witness, as well as any circumstances affecting the decision whether a prosecution is in the public interest. In cases of child sexual abuse, prosecutors rely heavily on the expertise of the specialist police officers who interview children alleging abuse to provide an indication of the child's credibility as a witness. As we saw in the previous chapter, child victims alleging other types of crime are unlikely to be seen by a member of any specialist unit. Although the police officer who interviews the child is supposed to include an assessment of the child's credibility as a witness in the case file, he or she often does not do so. The statement itself may not give the CPS any indication that the child was, for example, shy and might therefore be a difficult or unresponsive witness. Prosecutors varied about whether they would request further information from the police. One Branch Crown Prosecutor said that his office would only ask for the officer's assessment if it were 'reaching out', that is trying to get close to the 51 per cent line, and thus 'nudging the case over'. 'It is easier to find whether there is a realistic prospect of conviction if the injury speaks for itself and there is forensic evidence. This is likely to be the case where the child is too young to call. The evidential problems occur in sexual cases. A straight ABH does not have evidential issues.' Prosecutors also have to rely on the police to asses the parent's willingness for the child to testify (unless the parent is a defendant), and also to explain the implications of giving a statement because the parent may not realize that doing so means that the child could be called as a witness in court.

Prosecutors were unanimous in expressing confidence in the general truthfulness of children. They were, however, also unanimous in their reluctance to use child witnesses:

Children's recollections fade. You may have to try to bluff the defendant into plea bargaining, because you only call children as a last resort. You will accept less in order to avoid calling a child.

We would move heaven and earth to run a case without the child, but we will call the child, even if it is a case of sex abuse, if there is good medical evidence and half an admission.

Prosecutors observed that judges also provide an incentive for the children not to be produced as witnesses:

The judge will say he is giving the defendant credit for not making the child testify (though he may not really do so), as an undisputed guilty plea is supposed to be worth from one-quarter to one-third off the sentence.

Historically, in deciding whether to proceed with a case, the CPS had not only to consider what sort of impression the witness was likely to make but, where child witnesses were involved, whether the child was likely to be able to give sworn evidence.[19] Children called as witnesses in criminal cases either gave their evidence on oath or gave it unsworn: 'Although the criterion for whether a child should be sworn or unsworn is whether the child understands the importance of telling the truth in court, those under ten tend to be unsworn, and those over ten sworn.'[20] This theoretical distinction may have derived from the fact that a child under 10 cannot make a 'Criminal Justice Act Statement', that is, he or she cannot be prosecuted for not telling the truth. The prosecutors and barristers interviewed stated that they had known children sworn between the ages of 8 and 12: it depended upon the capacity of the individual child. There was no general guidance on how to test the suitability of the child to take the oath, or what questions to ask, though such questions generally focused on whether the child understood what it meant to tell the truth and recognized the gravity of the proceedings.

When a judge was determining whether a child understood the nature of the oath or was to give unsworn evidence, it was necessary for the child to be questioned not only in the presence but also in the hearing of the jury. Most prosecutors found fault with the oath-taking process: 'the goal is that children should give evidence without distress. The present situation with the oath is very unsatisfactory.'

If it was found that a child was too young or too immature to be sworn, it was still possible for him or her to give unsworn evidence. But this had to be corroborated by a witness under oath. In cases of sexual abuse or sexual assault the lack of corroboration meant that many cases were dropped even though it was felt that the child would have provided good testimony. However, research on child memory showed that fears about the reliability of child witnesses (relating to poor recall, suggestibility, and difficulties of distinguishing fantasy and reality) had been greatly exaggerated. A Home Office paper reviewing psychological studies in this area concluded that children should not be barred from testifying merely on the basis of age.[21] In the light of these findings, section 34 of the Criminal Justice Act 1988

[19] *Code for Crown Prosecutors*, para. 5(iv) and (x).

[20] C. J. Emmins and G. Scanlan, *Blackstone's Guide to the Criminal Justice Act 1988* (London, 1988), 80.

[21] C. Hedderman, *Children's Evidence: The Need for Corroboration*, Home Office Research and Planning Unit Paper, No. 41 (London, 1987).

abolished the strict corroboration requirement in so far as this was based on the minority of the child. However, judges still had the discretion to decide whether a child was competent to distinguish between truth and fiction, and continued to warn the jury of the dangers of convicting a person on the basis of uncorroborated evidence alone. If the case involved a sexual offence, the prosecutor would always look for corroboration.

Whilst welcoming this change, academic lawyers such as John Spencer pointed out the problems involved in retaining the competency requirement (under which children can only testify if they are of sufficient intelligence and understand the duty of speaking the truth).[22] Whereas young children may have difficulties in showing that they understand an abstract concept such as 'truth', they may, none the less, be able to give very useful information to the court.[23] The Criminal Justice Act, 1991 no longer assumes the child to be incompetent. However, in leaving judges with the power to 'stand down' a child witness on the same grounds as adults (lack of knowledge or intelligence necessary to understand the nature of the oath), the Act still allows them to pre-examine children, so effectively retaining the competency requirement.

After the 'reasonable prospect of conviction' test has been satisfied, the Crown Prosecution Service makes a further independent assessment of the public interest. That is, it has to decide whether the prosecution of an apparently guilty person is worth pursuing. Although factors leading to a decision not to prosecute vary from case to case, broadly speaking the graver the offence the less likely it is that the public interest will allow a disposal less than prosecution.[24] The *Code for Crown Prosecutors* states that sexual assaults upon children 'should be regarded seriously . . . In such cases, where the Crown Prosecutor is satisfied as to the sufficiency of the evidence, there will seldom be any doubt that prosecution will be in the public interest.'[25] However, prosecutors interviewed in the field-work areas felt that the public interest decision was an extremely difficult one in cases involving

---

[22] J. R. Spencer, 'Reforming the Competency Requirement', *New Law Journal*, 138(6346) (4 Mar. 1988), 147–8; B. Naylor, 'Dealing with Child Sexual Assault: Recent Developments', *British Journal of Criminology*, 29(4) (Autumn 1989), 399.

[23] G. S. Goodman *et al.*, 'Child Sexual and Physical Abuse: Children's Testimony', in J. S. Ceci *et al.* (eds.), *Children's Eye-Witness Memory* (New York, 1987).

[24] *Code for Crown Prosecutors*, para. 8.

[25] Ibid., para. 8(vi)(*b*).

child victims, since they must weigh the public interest against the possibility of causing even more harm to the child.

All the prosecutors agreed that, even though they may try to minimize the trauma to the child, heightened public interest in child sexual abuse has shifted the balance in the public interest decision even further towards prosecution. 'Greater public policy awareness outweighs the child's interest. Such awareness makes a difference to a jury, which is then less likely to chuck out a case. A prosecutor can use this public interest element in assessing the "realistic prospect" test.' Although they also said that they attached considerable weight to serving the best interests of the child, they all claimed to have access to very little information about the child's circumstances on which to make the public interest decision. One prosecutor said there were no guiding principles:

We would be happy to get comments about the effect of splitting up the family, the child's feelings of guilt, and the prevention of further offences— all of these must affect the public policy decision. But we have to rely on the police to provide information: we cannot solicit a psychiatric report about the child—there must be no compulsion of the witness.

Occasionally, information about the family is provided by the defence solicitor, but there is no obligation on the Crown Court to seek medical advice about the effect on a child of having to testify. Research conducted by the Vera Institute of Justice, New York, suggests that the information that is generally available to the CPS to make the public interest assessment is in fact extremely limited. The Institute therefore recommended that this assessment should take place early in every case and that the CPS should develop new systems to identify, assemble, present, and assess social and contextual information on a routine basis.[26]

Part of the public interest test is that the case must not be stale, whether the victim is a child or an adult. The CPS should be 'slow to prosecute' if the last offence was committed three or more years before the probable date of trial, unless, despite its staleness, an immediate custodial sentence was likely to be imposed.[27] Some prosecutors in the field-work areas noted that this provision is particularly relevant to late disclosures of child sexual abuse. For example, in one case a girl

[26] C. Stone, 'Public Interest Case Assessment and Diversion from Prosecution', Vera Institute, New York, 1987.
[27] *Code for Crown Prosecutors*, para. 8(ii).

alleged abuse by her grandfather and stepfather over a period of years. The grandfather made admissions, but there was no medical evidence. The case was over three years old, and the prosecutor thought that it was too stale to revive.

The Role of Counsel

The CPS may instruct counsel in certain cases which are complex or difficult in the magistrates court and will always do so when cases go to the Crown Court (CPS lawyers, whether barristers or solicitors, have no rights of audience in the higher courts). Although barristers do not usually specialize in particular types of case, a few barristers have built up considerable expertise in prosecuting rape and child abuse cases. One female barrister interviewed thought that the 'CPS would choose a woman first, but the most experienced women at the Bar cannot handle all the cases now sex crime is a real growth industry'. A Crown Court clerk felt that 'the consistent use of certain counsel can contribute to delays even if there is pressure to get a case on, because of the competing demands on popular barristers'.

Barristers often receive a brief or review it in detail only on the eve of court. However, in child abuse cases, counsel may be asked by the CPS to accept a case at an early stage. One barrister noted an increasing tendency of the CPS to send her papers for preliminary advice. Barristers also noted that in the child abuse cases they are asked more and more to appear at committal proceedings, and would try to ensure continuity by following a case through to trial, though this is not always possible.

If instructed sufficiently early, barristers may hold a conference with the police officer on the case and the CPS. It is often up to counsel to ask for a conference. There may be no one present who has seen the child and only one barrister mentioned asking for the social worker to be present where appropriate. Issues which may be discussed at conference include whether the child can be called as a witness; the availability of a video interview; the possible use of screens; and whether the child would understand the oath.

Barristers wish to avoid surprises at court. Accordingly, one noted that she would ask at the conference whether there was a possibility that the child's full story had not yet been obtained. She wanted to know whether there were likely to be any further disclosures. Only one barrister mentioned asking the officer in charge of the case if he or someone else would counsel the child about coming to court: 'for example, is someone explaining to the child that he will have to give testimony out loud—he may not understand this once his statement has been written down'.

A prosecuting barrister is not simply the agent of the CPS: he makes a further independent assessment of the decision to prosecute, and also controls how the case is presented. As one Branch Crown Prosecutor put it:

The man in the wig rules the roost. Even if the CPS is told about the child's requirements, and the case goes to the Crown Court, the barrister—even if instructed to the contrary—may not do as the CPS requests. For example, the barrister may decide that it is more important to let the jury see the fearful reaction of the child, than to make an application for screens. Over and above the evidence, emotional impact is important, and the Crown is at liberty to use this as much as the defence.

In assessing the strength of the case, barristers said that they not only look for corroboration and inconsistencies, but also take the public interest into consideration. One barrister said that if he was briefed after committal proceedings at which the child has appeared, and the case looked very difficult, he still felt that he owed it to the child to proceed: 'Child abuse cases are extraordinarily difficult—particularly challenging and frustrating. More cases of this type are lost than in comparison with other categories.'

Barristers emphasized that, unless they were very fortunate, they were usually faced with problems caused by lack of information about the child and had difficulties in obtaining it—'the child's context is lacking'. They also complained that they were not routinely informed about care or family proceedings: 'the child may have a motive to lie but if you are prosecuting you don't know'. Moreover, prosecuting counsel do not generally see any social work or psychiatric reports (considered useful in looking for further evidence) because these are considered to be beyond the ambit of the prosecutor.

In sum, although information discussed at the case conference may be relevant to the decision to prosecute, in practice there is no formal line of communication between Social Services and the CPS. The police make the ultimate decision whether to send the case forward to the CPS. If the police decide not to proceed, CPS do not review the case. When a case concerning a child victim is sent to the CPS, the decision to prosecute will usually be made by the CPS without any informed reference to the best interests of the child. The prosecutor has to make decisions—on the 'reasonable prospect of conviction' and the 'public interest'—which would benefit from personal knowledge of the child and the child's circumstances. He does not, however, see the child before the court, and has, therefore, to make these decisions solely on the basis of information contained in the police file. He may thus be denied basic information about the child essential for him to make an informed decision about the desirability of prosecution.

The Child Witness and the Court

As noted above, the stress which children who are victims of sexual abuse and violence may suffer when they are required to appear in court at witnesses has been pointed out by academic lawyers. It was highlighted in the *Report of the Advisory Group on Video Evidence* (the Pigot Report) and the Scottish Law Commission *Report on the Evidence of Children and Other Potentially Vulnerable Witnesses*.[28] As a result, a number of innovative procedures intended to alleviate stress in child witnesses to these crimes have been introduced. These have taken the form of the provision of support and preparation for the court appearance and modifications in court procedures before and during the trial.

Provision of Pre-trial Preparation and Support for Child Witnesses

It is now widely recognized among professionals that appropriate pre-trial preparation of the child witness can make a crucial difference to the child's ability to testify, as can the provision of support for the child before and during the trial itself. In the English and Welsh legal system, there is no single agency with special responsibility to provide support and preparation for child witnesses. However, in recent years, attempts have been made by a wide range of individuals and agencies to prepare children for the experience of giving evidence in ways which will not prejudice the rights of the defendant. Since very young children are now being called as witnesses, and are likely to be

---

[28] Home Office, *Report of the Advisory Group on Video Evidence*; Scottish Law Commission, *Report on the Evidence of Children and Other Potentially Vulnerable Witnesses*.

used more now that the competency requirement is abolished, issues of support and preparation are becoming increasingly important.[29]

There are now a number of aids available to prepare a child for a court appearance. A range of materials provide detailed information for children and their parents, for carers, and also for professionals providing help and support. The leaflet, *The Child Witness*,[30] provides information for persons dealing with child witnesses, and a video has been produced on court procedures for the training of social workers and health visitors involved in children's cases. No equivalent video has yet been produced for the children themselves in Britain, although a number of orientation videos for children do exist in the United States. Publications such as *Susie and the Wise Hedgehog*, *Being a Witness*, and *Going to Court* are available for child witnesses themselves.[31]

Admirable though these written materials and videoes are, they are not adequate in themselves as a means of explaining court procedures to children. In addition, child witnesses need individual preparation. In Scotland the prosecution is responsible for preparation for court. The Scottish Law Commission *Report on the Evidence of Children and Other Potentially Vulnerable Witnesses* acknowledged the value of this and concluded that the use of new procedures and techniques such as videotaped testimony were unlikely to be required in more than a few child witness cases if children were adequately prepared for a court appearance. It stated 'In the majority of cases—and provided that there has been careful and sympathetic pre-trial preparation of the child—we anticipate that children will be able to give evidence at trial by conventional means'.[32] It affirmed that 'a very great deal' is already being done by Procurators Fiscal in Scotland to prepare child witnesses, and continued: 'We understand that the results are already

---

[29] In *R. v. B.* (*The Times*, 1 Mar. 1990) the Court of Appeal upheld the decision of an Old Bailey Judge to allow a 6-year-old girl to give uncorroborated unsworn evidence about incest which took place when she was 5. The Court of Appeal referred to Section 38(1) of the Children and Young Persons Act 1933, and declared that the question at issue was whether the child was sufficiently intelligent and understood the duty to tell the truth. The judge in each case has discretion to decide this as statute laid down no minimum age.

[30] J. Plotnikoff, *The Child Witness* produced by *Childright*, the Children's Legal Centre (London, 1989).

[31] *Going to Court*, produced by Crown Office and Procurator Fiscal Service (1989); *Going to Court*, produced by West Yorkshire Police (1989); *Susie and the Wise Hedgehog*, produced by Madge Bray (1989); *Being a Witness*, produced by *Childright*, the Children's Legal Centre (London, 1989).

[32] para. 1. 8. *j.*

being perceived as beneficial in that many children are thought to have been better able to cope with the experience of giving evidence than would otherwise have been the case.'[33] By contrast, there are no Practice Directions or agreed guide-lines for England and Wales indicating what would constitute appropriate preparation of a child for a court appearance. Neither the *Report of the Advisory Group on Video Evidence*[34] (the Pigot Report), which recommended the admissibility of videotaped testimony which would remove the child from the court room, nor the Criminal Justice Act 1991, which provides for the admissibility of a video recording of an early interview with the child, mention the preparation of the child witness for giving evidence.

The issue of how—and indeed whether—a child should be prepared for court is controversial. There is a fine balance to be struck between 'coaching' a child witness and 'warming the child up' for the court appearance. It is permissible to refresh the child's memory. But the testimony should not be rehearsed nor should the child witness discuss this with another witness in case it appears they have colluded. However, children, like adult witnesses, are entitled to refresh their recollection before court by reading, or having read to them, their own statements or viewing video interviews in which they took part. In each case, the preparation of the child for court should be discussed with the police and the CPS, so that the methods used are not open to challenge by the defence.

The question has arisen whether or not, once the child is ready to testify, he or she should have a 'support person' or chaperon. The only official statement on this is contained in the Crown Court Rules, which states that child witnesses under the age of 14 may have a support person with them in the witness room when the video link is in operation.[35] The presence of a support person for the child witness was endorsed, with reservations, by the Court of Appeal in *R.* v. *X, Y,* and *Z.*[36] This decision upheld the use of screens to prevent child witnesses seeing or being seen by defendants in the dock, on the basis of a social work report that some of the children were unlikely to be able to speak if required to confront the defendants in open court. Lord Lane, the Lord Chief Justice, also commented on the use of

---

[33] para. 2. 10.
[34] Home Office, *Report of the Advisory Group on Video Evidence* (London, 1989).
[35] *Crown Court Rules 1982*, Rule 23A, para. 10.
[36] *The Times*, 3 Nov. 1989.

social workers sitting alongside the child witnesses 'to comfort and console them when necessary'. He said

plainly, to have anyone sitting alongside a witness was a course of conduct that had to be undertaken with considerable care. When it happened, the court had to be astute to see that nothing improper passes and no undue encouragement was given to the child witness to make him or her say something other than the truth. There was no suggestion that the social workers had done anything other than what was proper when they were sitting alongside the witness.[37]

The Lord Chancellor, Lord Mackay, commended the use of court ushers for this purpose[38] but it is clearly preferable for the support person to be someone with whom the child is familiar. Indeed, the Scottish Law Commission *Report on the Evidence of Children and Other Potentially Vulnerable Witnesses* endorsed the presence of a support person to accompany child witnesses to court and said that it was preferable that this person be someone well known to the child.[39]

Modifications in Pre-Trial and Court Procedure

During the pre-trial period, the listing of the case can be altered to take account of the needs of the child. Indeed, *The Victim in Court* drew attention to the fact that: 'At present listings tend in practice to be negotiated to take account of the competing interests of counsel and others, while victims and other witnesses are left out of consideration.'[40] In February 1988, the Minister of State at the Home Office, John Patten, announced that new guidance would be sent to the police and the CPS to ensure 'speedy progress' for child abuse cases: 'the damage done by child abusers to their victims must not be added to by avoidable delay in bringing criminal proceedings'.[41] This injunction was confirmed in a Home Office Circular sent to chief

---

[37] The Scottish Law Commission *Report on the Evidence of Children and Other Potentially Vulnerable Witnesses* (Edinburgh, 1990) considered the issue of support at the trial in some detail. 'There seems to be little doubt that the presence, close at hand, of a parent or some other trusted adult can, in some cases, give a young child the reassurance that is required for evidence to be given clearly and confidently; and for that reason we consider this practice should be encouraged as much as possible' (para. 2. 12).

[38] Speaking at the conference on Children's Evidence in Legal Proceedings Cambridge June 1989.

[39] para. 2. 12.

[40] National Association of Victims Support Schemes, *The Victim in Court*, para. 2. 21.

[41] Home Office News Release, 18 Feb. 1988.

officers of police. It stated 'Chief Officers will wish to bear in mind the need to deal expeditiously with such cases in the interests of the child, and so help to minimise the time before the case comes to court. The Director of Public Prosecutions is issuing guidance to the Crown Prosecution Service.'[42]

If care proceedings are instituted, case law indicates that, in the child's interest, these should precede any criminal prosecution and should not be delayed at the defendant's request until the outcome of the criminal case. The police and CPS can help to expedite care proceedings by providing the local authority solicitors with the necessary evidence. However, where civil proceedings are instituted first the criminal case may be delayed yet again, possibly to the ultimate disadvantage of the child.

Until 1991, child victims could be required to appear at old-style committal proceedings (under s. 6 (i), Magistrates Court Act 1980) in a magistrates court to determine if there was sufficient evidence to justify committing the accused for trial at the Crown Court. These proceedings were known to be extremely stressful in that they were used to test out witnesses to see if they came up to proof. Section 103 of this Act provides that in any proceedings before a magistrates court inquiring into a sexual offence, a child shall not be called as a witness for the prosecution but that a written statement shall be heard instead. This rule is subject to the following exceptions: where the defence objects to the child's statement being tendered in evidence; where the prosecution requires the attendance of the child for the purpose of establishing the identity of the accused; where the court is satisfied that it has not been possible to obtain a statement from the child; or where the inquiry into the offence takes place after the court has discontinued summary trial and the child has given evidence in the summary trial. Section 53 of the Criminal Justice Act 1991 provides for certain cases which are destined for trial at the Crown Court and which involve children, as either victims or bystander witnesses, to be taken over by the Crown Court without delay, bypassing committal proceedings.

On the day of the court appearance itself, a number of special procedures and facilities which are intended to alleviate the stress caused to child witnesses have been advocated. It is widely agreed that the child witnesses should be able to wait away from the public areas

---

[42] Home Office Circular 52/88, para. 25.

of the court-house and, in particular, that they should not have to be confronted by the defendant. The importance of special waiting provisions cannot be overestimated: children are often required to attend court for many hours, possibly even over a period of days, before being called to give evidence. If a child has spent several hours in a cell-like room or has seen the defendant in the hall, then even the provision of the video link discussed below may come too late to help their state of mind.

One of the most curious features of the court system in England and Wales is surely the convention that the prosecutor should not speak to any witness before the trial begins. In practice a number of prosecutors are now introducing themselves to the child before the trial in order to try to create a rapport with the child concerned. However, they remain conscious of the need to exercise extreme care when speaking to witnesses prior to the trial.

A number of modified procedures are now in use in some court rooms when children give evidence. These operate at the judge's or magistrates' discretion, subject to objections from the defence. Judges and magistrates have the power to exclude the public from the court when a child testifies. The prosecution normally starts by asking for the name and address of the witness. In sensitive cases, such as those involving children, this information may be written down at the discretion of the judge. At Crown Court centres around the country some judges now take off their wigs and robes before a child witness comes into court. Sometimes barristers also remove their wigs and gowns. Seating arrangements may be changed so as to allow counsel to sit next to the child during questioning, to enable the judge to come off the bench, and the child to be removed from the witness box and placed near the jury or alongside the judge. In some cases a soft-spoken child may be allowed to use a microphone.

The most radical of the reform measures are those that attempt to shield the child victim from direct confrontation with the accused at court: the use of screens to prevent eye contact between the witness and the defendant; broadcasting the child's live testimony into the court room via closed-circuit television; and the videotaping of an early interview with the child.[43] The first of these techniques to be

---

[43] The 1985 US Department of Justice report, *When the Victim Is a Child* (D. Whitcomb *et al.*, Washington DC, 1985), discusses various *ad hoc* techniques to shield child victims from eye contact with defendants, but does not mention the use of screens. In 1988, the Supreme Court struck down an Iowa law permitting the placement of a

introduced was the use of screens. These were first used at the Old Bailey in 1987 and applications for their use subsequently increased dramatically.[44] No statutory authority exists for the use of screens, but none is needed, for the judge may rely upon his discretion to do what is necessary to ensure that the trial is fair to both prosecution and defence. A judge in a case heard in the Court of Appeal in 1989 endorsed the use of screens holding that 'the trial judge had a duty to see that justice was done which meant that he had to see that the system operated fairly not only to the defendant but also to the prosecution and also to the witnesses'.[45] Although the usefulness of screens has to some extent been overtaken by video technology, they remain a valuable alternative in magistrates courts where the video link is not in use and for children who do not wish to use the video link where it is available.

Under the Criminal Justice Act 1988 children under the age of 14 are permitted, with the leave of the court, to give evidence by live television video link in trials for sexual offences.[46] This means that the child is seated in a separate room, testifying in front of a video monitor in answer to questions from counsel in the court room, the child's testimony being relayed on a monitor in the court room.[47] The Criminal Justice Act 1991 raises the age limit for the video link in cases involving sexual offences from 14 to 17.

screen between the defendant and a child testifying about sexual assault (the only state with this provision). The court ruling said that the use of the screen violated the defendant's Sixth Amendment right to confront witnesses. It left open the possibility that use of screens, testimony by closed circuit television, or other methods aimed at minimizing trauma to the child victim of sexual abuse might be permitted on a case-by-case basis where specific witnesses were found to need special protection. *Coy* v. *Iowa* [1988] US Supreme Court.

[44] The principle of screening a witness is much older than this. In *R*. v. *Smellie* [1919], Crim. App. Reports, the Court of Appeal held that if there is a fear that a witness may be intimidated, the witness can give evidence out of sight. Prosecuting counsel therefore has to establish a fear on the part of the witness. Common law requires that the defendant must hear the evidence given.

[45] *R*. v. *X*, *Y*, and *Z*, Court of Appeal Criminal Division: The Lord Chief Justice, Hutchinson, and Rougier JJ: 31 Oct. 1989, quoted in *Criminal Law Review* (1990), 515–16.

[46] J. Spencer and P. G. Tucker, 'The Evidence of Absent Children', *New Law Journal*, 137(6320) (28 Aug. 1987), 816–17; J. Spencer, 'Child Witnesses and the Criminal Justice Bill', *New Law Journal*, 137, 6330 (6 Nov. 1987), 1031–3; E. Woodcraft, 'Child Sexual Abuse and the Law', *Feminist Review*, 28 (Spring 1988), 124–32.

[47] Of the 226 applications to use video links made between the passing of the Act in 1988 and July 1989, 207 were granted by the judge. A guilty plea followed in 67 cases making it unnecessary for the child to give evidence. *Guardian*, 14 July 1990.

The Pigot Committee on Video Evidence, which reported in December 1989, argued strongly that children should not be required to appear in court even if protected by screens or cross-examined by means of the video link.[48] It recommended that in cases of alleged sexual abuse, violence, or cruelty the court videotape their testimony at an out-of-court hearing with judge and lawyers for both sides, in advance. The initial interview would be carried out by a trained examiner following a Code of Practice intended to ensure fairness for the accused. Soon after the initial examination defence counsel would cross-examine the child before the trial judge. Both interviews would be videoed and at trial the tape of the first interview would replace the child's examination-in-chief and the second would replace cross-examination.[49]

The Criminal Justice Act 1991 accepts that a video recording of the first interview should be admissible as the child's evidence-in-chief in cases involving a sexual or violent offence.[50] The tape is not admissible automatically: it must be shown in advance to the judge, who has the power to refuse leave if he feels the interests of justice require it to be excluded. A code of practice for conducting interviews with child witnesses which will be videotaped and presented in evidence in criminal courts is being drawn up by the Home Office.[51] Where the tape was admitted, the court would know exactly what the child had said when the case first came to light. Thus, the child would not have to retell the story from scratch at the trial. In addition, there would be no need to delay the start of therapy for fear that at the trial the defence

---

[48] For a fuller analysis of the recommendations of Pigot see J. McEwan, 'In the Box or on the Box? The Pigot Report and Child Witnesses', *Criminal Law Review* (1990), 363–70; R. White, 'The Pigot Report', *New Law Journal*, 140(6445) (2 Feb. 1990), 300–1.

[49] On the videotaping of children's evidence see G. Williams, 'Videotaping Children's Evidence', *New Law Journal*, 137(6290), (30 Jan. 1987), 108–12; 'More about Videotaping Children', *New Law Journal*, 137(6300) (10 Apr. 1987), 351–2; 'More about Videotaping Children: 2', *New Law Journal*, 137(6301) (17 Apr. 1987), 369–70.

[50] J. Temkin, 'Child Sexual Abuse and Criminal Justice: 1', *New Law Journal*, 140(6447) (16 Mar. 1990), 352–5; 'Child Sexual Abuse: 2', *New Law Journal*, 140(6448) (23 Mar. 1990), 410–11.

[51] Contrary to the proposals of the Pigot Report, the Criminal Justice Act 1991 did not make provision for an official Code of Practice for conducting video interviews. This inevitably raised doubts about when and why a judge would be expected to exclude a tape. The Home Office is therefore planning to issue its own code of practice, which will refer to the conducting of interviews (e.g. techniques), the videotaping of the interviews (including what should be available on the monitor to observers of the video recording, and the location of such interviews), and the admonition given to the witness (i.e. what the child should be told about telling the truth).

will object that the therapist put the accusation into the child's head. However, the Criminal Justice Act 1991 did not include the Pigot Committee's second main proposal that a pre-recorded examination by the defence counsel should replace cross-examination in court. The government felt that, however informal such hearings could be made, the system risked facing the child with several taxing and perhaps confusing rounds of questioning and additional delays. The Act provides that the tape of the initial interview can only be admitted in evidence if the child later attends trial for live cross-examination in the court by video link. Although the Act, therefore, preserves what is arguably the most harrowing aspect of the trial, it does prohibit an unrepresented defendant in a child abuse case from cross-examining the child victim, or bystander witness, in person.

Innovative Procedures in Practice: Oxford and Bedfordshire

In England and Wales, pre-trial preparation of child witnesses and orientation, where provided, is most likely to be carried out by social workers or specialist police officers who may lack experience of court procedures. There is a great suspicion amongst the legal profession that if social workers were charged with helping child witnesses they would end up coaching the child to give evidence. Many barristers were, therefore, reluctant to give a child's statement to a social worker for the purpose of going over it with the child. It was thus not surprising that some of the social workers interviewed mentioned that they had experienced considerable difficulty in obtaining such statements, although very few had dealt with these issues or been sensitized through training to the problems involved.

One effective way of reducing the anxiety of a potential child witness is to take the child to the court prior to the date of the hearing. These visits would, of necessity, be to an empty court if the child was under the age of 14, as young children are not permitted to observe a court in session. Court clerks felt that such visits would help to put the child at ease, but very few such requests had ever been received at either magistrates courts or the Crown Court centres in the field-work areas.

The difficulties faced by those seeking to help prepare child witnesses are well illustrated by the following case which involved several boys who were scheduled to testify in a sexual assault trial involving a single defendant at Crown Court. One of the boys, aged 10, was in care, and a child psychiatrist advised the local authority solicitor that the boy was extremely anxious, and that consideration needed to be given to his emotional plight. The psychiatrist recommended that the residential social worker contact the CPS in order to get help concerning support for the boy in court. She did so, but felt that the prosecutor to whom she spoke was dismissive of the whole issue. He told her that the boy would be treated kindly in court, and that he had nothing to worry about if he told the truth. He added that the boy was too young to visit the court in advance, and anyway the least said the better until the day of the trial. The social worker was told that there would be people to help the boy in court, but that 'there are too many people holding his hand if you ask me'. The psychiatrist considered that the prosecutor's approach consititued 'secondary abuse of children'.

The majority of those Crown Prosecutors and barristers interviewed were in favour of the idea of a 'support person' who would accompany the child into the court, sit by his or her side during the hearing, explain the court verdict, and debrief the child afterwards. They considered it anomalous that a court would certainly not allow a juvenile defendant to appear without a suitable adult to provide support and protection. Naturally, to provide this for a witness would involve advance planning and would need the support person to understand the constraints of his or her role.

It is the prosecution's responsibility to apply to the court for permission for a support person to undertake these tasks, but there are no formal procedures whereby the CPS would receive information that such a person was necessary. The fact that the defence may object to the person chosen and that the judge has to give his approval means that in many cases the decision about who might be a suitable support person is left until the day of the hearing. At that time, it may be difficult to find someone to whom none of the parties objects.

Lack of co-ordinated planning can lead to the proposed person being rejected by the court at the last minute. As a result, the only one present who could act as a support person is often a parent or social worker who may be required as witnesses in the case. It was found that frequently they had not been advised that a witness who has not yet been called cannot accompany the child into court. Even after testifying, witnesses are likely to be considered unsatisfactory support persons for the child, as they may themselves be thought to have an emotional investment in the outcome of the trial. All the professional personnel concerned with the court who were consulted agreed that this was most unsatisfactory and that the support person should not be the parent but someone of obvious neutrality with whom the child is familiar. When support is provided in the court room, this role is often performed by a woman police constable or social worker; in the relatively few cases where Victim Support volunteers are involved they may also provide support in court for the child victim.

The only court in the field-work areas with some special provision was the Crown Court in St Albans where the Women's Royal Voluntary Service were on duty every day and were allowed by the judge to sit by child witnesses when they testified in court. One interesting case was observed in which two young girls aged 8 to 10 were required to give evidence of sexual assault against them. None of the court procedures had been modified and their mothers and the social worker were not allowed to sit with them as they too were required as witnesses. The WRVS volunteer sat by each girl in turn as she gave evidence. Both girls were in tears under cross-examination and clearly appreciated the comfort provided by the volunteer, who was also available to look after them during a long adjournment.

The importance of victims being told the outcome of their case and, where necessary, having this explained to them has been stressed in research studies and forcefully endorsed in *The Victim in Court*.[52] However, since there is no longer automatically a police presence at the magistrates courts, the police themselves often do not know the immediate outcome. The Oxford Police Prosecutions Department sends a very brief letter with court results to victims. Bedfordshire Police do not have a routine procedure for informing victims. No one is given responsibility for debriefing a child witness or explaining the outcome of the trial to them.

Innovations and modifications in court procedures were also examined in Oxford and Bedfordshire. The field-work was carried out before the implementation of the Criminal Justice Acts 1988 and 1991. This said, in the field-work areas innovative procedures were not available in all courts. Even where they were, they were applied in an arbitrary way or often not at all. With regard to listings, the Home Office directive requiring 'speedy progress' in child abuse cases has had widespread endorsement, but has proved difficult to implement. Cases were not earmarked for priority: no one in particular had

---

[52] National Association of Victims Support Schemes, *The Victim in Court*.

responsibility to speed things up. While acknowledging that cases involving child witnesses should be handled more quickly, the police and CPS in the field-work areas did not single out cases involving child witnesses for faster treatment. There were difficulties in placing trials with child witnesses on a 'fast track' at court not least because the listing officers in the magistrates courts were dependent on the police (and in the Crown Court on the CPS) to alert them to the fact that a child might be called as a witness. Even where it appeared likely, from the nature of the offence and the plea, that a child would probably be required to testify, listing officers said that they did not take the initiative in allocating an early court date to such a case. The prosecutors we interviewed conceded that it was up to them to try to move cases on more quickly, but all concurred that this was very hard to do.

A further complication is that certain cases (including rape, sexual intercourse, or incest with a girl under 13, and incitement, attempt, or conspiracy to commit any of these offences) have to be tried by a High Court judge.[53] This is obviously likely to contribute to further delay. At the Crown Court in Oxford and in St Albans (the Crown Court centre for the majority of cases in South Bedfordshire) a High Court judge sits three times a year for about two weeks at a time. In St Albans a case involving a child witness was put back from the list of one High Court judge until the next High Court judge's visit; in Oxford a trial involving a child witness was put back from February until the next visit of the High Court judge in July. The child was at court expecting to testify on the day in February when this occurred and was greatly distressed by news of the delay.

In selecting a court room in which a trial was to be held the child's interests were rarely paramount. In order to identify the most suitable (generally, the less formal) court in which to put a child witness, forward planning is needed. Yet this is often not possible. Even if arrangements are made to obtain the most suitable court, the child's interest will be overridden if it is believed that a secure dock is needed for the defendant, as these are not available in court rooms used for juvenile or domestic work. Court staff stressed that the choice of court room is often limited. It is desirable for the case in which the child is to testify to be put on early and for the child to be called as quickly as

---

[53] Unless released by the presiding judge for trial by a circuit judge who has been approved for the purpose by the Lord Chief Justice.

possible. Yet court officers and prosecutors did not routinely attempt to arrange this.

On the day of the trial itself, despite all the innovations suggested, in practice very few procedural changes or modifications had been implemented. Space in most courts is at a premium, and no court in the field-work areas had a room specifically set aside and equipped for child witnesses. Court staff expressed a willingness to improvise, but stressed the need for advance notice of special witness requirements.

Although judges and magistrates have the power to exclude the public from the court, this discretionary power is infrequently used. Magistrates, in particular, seem reluctant to make such an order. Indeed, in the field-work areas, there were few attempts to modify procedures in magistrates courts, although child witnesses were not always required to testify from the box. No examples were provided of magistrates coming off the bench. Magistrates seemed content to rely on the clerk's skills to make the child feel comfortable.

Screens were used in the field-work areas in a few cases at Crown Court involving children who were witnesses to sexual offences. They had also been used at some magistrates courts in old-style committal proceedings, but they did not appear to have been used for child witnesses in trials of other categories of offence or in trials at magistrates courts. In cases where screens were allowed, it was impossible to predict at the beginning of the legal process whether they would actually be available if the child had to give testimony.[54] Other difficulties resulted because the screens were not purpose-built and the CPS has no financial responsibility to provide them; because courts were not designed with screens in mind; or because the position in which screens were placed varied widely and screens are not equally effective in every type of court room. Responsibility lay with the CPS to make the application to the judge, but they did not always have the necessary information to know whether screens would be needed.

Although the use of screens has spread, there has been no official ruling about the circumstances of the cases in which they should be used. The extent to which these applications were made and granted by the judge varied from court to court and judges appeared to take into consideration two factors: the child's age and whether the

[54] As has been seen, in 1989 the Court of Appeal endorsed the use of screens. *R* v. *X, Y* and *Z* (*The Times*, 3 Nov. 1989). A judge has the duty to see the system by which screens are used operated fairly not only to the defendant, but to the witness.

defendant was known to the child.[55] This may not require a blood relationship. Thus, in Oxford a request for screens was granted for an 11-year-old boy who was the defendant's neighbour.

Child Victims' Experiences as Witnesses

Although the number of children in our study who were warned to appear as witnesses in court was small, the information which they provided was so interesting that it is worth describing their experiences in detail. Those children who actually appeared as witnesses in court were all teenagers who had been victims of physical assault. The stress suffered by all of them, not only during the trial but during the period leading up to it, was very evident. The mother of a teenager who had been attacked by a group of girls described her daughter's feelings after they received the letter informing them that their daughter had to go to court:

She was very worried by this, about seeing the attackers again and about having to stand up and say something. The offence had happened some time before, and she was beginning to forget it.

According to the mother:

No one explained who the people in court were, but the solicitor in charge of [prosecuting] the case chatted to us beforehand and told us what kind of questions he would be asking. My daughter was sworn in and went into the witness box. She could only be heard with difficulty, and was asked once or twice by the magistrates to speak up. She had been totally unprepared for the cross-examination by the defence solicitor and was very upset by it. She was made to feel that she was the guilty party. The whole family was upset by the experience and would never have agreed to go through with it had we known what it would entail. It would have been a great help to have had someone to explain in advance the court procedure.

One 14-year-old assault victim said he had been worried about going to the magistrates court. An official whom he could not identify gave him his statement to read before the hearing. He found this helpful. However, he described his appearance in court as follows:

---

[55] However, in a case of a 5-year-old Leicester girl whom the CPS proposed calling as a witness, the court 'indicated that it was not prepared to provide screening facilities in the event that she appeared in court'. 'Protection Needed for Young Witnesses in Sexual Abuse Cases', *Childright*, 49 (1988).

I had to say my name and address out loud. The offender probably knew where I lived. I was only in the witness box for a few minutes. The lawyers were polite. They told me to speak up. No one introduced anyone or explained who the different people were. It would have helped to know the time of the hearing. Both times I went to the court at 10 a.m. as required by the court letter. The first time I had to wait till 11.30 a.m. and the second time till after lunch. My friend and his mother were both upset about the confusion over the time. In the court letter, we were told we could wait in a separate waiting-room but in fact we were in a big hall where the gang members also waited. No one came to tell us the result.

Another assault victim, a teenage boy, said he had been very nervous about the prospect because he had never been to court before. His mother described her son's ordeal:

He had to wait about half an hour and during this time he cried. I thought he was going to pass out, he was so nervous. In court the chairman of the bench explained what would happen and introduced the key personnel. When he [the victim] went into the witness box and was sworn in he was allowed to sit down, but he had to say his name and address out loud. He whispered, so he had to repeat it. The defence started to try to confuse him. He had not been prepared for what would happen. He just thought someone would ask him a few questions and that would be it.

The offender was eventually found guilty, but at the time of the interview the victim and his family still did not know the sentence. His mother had been to the police station a few times to ask but had been told that they did not know. The victim and his mother both affirmed that the worst part of the whole incident was going to court.

The trauma of being a witness in court was not confined to those children who had actually appeared there. It was also experienced by the children and their families who had been warned to appear. Because in many cases the defendant does not enter a guilty plea until the last minute, children may suffer the fear of an expected court appearance which never actually materializes. The trauma which may be caused in such cases is well illustrated by the experience of a boy who had been assaulted. The mother said

No one explained anything about going to court. My son was extremely anxious and did not want to go. On the day, he cried his eyes out when he was made to sit in the big waiting-room, but after we had waited half an hour, we were told that the offender had pleaded guilty. We went home, but found out from the paper that the case had been adjourned for reports.

This case had taken four-and-a-half months to come to court and the family still did not know the result at the time of our interview. The mother said that the offender was still walking around, and that her son was terrified to go out for fear of meeting him. Anxieties generated by the lack of information about the criminal justice process, fear of having to appear as a witness in court, and uncertainty about the outcome of the trial are, then, all major sources of distress to child victims. In a few cases this 'secondary victimization' by the criminal process actually outweighed the trauma of the crime itself. One mother whose daughter had been sexually assaulted said 'the wait for the case to come up [ten months] was interminable'. Another put it more strongly still: 'the worst thing about the whole affair at present for my daughter was thinking about having to go to court and the wait. If she'd known it would be like this she would never have reported it.'

Conclusion

The innovative procedure now being implemented for child witnesses in cases of violence or sexual assault before and during trial represents an important advance in that it signifies recognition of the particular vulnerability of the abused child. Whilst the availability of special procedures and facilities at court for child witnesses in abuse cases is becoming more common, its development is as yet entirely *ad hoc*. Provision varies not only among different courts but also according to different personnel and judges. It is to be hoped that the legislative provisions contained in the Criminal Justice Act 1991 will help these children. However, it is not known which, if any, of these reforms actually have the intended beneficial effect on the child's well-being or whether they are effective in reducing the stress of testifying.

No one inside or outside the criminal justice system has a clear responsibility to provide information about the court process to child victims and their families; to liaise with others about the child's needs; to assist the child required to give evidence (by arranging an advance visit to the court or by reading the child's statement); to support the child in court; or to explain the court verdict. Support, where offered, is often marred by lack of continuity or by the inexperience of those providing it.

The US report *When the Victim Is a Child* suggests that children who are supported throughout may be effective witnesses at trial even without innovative techniques.[56] The report recognizes that giving evidence is not the only cause of anxiety for the child, the period leading up to the trial can also be extremely stressful; the use of innovative or modified procedures during the court hearing may not help a child who is already upset. Although in the US many states have adopted laws that permit the use of innovative techniques in court when children testify, in fact the report states: 'Alternatives to traditional in-court testimony have only been used as a last resort. Other reforms, aimed at reducing the burden on child victims throughout the investigation and adjudication process, can substantially reduce the need for radical departures from tradition in the courtroom.'[57] Active victim assistance programmes in America aim to provide support and comfort to child victims throughout the adjudication process. The 'victim assistant' explains the adjudication system, prepares child witnesses for giving testimony in court, and accompanies them on the day of the trial. Many victim assistance programmes have developed videotapes, colouring books, dolls'-house-sized court rooms, and other child-friendly techniques to complement their support efforts.[58]

In Britain there is no tradition of independent representation of a witness in a criminal case. The guardian *ad litem*—an independent representative who advocates the best interests of the child—is only available to children in civil proceedings. In the US, in a small number of states, the role of guardian *ad litem* has developed to include the role of safeguarding the child's interests in the criminal courts. In practice the role of the guardian *ad litem* is quite similar to that of a victim assistant, but the guardian has the power to communicate directly with the court.[59] In all ways, the American example offers much that may usefully be adopted in tailoring the British criminal justice system to the special needs of child witnesses.

---

[56] Whitcomb *et al.*, *When the Victim Is a Child*, 111 ff.

[57] D. Whitcomb, 'When the Victim Is a Child', in J. R. Spencer *et al.* (eds.), *Children's Evidence in Legal Proceedings: An International Perspective* (Cambridge, 1990), 133.

[58] Whitcomb, 'When the Victim Is a Child', 142.

[59] Ibid. 142–3; M. Hardin, 'Guardians *ad litem* for Child Victims in Criminal Proceedings', *Journal of Family Law*, 25(4) (1986–7), 687–728.

7

The Social and Welfare Agencies: Provision and Response

There are a considerable number of agencies outside the criminal justice system which can provide help for victims of crime. They range from organizations which provide specific assistance—the emotional advice, practical help, and information provided by Victim Support Schemes, helplines, and Rape Crisis organizations—to the shelter provided by women's refuges. In addition, community-based professionals, such as doctors, psychiatrists, and social workers, can and do offer help to crime victims. Much has already been written about the range of support and help offered by these agencies to adult victims and how far they meet victims' needs. Conversely, discussion about the effects of crime on children, the types of help they need and the extent to which it is available has hitherto been comparatively meagre. Despite the prominence given in the media and elsewhere to the problem of child abuse, the professional response has focused on the diagnosis and management of such cases, with little attention being given to the provision of support to abused children and their families. There are only a handful of studies of locally organized projects set up to help abused children, all of which emphasize the need for long-term support for these children and their families both in the community and by psychiatric professionals.[1] What little information exists about the provision of help for children who are victims of other crime is contained in American studies of children who are the indirect or 'bystander' victims of extreme violence perpetrated on their mothers—domestic violence, rape, and homicide. These studies have, in the main, been carried out by

---

[1] Calam and Franchi, *Child Abuse and its Consequences: Observational Approaches* Bagley and King, *Child Sexual Abuse: The Search for Healing*; A. C. Salter, *Treating Child Sex Offenders and Victims: A Practical Guide* (Newbury Park, Calif., 1988); P. Dale *et al.*, *Dangerous Families: Assessment and Treatment of Child Abuse* (London, 1986).

clinicians who have developed an understanding of the experiences which people are likely to undergo after suffering serious victimization. As noted above, they have coined the term 'posttraumatic stress disorder' to describe the experiences of these victims and their findings have contributed to the development of 'Special Crisis Intervention' programmes and therapeutic counselling for such children.[2] Thus, such information as is available about the type of help needed by child victims relates to support for very serious crime. Little is known about the types of agency which exist to help child victims on a broader basis and whether or not they are in fact meeting the needs of such children.

The key role of the family in providing for children is one which has been assumed since the invention of the term 'childhood'.[3] Where children are victims of crime it may be thought that responsibility for help and support could safely be left to their family. In cases where the family network breaks down, such as those involving child abuse, it has long been assumed that the State will assume a parental role and Social Services, who have a statutory responsibility for the welfare of children, will provide the necessary support. But what of children who are victims of other types of crime? There is, in fact, a wide range of community-based organizations which do, or could, provide services for child victims and their families, whether or not children are central to their concerns. There are those agencies which cater especially for child victims: the most obvious of these is the Social Services, but the NSPCC, helplines, and Victim Support Schemes can also provide help. There are also other agencies which exist specifically for children—schools and their support services including school nurses, school counsellors, and education welfare officers. In addition, there are agencies which come across children in the course of their work—health service professionals such as health visitors, GPs, and hospital casualty staff; also probation officers, and voluntary organizations such as women's refuges.

National policies do exist on how such agencies should respond to abused children. The policy document *Working Together* advises all

---

[2] R. S. Pynoos and K. Nader, 'Children who Witness the Sexual Assaults of their Mothers', 567–72; Davis and Carson, 'Observations of Spouse Abuse: What Happens to the Children?', 278–91; Silvern and Kaersvang, 'The Traumatized Children of Violent Marriages', 421–36; Grusznski *et al.*, 'Support and Education Groups for Children of Battered Women', 431–44; K. Johnson, *Trauma in the Lives of Children* (Basingstoke, 1989).

[3] P. Ariès, *Centuries of Childhood*.

statutory, professional, and voluntary agencies of their duty to be alert to signs of child abuse; to pass on information about any child whom they suspect is being abused to the local investigating agencies (the police, Social Services, or the NSPCC); and to refer such children and their families to statutory and voluntary agencies for help. Social Services have a responsibility to plan and co-ordinate longer-term support.[4] There are, however, no guide-lines for how agencies should respond to children who are victims of other crime. This chapter will examine the type of help which these organizations offered to child victims in the field-work areas of Oxford and Bedfordshire and the types of help sought by or offered to children and their families in the study sample. Victim Support Schemes and helplines were the only bodies which were able to provide more than anecdotal evidence of the numbers of child victims supported, and in the case of Victim Support, considerable information about the type of help provided to child victims. Thus, using the data obtained from studying Victim Support files in Oxford and Bedfordshire and from a monitoring exercise of all Victim Support Schemes, a fuller account of the services offered to child victims than that provided by other agencies is included.

Community-Based Help for Child Victims in Oxford and Bedfordshire

Social Services

The foremost agency with a duty to protect the welfare of children is, of course, the local authority Social Services Department. This has a statutory responsibility to investigate allegations of child abuse and reports of children considered to be at risk as well as to monitor the progress of those listed on the 'At Risk' Register. In addition, Social Services have a duty to safeguard and promote the welfare of children within their area who are in need, to promote the upbringing of children by their families, and, where necessary, to provide accommodation.

In the field-work areas the main types of children who came to the attention of Social Services were victims of abuse (emotional, physical, or

---

[4] DHSS and Welsh Office, *Working Together: A Guide to Arrangements for Inter-agency Co-operation for the Protection of Children from Abuse* (London, 1988), 21.

sexual) or neglect and also children in households where domestic violence or even homicide had occurred. At present, all Social Services Departments give priority to cases of child abuse within the family, and a major part of their resources are devoted to this work. In both Oxford and Bedfordshire, training officers had been appointed during the late 1980s to oversee this work and to provide regular training, monitoring, and assessment of staff dealing with these cases. However, all social workers emphasized that, at present, resources were being concentrated upon identification and investigation of such cases. Although abused children were in great need of therapy and support, Social Services were able to provide only very limited assistance. One social work team leader summed up the general view: 'For social workers, the investigation of the allegation is the most important stage when an allegation of child abuse is made. When this is completed, there is a collective sigh of relief from the agency. Support for the child and family is not a priority.'

Whenever an allegation of abuse or neglect was brought to the attention of Social Services, formal 'child protection procedures' were generally followed. After the investigation of any allegation of child abuse had begun, the Social Services Department convened a case conference to formulate a plan for the future of the child and its family. A key worker was appointed to notify the relevant agencies and organize support on behalf of the child. In both Oxford and Bedfordshire a number of residential homes were available where abused children could be sent as a place of safety. Where specialist help was required social workers could refer those under the age of 5 and their mothers to Family Centres where play facilities, training in parenting skills, and the mutual support of other mothers were available. Children aged between 5 and 12 could be referred for a variety of psychiatric treatments or therapies to specialist hospitals, such as the Park Hospital for Children in Oxford or to Great Ormond Street in London.

For older children, there was much less specialist help available. Social workers, in both Oxford and Bedfordshire, organized groups for sexually abused girls. The main aim of these groups was to provide a forum for overcoming the trauma created by abuse and, to a lesser extent, by the events consequent on its disclosure. Social workers considered these groups to be very important in providing a means to raise levels of self-esteem, to increase assertiveness, and to teach self-protection strategies. They employed various therapeutic techniques including role-play, games, physical activity, and group discussion to try to overcome or release the powerful and destructive emotions engendered by sexual abuse. However, these groups were run by social workers on a voluntary basis with scant resources to fill what they perceived to be a gap in the provision of support. All these social workers could think of few, if any, agencies to which they could refer teenagers and they were aware that this age-group suffered through lack of specialized help and treatment. Thus, although some support was available, all social workers were aware that abused children were not receiving as much help as they required to assist their recovery from the crime. They acknowledged that they themselves were not able to provide it, given their limited resources, nor were they able to undertake any preventive work. They were also aware that the agencies to which they were referring such children were over-stretched. In addition, they could provide very little in the way of monitoring and support for children whose names appear on the 'At Risk' Register. All of them recognized the need to monitor these families, the dangers inherent in failing to do so, and the futility of maintaining such registers without taking precautions to reduce the risks which they had identified.

Social workers were very much aware of the help needed by children who were victims of other crimes, but any help provided was necessarily entirely discretionary and dependent upon the limited resources available. The majority of social workers made special mention of the need to provide support for children in households where domestic violence was occurring or where a homicide had taken place. Indeed, American, and more recently British, research has drawn attention to the particularly traumatic consequences for children who live with violence within the home and the need for professional therapeutic intervention. Pynoos and Eth, researching in the United States, found that 'witnessing such events resulted in signs and symptoms of post-traumatic stress in nearly 80% of some 100 uninjured child witnesses we have studied'.[5] As a result of their findings, innovatory support programmes were established in the United States to provide counselling and therapy and to promote

[5] R. S. Pynoos and S. Eth, 'Programs for Child Witnesses to Violence. Special Interventions', in M. Lystadt (ed.), *Violence in the Home* (New York, 1986); see also Pynoos and Nader, 'Children who Witness the Sexual Assaults of their Mothers'; R. S. Pynoos and S. Eth, 'Children Traumatized by Witnessing Acts of Personal Violence: Homicide, Rape and Suicidal Behaviour', in S. Eth and R. S. Pynoos (eds.), *Posttraumatic Stress Disorder in Children* (Washington, DC, 1985).

liaison between agencies. Indeed, the need for the helping agencies to recognize that, in cases of spousal abuse, children as well as their mothers might be victimized has been underlined by several American researchers. They have also stressed the need for intervention with such children to become a professional priority.[6] A number of social workers mentioned difficulties which they had faced when attempting to provide support for children in households where homicide had occurred. Black and Kaplan's findings based on research they carried out in England suggest that children in such situations are deeply traumatized. They recommend that

All children who are deprived of two parents suddenly by one killing the other should be seen in a child psychiatric department for crisis intervention to minimise post-traumatic stress, and for bereavement counselling by experienced and expert professionals. This work should be done in association with the social worker, who can help to construct a life-story book and help them by revisiting their home, school, mother's grave, etc. We believe a child psychiatric team should be involved in every case—the rarity and complexity of these events requires the most expert advice and intervention available.[7]

In the field-work areas, the combination of insufficient resources and the lack of relevant expertise made it difficult for social workers to provide help for such children. However, while recognizing their own inability to respond adequately, Social Services do not refer such children to other agencies. Indeed, they had very little knowledge of other agencies which could provide support for such child victims.

The NSPCC

The NSPCC, although a purely voluntary organization, does possess statutory powers which embody the authority to remove children from homes where they have been or may be abused. In 1972, the Society set up twelve special units in England and Wales for the assessment and treatment of families where serious or repeated child abuse had occurred. In addition, there is a network of thirty-four child protection teams, whose members are child care specialists and

[6] Silvern and Kaersvang, 'The Traumatized Children of Violent Marriages'; Grusznski *et al.*, 'Support and Education Groups for Children of Battered Women'; Davis and Carson, 'Observations of Spouse Abuse'.

[7] Black and Kaplan, 'Father Kills Mother: Issues and Problems Encountered by a Child Psychiatric Team', 629.

who provide a twenty-four-hour service in response to calls from families, the general public, and other professionals. In April 1987 the NSPCC launched a £4 million programme to expand and develop these teams. One of the purposes of this initiative was to replace the NSPCC's traditional preventive methods of working, based on deploying local inspectors, with child protection teams which are intended to be more responsive to local needs and more flexible in co-operating with other agencies. Through these teams and their family centres, the NSPCC deals with many different kinds of problems in families. These range from long-term neglect to serious, even fatal, physical abuse and sexual abuse, and to marital and other emotional difficulties. They also offer education and consultation to organizations and professions concerned with child abuse.

In addition, the NSPCC receives referrals from professional agencies including Social Services, from the general public, and self-referrals. However, the NSPCC primarily sees its duty as being to provide protection for child victims of assault, ill-treatment, or neglect but does not extend this to other child victims. The NSPCC had no branch in the Oxford area and was only just establishing itself in Bedfordshire. It is not surprising, therefore, that none of the children in the study sample had sought or were offered its help.

Victim Support

As has been seen, over half of the 350 Victim Support Schemes in England and Wales offer help and advice to children who are the direct victims of crime. The remainder inevitably come across children who are indirect victims in households in which crimes have occurred. Victim Support national guide-lines issued in 1990 advised schemes to accept referrals of children with parental consent if they have experienced volunteers backed up with professional support. They excluded victims of abuse within the family, on the grounds that they are the statutory responsibility of Social Services. Children who are the direct and indirect victims of a wide range of crimes come to the attention of Victim Support Schemes. In the month of October 1988 alone, for example, 76 (of 350) schemes provided support for 367 cases which involved child victims. Nearly half of the cases were domestic burglaries in which the children were members of the household. Of the rest, the majority were cases of physical assault against either the child or an adult member of the family. These ranged from relatively minor attacks through more serious physical and sexual assaults to 10 cases of murder all occurring within the family. In the course of a year the two schemes in the field-work areas of Oxford and Bedfordshire responded to 328 cases involving children who were either direct or indirect victims of a wide range of crimes. The majority of the cases involving direct child victims were physical or sexual assaults. Of the indirect cases, most concerned children in households where burglaries had taken place.

Victim Support is the only agency which provides 'outreach' help for victims of crime, including child victims. It lays emphasis on personal contact and upon 'reaching out' to victims rather than leaving them to ask for help, aiming to establish contact as soon as possible after the event, to provide assistance in a crisis, and to act as referral agents to appropriate sources of support or professional or specialist help. In so far as Victim Support volunteers provide support to child victims, they do so in the context of providing support to the family as a whole. They are able to provide emotional support, advice, and information, particularly about the criminal justice system and compensation. Where younger children were concerned, Victim Support volunteers usually provided advice and support to the parents in the hope that by doing this they were helping them to support their children. In the case of teenagers, on the other hand, volunteers were often asked by parents to talk to them on their own. In the vast majority of cases the volunteer's help is confined to one visit. However, where necessary they also provide long-term support, often working alongside other agencies, or refer victims to other agencies for specialist help.

It would be an error to assume that Victim Support provides a comprehensive support service for all child victims. In the first place, as we have already seen, it is heavily dependent upon the police for referrals. The service which it can offer to child victims is not widely known about by other agencies. In any event, not all cases involving child victims come to the attention of the police. Even when they do, by no means all of the children involved are referred by the police to Victim Support. In both Oxford and Bedfordshire there was an agreed policy that the police should automatically refer to Victim Support all crimes involving children which came to their attention (except child abuse and sexual assault: the latter would only be referred with the agreement of the victim's parents). However, an examination of Victim Support Scheme and police records in the two field-work

TABLE 2. *Direct child victims recorded by the police in Oxford, 1987, and in Bedfordshire,[a] 1988, and referrals to the Victim Support Schemes (VSS)*

Offence	Oxford			Bedfordshire		
	Number recorded by the police	Referrals to VSS		Number recorded by the police	Referrals to VSS	
		No.	%		No.	%
Murder	—	—	0.0	1	1	100.0
Grievous bodily harm	2	1	50.00	12	7	75.0
Actual bodily harm	37	15	40.5	114	86	75.4
Robbery[b]	6	—	0.0	19	16	84.2
Kidnapping	1	—	0.0	4	2	50.00
Blackmail	—	—	0.0	1	1	100.00
Sexual offences[c]	51	2	3.9	58	28	48.2
Burglary	—	—	0.0	3	1	33.3
Theft	49	—	0.0	23	5	21.7
Cycle theft	210	—	0.0	84	21	25.0
Criminal damage	3	—	0.0	4	2	50.0

[a] Luton, Leighton Buzzard, and Biggleswade.
[b] and attempted robbery.
[c] Rape, buggery, indecent assault, gross indecency, unlawful sexual intercourse.

areas over the period of a year confirmed that the Victim Support Schemes were not receiving referrals of all cases.

The Oxford scheme had had referred to it only 5 per cent of the total number of cases involving direct child victims recorded by the police in 1987. This was partly because cycle theft (which in Oxford accounted for 57 per cent of the recorded offences) was excluded by agreement with the police, even though, as we have seen, cycles are regarded as valuable items and children are upset by their loss. Yet, even if cycle thefts are ignored, the referral rate in Oxford was still only 12 per cent.

Only offences of physical violence or indecent assault were referred, the former category accounting for nine-tenths of the cases. In contrast the Bedfordshire scheme received information on about half (52 per cent) of the crimes recorded. Cases of violence still accounted for 55 per cent but there was a much wider range of offences referred, including sexual crimes, robbery, and cycle theft.

In addition, as we have seen, a further problem which reduced the population of child victims eligible to be referred to Victim Support was the fact that the police did not routinely record the presence of children in households which they visited where the parent was the 'named victim'. The majority of police officers were unaware that children in such households may be in need of support and that they should be brought to the attention of Victim Support. An examination of Victim Support Scheme records in Oxford and Bedfordshire over the period of a year revealed 141 cases which involved children as indirect victims; none of them was named on a police crime report. Identification by a Victim Support Scheme of children who are potentially indirect victims is dependent, first, upon a volunteer visit being made and, secondly, on the awareness and ability of the volunteer to investigate whether there are children in the household. However, there are many reasons why the presence of children may not be noticed. Only a very small percentage of victims referred to Victim Support received a visit from a volunteer (in Oxford 21 per cent of the referrals were visited and in Bedfordshire 9 per cent, the rest being sent a letter offering the services of the scheme). Moreover, it is not always possible to plan a visit at times when children may be present and a number of volunteers felt it to be unacceptably intrusive to enquire after other members of the family if they were not there.

It is clear, therefore, that in neither area was the automatic referral of cases involving child victims being carried out. Like all Victim Support Schemes, Oxford and Bedfordshire are heavily dependent upon the police for their referrals, indeed, 99 per cent come from the police. The rapid turnover of civilian referral officers meant that a number of the newer civilians were ignorant of the policy agreed. In addition, the co-operation of police officers who dealt with victims was essential to the success of Victim Support in that they were able to inform victims about the availability of this service. However, across the ranks, the majority of police officers were unaware that child victims were included in their force's policy of automatic referral of victims recorded on a crime report. When they were told, many were ambivalent about this. The majority considered that Victim Support was not a suitable organization to provide assistance for child victims. The specialist officers in charge of child abuse and sexual assault in Oxford were the only ones who claimed that they asked child victims and their families whether they would like to be visited by Victim Support. They recognized that the Social Services were often not involved with children who were sexually assaulted outside their own families. Even when they were involved with an abused child, some mothers also needed support. It was only in cases such as these that the police informed their mothers about the existence of Victim Support. In neither of the field-work areas was the referral system monitored or reviewed regularly by Victim Support. None of the co-ordinators had any idea of the total number of offences against children recorded by the police in their area. During the period of our study the area co-ordinators in both fieldwork areas began to make vigorous attempts to gain knowledge of child victims by visiting police stations daily to examine the crime reports and collect cases. This undoubtedly was responsible for boosting the proportion of cases known to them and a good omen for the future.

Even if child victims and their families were told about Victim Support, by no means all those who were offered help accepted it. An examination of the records of the Victim Support Schemes in Oxford and Bedfordshire over the period of a year showed that the parents of 164 of the 187 direct child victims referred by the police were contacted and offered the services of the schemes (the additional 23 were either referred to another Victim Support Scheme or were already being dealt with by Social Services). Once a victim is referred to a Victim Support Scheme, the co-ordinator has the responsibility for establishing initial contact with the victim. He or she usually does so in one of three ways: by asking a volunteer to make an unannounced visit to the victim's home; by making a telephone call; or by sending a letter to the victim (or, in the case of a child, the child's parents) offering the services of the scheme.

By far the most effective way of ensuring that the offer of help is accepted by the victim is for them to be visited by a Victim Support volunteer as soon as possible after the event. However, in practice a number of constraints operated which prevented schemes from adopting this method of contacting all victims. In both Oxford and Bedfordshire there were not enough volunteers to visit every victim referred.[8] This meant that a system of priority for visits for victims had been worked out in each area. In Bedfordshire, the scheme's priority was for visits to be made to single and elderly victims; in Oxford, emphasis was placed on victims of serious crime. In neither area was priority given to child victims. There were a number of reasons for this. First, the co-ordinators in both areas were unsure about making initial contact with child victims and their families by an unannounced visit. A number of them felt that this would be too intrusive a way of approaching child victims. In addition, a further problem was that of obtaining a volunteer whom the co-ordinator felt was suitable. It is, therefore, hardly surprising that very few children referred to Victim Support in the field-work areas were contacted initially by an unannounced visit by a volunteer: 6 out of 18 in Oxford and 24 out of 146 in Bedfordshire. In all the remaining cases, a letter was sent to the child's parents offering the services of the scheme. All of those visited took up the offer of support but there was a lower response rate to letters: 2 out of 10 in Oxford, both requesting a visit, and 19 out of 120 in Bedfordshire, 9 requesting a visit and 10 asking for help or advice over the telephone. Thus, only 51 of 164 children whose parents were contacted took up the offer of Victim Support. It is impossible, of course, to tell how far children were responsible for deciding not to avail themselves of the service offered or how far parents ignored or rejected it on their behalf. However, it would appear that the method of contacting child victims and their families is a key factor in determining whether an offer of help is taken up, and this needs to be reviewed by Victim Support.

In addition, not all those child victims referred actually obtained help from Victim Support because a number of constraints operate against volunteers providing an effective service to those children they visit. To begin with, they were dependent upon parental co-operation. If this was refused, there was nothing they could do to help the child even if they felt help was needed. Often, particularly where the children were indirect victims, parents disputed that their children needed additional help. In many cases parents had not even considered that their children might be affected. Gaining parental permission was further complicated in those cases where parents were unable to speak English. Here the volunteers found that the only way in which they could communicate with the parents was through the children, who

---

[8] The Oxford scheme had 45 volunteers on its books; Luton had 14 volunteers; and Leighton Buzzard and Biggleswade had 14 between them.

could usually speak English. Attempts had been made to recruit volunteers from ethnic minorities and an increasing number were coming forward.

Another factor mentioned by all those co-ordinators and volunteers interviewed was that they had not received enough training about the specific needs of child victims. Although all volunteers had initially received six to eight weekly training sessions in counselling skills, the support of child victims had been mentioned only briefly. A number of one-day training workshops on children had been organized in Oxford but volunteers felt far from confident in their abilities. In the absence of specialized training, all the co-ordinators we spoke to said that the criteria they used in selecting suitable volunteers to visit direct child victims was that the volunteer had children of his or her own, or else worked in a profession, such as teaching, which brought them into frequent contact with children. They recognized, of course, that it was not possible at present to select volunteers on the basis of their suitability to visit children who were indirect victims as the presence of children in families is not usually noted by the police. This was a particularly strong argument for this information to be provided.

The primary task of volunteers upon visiting a child victim is to make some estimate of the degree of disturbance suffered by the child and family in order that they may establish the extent of the victim's needs for support and assistance. All the co-ordinators and volunteers admitted that they did not have the required expertise to gauge the psychological impact of the crime on children. They needed to be better informed about the likely effects of crime on children, so as to be better able to advise parents about what kinds of reaction they may expect from their children and how to cope with them. Co-ordinators and training officers of the schemes provided a good deal of support for their volunteers but they all expressed the view that it would be far better if the schemes could draw on professional supervision and support from properly qualified persons.

A further constraint arose in cases where volunteers felt that the child's needs were such that they would be better met by another agency. In general there was a dearth of knowledge about sources of more specialist help or the willingness of such agencies to take referrals of child victims. One co-ordinator summed up the general view: 'Who do you refer on to? If you can't refer the only thing you can do is to stay in there.' Even where an appropriate agency could be identified, both volunteers and co-ordinators saw referral as problematic. It was often difficult to get parents to accept that their child needed further help. A primary concern here was that, having promised confidentiality, co-ordinators were unwilling to betray that trust. Many co-ordinators felt unclear about their legal and moral obligations in such cases: this was a particularly difficult issue in suspected child abuse cases. As a result Victim Support has produced national guidelines which make clear the kinds of instance when confidentiality may be breached.[9]

Generally, working with other agencies could be problematic. It was clear that the sharing of information with another agency was not always reciprocated by the agency concerned. A number of co-ordinators cited instances where Victim Support had been involved in a case in which Social Services had also been involved. An example might be a case of child abuse where Victim Support had been called in to provide help for the mother. In such a case difficulties arose over where the precise boundaries between the two agencies lay. Whilst the social workers were only too anxious to make full use of information provided by Victim Support, they did not take Victim Support into their confidence in return nor did they reciprocate in sharing information. Such experiences as these led co-ordinators to feel that Victim Support was not taken seriously as an agency in its own right by the Social Services Department.[10]

In order to counter all these difficulties, Victim Support set up a 'Demonstration Project' which was carried out by Victim Support in Bedfordshire in 1988 and which aimed to raise awareness of child victims and to improve services for them. It had several main objectives. These included improving liaison with the police to ensure referrals of all direct child victims; developing training and support for volunteers; formulating a 'checklist' for the use of volunteers when visiting families with children; producing literature to help child victims and their families cope with the experience of victimization,

---

[9] National Association of Victims Support Schemes, 'Confidentiality Guidelines', 29 Nov. 1988.

[10] In a report published in 1987, the British Association of Social Workers drew attention to the fact that 'An important component of helping and supporting people in the community involves the contribution of volunteers, self-help groups and informal carers.' It emphasized the need for social workers and others in helping professions to work alongside them. It does not appear that this exhortation had been heeded in the field-work areas. British Association of Social Workers, *Towards a Better Partnership: Social Workers and Volunteers* (Birmingham, 1987), p. v.

and raising the awareness of other agencies of the services which Victim Support could provide for child victims.[11] As a result of this project, Victim Support are producing well-defined policy guide-lines which will both determine the nature of the service which volunteers can be expected to offer to child victims and provide training materials to this end.

Helplines

Helplines have been set up, both nationally and locally, and a number of these offer services to child victims and to any person who wishes to ask about a problem relating to a child. Perhaps the best known helpline for children is Childline. Other helplines which also receive calls from children include the Samaritans, Incest Crisis Line, Rape Crisis Line, and local helplines such as the National Children's Home Careline in Luton. These helplines aim to befriend, advise, and assist their callers by giving them time to talk confidentially over the telephone to a sympathetic adult. A Code of Practice has been drawn up—*Telephone Helplines: Guidelines for Good Practice*—which sets standards for the selection, training, supervision, and support of volunteers in an attempt to safeguard children telephoning in.[12]

Of all the helplines, Childline receives by far the largest number of calls involving children. Between its launch in October 1986 and November 1990, Childline counselled more than 102,000 children and advised 19,000 adults. By far the largest category of problems about which children telephoned concerned physical and sexual violence and abuse. Incest Crisis Line was set up in 1978 as a twenty-four-hour counselling service for victims of sexual abuse. It now receives approximately 1,500 calls per week from abused children, and provides confidential counselling over the phone. Whilst the Samaritans offer a service to anyone who is in need of help or support, of the 15,000 calls received by the Samaritans in Oxford over the course of one year (1988) approximately 20 per cent were from persons under the age of 17. The majority of these calls concerned

---

[11] A leaflet, *Coping with Burglary: Your Child's Reactions* (Bedford, 1989), and a publicity leaflet for children about Victim Support have been distributed to children in schools and left with children on volunteer visits.

[12] Telephone Guidelines Working Party, *Telephone Helplines: Guidelines for Good Practice* (London, 1989).

problems arising from parental domestic violence and child abuse. The National Children's Home Careline provides a general service for those having problems in their family life. In Luton this helpline received just under a quarter of its 1,800 calls from children during 1987. The majority of these concerned sexual or physical abuse.

In addition to these national helplines, a growing number of helplines have been set up as a result of local initiatives to serve specific sections of the community in recent years. Of these, perhaps one of the best known is the Leeds Touchline, which specifically targets children who are victims of abuse. In Bedfordshire, an Asian Women's Helpline has been established to cater for the problems faced by many Asian women whose poor command of English isolates them from other sources of help. The organizers of this helpline were particularly concerned about the large number of calls from children reporting instances of domestic violence in Asian families. Indeed, the children in such families were often the only family members who could speak English fluently and the onus fell on them to help their mothers in their plight, perhaps at more risk to themselves.

The response to the setting up of helplines specifically for children has been overwhelming. The level of demand for such services is extremely high and the difficulties of coping with it are immense. Nevertheless, the helplines are offering a valuable service to child victims. All the counsellors interviewed were convinced that they were not dealing with the same population of victims who reported to the police. If this is so, then helplines are enabling children, who perhaps would not previously have disclosed their victimization, to seek help they would not otherwise have received.

However, there are a number of major drawbacks to this form of help for child victims. Helpline personnel are dependent upon children making contact with them. The majority of their calls came from older children and especially teenagers rather than the younger age-group. All those we interviewed were well aware that their service was of limited value for younger children, who could not get access to telephones or were too young to make calls themselves. Helpline counsellors were also well aware that, in providing children with information about possible solutions to their problems, they placed responsibility for deciding how to resolve the problem on to the child himself or herself. They were aware of very few agencies, other than Social Services, to which they could refer children for wider forms of assistance.

Schools

Schools play a major role in the lives of all children. The majority of a child's waking hours are spent in school and schooling makes a significant contribution to a child's socialization in the community. Children's experiences both inside and outside school affect their educational performance and the life of the class generally. Of all those who deal with children, schoolteachers and their support staff (school counsellors, education welfare officers, school nurses, and the educational psychological service) are perhaps best placed to identify and provide support for child victims in the course of their daily work. All the schools in the field-work areas were provided with support staff although only two had a school counsellor. These staff said that they were willing to provide support for child victims and refer them to the appropriate agency, should further help be needed. However, providing such support necessarily relies on schools knowing when their pupils have been victimized or identifying such children. As Chapter 5 has shown, school staff appeared to be reluctant to take action in cases involving the victimization of children.

At present, the focus of attention in schools is on the identification of abused children, with a particular emphasis on sexual abuse. This is hardly surprising, given that this is the one area where policies for responding to such children exist. Training sessions for teachers and school support staff in identifying and responding appropriately to child abuse, particularly sexual abuse, have been conducted. However, only a handful of the teachers interviewed had received any training in this area. Schools and their support staff had provided support for such children and referred them to Social Services. However, the majority emphasized that they found the identification of abused children fraught with difficulties, given that such cases were rarely clear-cut: children seldom disclosed the abuse and there were few, if any, visible or identifiable external signs. The majority were extremely wary of contacting the investigating agencies even in cases where they suspected abuse, because of the consequences for the child and family which they thought would ensue. A number had, in fact, sought advice from Childline about this problem. In one case, where a headmistress of a primary school suspected a child was being sexually abused she telephoned Childline, who sent down a representative to the school to talk to the staff about child sexual abuse and its identification—an experience which they all found helpful.

With the exception of abuse, school staff in the study areas were unlikely to enquire about children who were victims of other crime. They would have no means of knowing about crimes committed against children or their families unless informed by the child or their parents. In practice this almost never happened. Where incidents of theft, assault, or bullying occurred in or around school, the emphasis was invariably on investigating the offence, punishing the offender, and, where possible, restoring any stolen goods. In the case of more serious incidents, the school would generally involve parents or the school's police liaison officer. However, the role of the police school liaison officer is an ambivalent one. These police officers were very aware of the difficulty of trying to reconcile the educational and law enforcement aspects of their role within schools. In order to maintain access to schools, to ensure continuing good relations and avoid difficulties with teachers, the majority of these officers encouraged the teachers themselves to deal with crimes committed within the school under its own regulations. The desire to divert young offenders away from the criminal justice system may be laudable. But, such a policy often had adverse implications for the victim. It was evident that, in acting in this way, schools were not always sensitive to the need of the injured party to be recognized and responded to as a victim. One head of pastoral care summed up the general view when she said 'All we do is to try to get to the bottom of the problem and sort out the offender. We do nothing for the victim.'

Although a number of teachers had approached child guidance and educational psychological services on behalf of children with behavioural problems which may themselves have stemmed from victimization, the majority of schools were not aware of the fact that child victims might need additional, specialist help. When alerted to this fact, most were unaware of agencies to whom they could refer such children.

The members of the educational psychological service we interviewed emphasized that they were able to provide treatment for children who were victims of crime. However, there were limits to the support they could provide for such children. The reason for this was that they were dependent upon other agencies to refer child victims to them. The majority of those referred to them by doctors, schools, and Social Services, were children with a wide variety of behavioural problems. Although some of these problems were the result of bullying and domestic violence, the educational psychologist would not be aware of this unless he or she probed further. The educational psychologists we interviewed said that they were receiving more referrals of children who were victims of rape and indecent assault. This was because of the demand for reports for the purposes of assessing compensation payable either by the Criminal Injuries Compensation Board or ordered by the courts.

It is, however, significant that the majority of schools in the study areas did undertake some preventive work with child victims. There has been a recent flood of child abuse prevention videos aimed at 4- to 12-year-olds, produced mainly in the United States and Canada.[13] These are intended to make children feel confident in dealing with the possibility of inappropriate advances by adults. A number of schools had adopted the Kidscape programme of 'Good Sense Defence', which aims to teach children assertiveness techniques to help protect them from crime generally. In upper schools, older children were often taught about crime and victimization, especially bullying, in the course of lessons on 'personal and social responsibility'. In addition, a number of schools had adopted the Health Education Authority's 'Teenscape Programme', which gives teenagers tips on self-defence and the 'Kidscape Bullying Programme', which is a practical guide on how to cope with bullying in schools.[14] All these programmes, however, have one thing in common: they place the responsibility for the child's protection firmly on the child himself or herself. None provides advice for those dealing with children on their likely needs if victimized, nor do they suggest strategies for support.

Health Authorities

The key role which health authority professionals—GPs, health visitors, and staff in hospital departments—should play in providing a comprehensive service for children is emphasized in *Working Together*. The fact that they are well placed to identify abused children is also underlined. Although the difficulties of diagnosing child sexual abuse were referred to by all those interviewed, all these agencies are now highly sensitive to the problems of child abuse, particularly sexual

[13] Videos currently available include *Child Molestation: Breaking the Silence* and *Now I can Tell my Secret*, both by Walt Disney, *Strong Kids, Safe Kids*, by CIC Video, *Say No to Strangers*, by the Home Office.

[14] M. Elliot, *Teenscape: A Personal Safety Programme for Teenagers* (London, 1990); M. Elliot (ed.), *Bullying: A Practical Guide to Coping for Schools* (London, 1990).

abuse, and the need to look out for signs of it and refer such children to social services. All the GPs we spoke to said that they were able to provide support for children who were victims of other crime; they tended, however, to be far less aware of the symptoms of other types of victimization. They all mentioned that they had provided treatment for children with physical, emotional, and behavioural problems arising, for example, from assaults or bullying. The majority of both GPs and health visitors said that domestic violence was a very common cause of upset and trauma in children. However, most said that in such cases they would deal with the symptoms not the cause.

Only a handful said that, in cases where a child appeared to be suffering serious psychological disturbance, they would suggest referral to child guidance or psychotherapy. The majority were unaware of other agencies to which child victims could be referred or to which they could turn for help in working with the child. These findings confirm those of Balint's definitive study of adult doctor—patient relationships. He found that one of the major problems which face doctors is that they are trained to deal almost solely with physical or organic illnesses. He noted that because of this training doctors feel inadequate when they are called upon to 'enquire into the intimate details . . . or into any other "psychological" problem'. He further maintained that 'medical training does not offer the future doctor sufficient experience in this skill, though it is a necessary skill in dealing with at least a quarter of his patients, if not more'.[15]

Hospital casualty department staff did not observe any special procedures for child victims, other than for victims of abuse. Whilst they recognized that they did treat children who were suffering from physical injuries as a result of victimization, they admitted that they tended to treat the injury alone without regard for its cause or its possible psychological repercussions. They did not think of referring children who were emotionally affected as a result of crime to other agencies for help.

The Probation Service

The Probation Service has been closely linked with the inception and growth of Victim Support Schemes. Although its work is mainly concerned with offenders, probation officers are well placed to help

[15] M. Balint, *The Doctor, his Patient, and the Illness* (London, 1968), quoted in Dobash and Dobash, *Violence against Wives*, 184.

victims through their close links with the police and other agencies. All the probation officers said that they might come across children who were victims of crime in the course of their work with offenders and that they could provide support for these children in the context of working with their client and his or her family. However, at present, in so far as they thought about child victims at all, it was in terms of those who had been abused within their own family. If they identified such children, they could cross-check with the 'At Risk' Register to ascertain that they were known to Social Services. If this was not the case, all claimed that they would refer them to Social Services. None could remember having provided support for a child who was a victim of another crime or having referred a child victim to another agency. Indeed, all of them were unsure about agencies to which they could refer child victims, other than Social Services. Although all were aware of the help which Victim Support could provide for victims, none realized that this service extended to children.

Women's Refuges

The growing willingness of women to seek help or refuge from violent husbands or partners has also drawn attention to the needs of their children.[16] Yet the provision of support has not kept pace with demand. The services of advisory bureaux such as Relate (formerly Marriage Guidance) and of women's refuges are heavily over-subscribed. The staff of these organizations in Oxford and in Bedfordshire are all aware of the problems which domestic discord, above all marital violence, can create not only for the spouses themselves but also for their children. All of them emphasized to parents the effects which marital disharmony may have on their children. Indeed, staff in women's refuges were keen to point out that there are usually more children than women in refuges since most of those seeking shelter were mothers with several children. These children are often extremely distressed both as a result of living in households where violence has been common over a long period of time and also because of the disruption of being taken from home to live in a refuge—a traumatic experience in itself. The upheaval of leaving their father, their home, and all that was familiar to them, of living in a communal setting

---

[16] See Smith, *Domestic Violence: An Overview of the Literature.*

with strange people, often in cramped conditions, having to attend a new school and make new friends, whom they felt unable to bring home to the refuge, all combined to intensify these children's sense of insecurity. Not surprisingly, the behaviour of children in refuges is often very disturbed.

The staff of women's refuges tried to encourage mothers to recognize the effects which domestic violence may have on their children. They were anxious not to take over providing support for children in such circumstances. Rather, they encouraged mothers to shoulder this responsibility themselves. They provided advice about the signs to look for and the sort of help which they could give their children. In addition, many women's refuges now employ a 'children's worker', to cater specifically for the needs of children. In the Oxford and Luton refuges the children's workers were, in fact, qualified social workers who worked with children directly; they also sought to raise their mothers' awareness of their needs. This latter role is particularly important, given that many of the women seeking refuge from domestic violence tend naturally to be preoccupied with their own problems, to the possible exclusion of those of their children. Several authors have drawn attention to the need for professional intervention with children of battered women, not least to help them to develop more effective coping strategies.[17] Although the refuge co-ordinators in the field-work areas recognized that the psychological damage to children in such circumstances could be serious and enduring, they were not aware of organizations whom they could work with or to whom children could be referred for specialist long-term help.

Compensation

As has been seen in Chapter 4, financial aid in the form of compensation from the courts and from the Criminal Injuries Compensation Board (CICB) is available for child victims. Very few of the agencies were aware of the existence of such compensation. Those who were felt unsure about the criteria which had to be satisfied before children were eligible, and the majority were not aware of the desirability for the offence to be reported to the police.

---

[17] Davis and Carlson, 'Observations of Spouse Abuse'; Gruszinski *et al.*, 'Support and Education Groups for Children of Battered Women'; Silvern and Kaersvang, 'Traumatised Children of Violent Marriages'.

The records of the CICB show that in the past very few claims were made on behalf of child victims. The Board did not collect statistics on the numbers of claims it received relating to children, except within the overall category of 'family violence', and it discontinued collecting data about this category of cases in 1985. Table 3 demonstrates that in the years for which information is available, very few applications on behalf of child victims of family violence were finalized: presumably very few such applications were made. However, during 1989 considerable publicity was given to the fact that children who were victims of violence were eligible for compensation. Partly as a result of our research, in late 1989 the CICB produced a leaflet about claiming compensation from the CICB on behalf of child victims. As a result the number of claims by or on behalf of children increased markedly. The total number of such applications received during the period 1 April 1989 to 31 March 1990 were:

All cases (including those of a non sexual nature)	4,825
All sexual assaults	1,318
Sexual abuse within the family or by a relative	802

TABLE 3. *Claims finalized for child victims*

Year ending 31 March	Cases of family violence finalized	Claims for children finalized
1983	165	5
1984	226	15
1985	239	12

Thus, there are many community-based organizations which can provide emotional help, advice, and information and also medical help for physical injuries for child victims and their families, and can refer them on to more specialist agencies for more specific help. At present the focus of attention of the statutory and professional agencies is on child abuse. This is not surprising as it is the one area of child victimization for which guide-lines are available on how agencies should respond. However, the statutory responsibility of Social Services for the welfare of abused children has, to a large extent, obscured the need for these agencies to identify and provide support for children who are victims of other crime. The same is true for other statutory and professional agencies. The main support for such children comes from the voluntary sector—from helplines, women's refuges, and Victim Support Schemes. However, these agencies are in no way making full provision for these children. They are dependent upon children identifying themselves and their needs or upon others contacting them on behalf of such children. There are difficulties for children, particularly those in the younger age-group, preventing them from making contact with agencies themselves, and other agencies are not referring such children. Indeed, the assistance which these agencies can offer is not widely known about by other agencies so it is hardly surprising that few referrals of child victims from them are received. As noted, Victim Support receives all but a handful of its referrals from the police and even here by no means all child victims who come to the attention of the police are referred.

Seeking Help: The Experiences of Child Victims and their Families

The Role of the Family

Research on vulnerable groups such as rape victims or women who have been subject to domestic violence has shown that most of them turn first to families and friends.[18] It is perhaps not surprising that the vast majority of children in all the 212 cases we studied also appeared to be primarily concerned with eliciting emotional support and sympathy for their plight from family and friends, over and above any formal response from other agencies. As noted in Chapter 5 in most cases children told their parents first; the remaining children told other relatives, friends, or their GP, schoolteacher, or school counsellor, and one telephoned Childline. Only one case, that of a 3-year-old girl who had been sexually abused by her father, was discovered by a social worker. The majority talked at length to their parents about their fears and anxieties. These might concern the offence, the offender, the possibility of a recurrence, or other worries

---

[18] Smith, *Domestic Violence*, 72; L. L. Holstrom and A. W. Burgess, *The Victim of Rape: Institutional Reactions* (Boston, Mass., 1978), 32–4. Research amongst adult victims has shown that 94% told all those in their household about the offence; well over half told friends and neighbours; 84% found them to be 'very' or 'fairly' sympathetic: M. Maguire and C. Corbett, *The Effects of Crime and the Work of Victims Support Schemes* (Aldershot, 1987), 71.

generated by the crime. In almost three-quarters of these cases, the victims and/or their families said that the immediate family had been very supportive, while a half also mentioned help from friends and neighbours. One family whose daughter had been a victim of a serious physical assault expressed a view that was widely held: 'the most important thing is to talk about it within the family. A trouble shared is a trouble halved. You can get the problem into perspective by talking about it.' Even in the case of less serious offences, families felt that the support they could provide was important. For example, a family whose son had been the victim of theft advised as follows: 'Talk the whole thing over. Try to make the child understand the crime and why it happened.' Some quite young children helped each other. Two siblings agreed: 'The best support we had was each other, but it was good to have Mum and Dad nearby if you wanted them.'

In the case of indirect child victims, the emotional support given by friends and neighbours was, in all instances, directed primarily at their parents. Three-quarters of the families where children were indirect victims claimed to have provided a supportive environment, but there were strong indications that it was the interview itself which stimulated many parents to think for the first time about the effects of the crime on their children. This is, perhaps, not surprising since many of the children had not thought of themselves as victims. However, support provided for parents by friends and neighbours could also have benefits for the child too. For example, one mother said she was thankful she lived in a community where she knew a lot of people well. She added 'I was very surprised at the sort of concern other people showed and J [her daughter] liked this as it made her feel important.'

However, it also emerged that a quarter of child victims had found very little support from within their own families. All of them were cases of sexual abuse or sexual assault on children or cases of rape or physical assault on parents. There were a number of reasons for this. Where the child had been sexually abused in the family by her father or stepfather (as four of the girls in the study sample had been), their mothers were badly disturbed, even devastated, after discovering the abuse. The whole family was deeply affected. In such cases, the ability of the mother to give emotional support to the child was seriously impaired since she, too, needed help. Self-blame and guilt at not noticing that the abuse was occurring was the most common reaction amongst mothers of abused children. For example, the mother of a

10-year-old girl sexually abused by her stepfather, who had been violent and threatened to kill her if she told anyone, was deeply depressed at these revelations and completely unable to provide support of any kind for her daughter. Her depression was compounded by the fact that she had had to take out an injunction against her husband, not only to keep him out of her house but to prevent him seeing her family, who had threatened to kill him. When the mother of a 3-year-old girl abused by her father found out about this, she was unable to comfort her daughter because of her own emotional trauma. It revived memories that she was herself abused by a friend of the family as a child, and she found herself unable to cope. Discovering that their child had been abused by their husband delivered a double blow to these mothers, all of whom were too preoccupied with their own feelings to provide sufficient support for their children.

Where a child was sexually assaulted outside the family, all the parents were extremely disturbed. This was particularly so when the offender was known to them. The family of a girl who had been sexually assaulted by one of their neighbours said 'We could have handled it better if he had been a complete stranger but he was a friend of the family. We are extremely isolated and all need help.' They expressed the wish to talk to someone outside their own family 'whom we knew would not repeat anything we said but who would be supportive'. They had not been able to talk about what had happened to their daughter and said that this was one of the reasons they were finding it so hard to cope. In another case of a teenage girl sexually assaulted by a teenage neighbour, the parents were so distressed that they had to move house. They affirmed that the event had 'wrecked our lives'. A mother of a boy who had been sexually assaulted said that she was worried about herself and her husband as 'we do not know how to deal with our feelings of anger'. The parents of a 12-year-old boy who had been indecently assaulted said 'we did not know where to turn for help'. Angry or confused about crimes against their children, many parents seemed preoccupied with their own need for support, often to the exclusion of the needs of the children themselves.

Similar feelings were also expressed where the parents had been the victims of assault or rape and were so distressed as to be unable to provide support to their offspring. Where the parent remained deeply upset, children were less likely to be able to put the incident behind them or ignore its continuing impact. Given that the emotional needs of children are often met mainly by their mother, in cases where she had been victimized children often found themselves without a basic source of support. In severe cases, for example where the mother had been raped or had suffered prolonged domestic violence, her own emotional trauma made it impossible for her to comfort her children. In general, women who had been raped found it almost impossible to conceal their continuing distress. Two of the mothers interviewed admitted that this had further upset their children. One said that 'although the children have not been told what happened I have not tried to conceal my feelings at all from them. When I cry I cuddle the children and that's how D knows I am upset . . .' The other recognized that 'B was affected by what he saw at the time and also my later distress. I have been crying a lot—I couldn't help it and I couldn't conceal it—I was shaking like a leaf.' Children may be deeply disturbed by their mother's plight and need reassurance that she will recover. But, as Silvern and Kaersvang point out, 'providing such help is expecting a lot from abused, often recently traumatized women'.[19] Their problems are likely to be exacerbated where they feel unable to discuss the offence with either members of their own family or friends. In these cases, women may require outside help, both to overcome their own trauma and to recognize that the 'children as well as their mothers have been victimized'.[20] The work of Pynoos and Eth in the United States on the impact on children of witnessing parental murder, rape, or suicide, has shown that the psychological needs of child witnesses are commonly neglected by the family, school, law enforcement agencies, and mental health professionals.[21]

Even in the aftermath of apparently less serious offences like burglary, the speed of the parents' recovery played a large part in determining the child's ability to put the experience behind them. One mother whose children continued to worry about intrusion by burglars eight months after the event admitted that 'I feel unsafe now . . . my nervousness is communicated to the children.' Parents who managed to conceal their distress were less likely to report continuing problems with their children. Another mother whose house had also been burgled reported that 'I did feel quite upset myself but was careful never to let it show to the boys' and she observed that after the same period of time (eight months) they appeared to have more or less forgotten about the incident.

---

[19] Silvern and Kaersvang, 'The Traumatized Children of Violent Marriages', 428.
[20] Ibid. 429.
[21] Pynoos and Eth, 'Witnessing Violence: Special Interventions with Children'.

It is clear that, for the majority of child victims in the sample, the family was the key source of immediate and continuing emotional support. However, children or parents in three-quarters of the cases in the sample—cases of sexual abuse or sexual assault, physical assault, and burglary and cycle theft—expressed the need for help outside the family. The circumstances where such help was needed included those where the child was particularly badly affected; where the parents themselves felt incapable of providing the level of support needed; where medical or psychiatric help was required; and where advice or specialist skills were needed. In all these instances, professional or voluntary agencies could play an important role in addition to the family network. Despite the high proportion of victims and their families who expressed the need for help, in fact in only half the cases in the sample did child victims and their families actually seek or were offered assistance. It is interesting to note that Social Services were involved with only 11 of the children and families in the 212 cases in the study sample—all of them children who were the direct or indirect victims of sexual abuse or sexual assault. Agencies from which help was requested were school staff, hospital casualty departments, family doctors, and helplines. Unsolicited help was offered to children and their families by only one organization—Victim Support. In a number of cases help was solicited by the same family from several of these agencies.

We will now go on to examine the types of help which these agencies provided.

Help Sought by Child Victims and their Families

Assistance was sought from health professionals by the parents of over half the 73 children who were direct victims of physical or sexual abuse or assault. Medical treatment for injuries such as cuts, wounds, and broken bones and concussion was sought from their GP or hospital casualty department by half the 53 children who were victims of physical assault. Four of these children were referred by their GP to the police, but in no case did the doctor or hospital casualty officer refer a child who was injured as a result of an assault to any other agency for emotional help. The parents of just over half of the children who had been sexually assaulted consulted their GP for emotional help for their child. In all these cases GPs referred children to a child psychiatrist.

Thirty of the parents of children in the study sample contacted their schools for advice and information about what to do about the offence. As has been seen in Chapter 5, the response from schools was generally negative. In only 10 of these cases did the school inform, or suggest parents inform the police, and in no case was a child or his or her parents referred to another agency for help.

Only a handful of the victims or their families in our sample had sought assistance from any of the many helplines now available. In a couple of cases of sexual offences against children the mother had telephoned Childline. One got through only to a recorded message, which she found most disconcerting. Another was simply told to report to Social Services, advice which she did not find helpful. Other helplines such as the Samaritans and Rape Crisis were reported upon more favourably. One mother whose daughter had been sexually abused by her husband, her daughter's stepfather, found much comfort in phoning the Samaritans in the middle of the night when she was very depressed. In another case a teenage girl who had been sexually assaulted was told about Rape Crisis by the police. She contacted them herself and praised the sympathy and advice that she received.

Thus, in most cases where parents sought help they did so on behalf of children but in a few cases for themselves. A very limited number of agencies were used, and the help which they received focused on the symptoms of their victimization, rather than seeking to help them to recover emotionally. This confirms the view that children are, in the main, dependent upon others to seek help on their behalf: only one teenager sought help herself. The parents of child victims have very little knowledge of the kinds of services which are available to help child victims and consequently did not consider Victim Support as a possible source of help. Apart from children who were victims of sexual abuse or sexual assault, there was very little referral of child victims to the police or other helping agencies.

Help Offered to Child Victims and their Families

Help was offered to child victims and their families by two agencies— Social Services and Victim Support. Although this help was not sought by the victims themselves, in all cases the police had been the referral agent.

Social Services were (as noted above) involved with 11 of the 212 cases in the study sample—all of them cases of sexual abuse or sexual assault. Social workers visited all 4 of the families where abuse had taken place within the family and also 4 of the 14 families in which the children had been sexually assaulted by someone outside their own family and 3 families where the mother had been raped. Parents tended to look to social workers as a useful source of advice, and for information about other agencies which could help them and their children. Children under the age of 12 were referred by their social workers to the child psychiatric services—to the Park Hospital in Oxford, to the local child psychiatric services in Bedfordshire, and to Great Ormond Street Hospital for Children. Although they were greatly in need of immediate help they all had to wait at least two months for an appointment. The mothers of 3 of these children had been referred by the police to Victim Support.

However, only 1 of the children over the age of 11 was referred by her social worker to a child psychotherapist. The remainder were not referred to any other agency for support by Social Services. Yet in all of these cases the children and their parents said they were in desperate need of further help. The parents of one teenage girl who had been assaulted by a family friend said that the whole family was extremely upset as a result and 'would have liked to have more information about self-help, including a therapy group for girls which we have heard is available'. Another teenage girl said that her social worker had talked about 'groups for girls like me but so far she has been unable to organize one'. Three of these girls were, in fact, referred by the police to Victim Support.

It is significant that there was no involvement of Social Services in the other 12 cases of sexual assault though in over half of these cases parents said that they were in need of support and their children in need of specialist treatment. In all these cases parents sought help for themselves and their children from their GPs and in all but one case were referred to the Child and Family Psychiatric Service.

The police referred 79 of the cases involving child victims in the study sample to Victim Support. Of these, 39 involved children who were direct victims of physical or sexual abuse or assault or burglary. The remaining 40 cases involved children who were indirect victims. In the majority of them, children were members of households where a burglary had taken place, but 8 were cases where children were the indirect victims of physical assault and 4 where children had witnessed the sexual assault of their mother. Of the direct victims and their families who were visited, one-third declined help from Victim Support, most of them saying that, although they appreciated the offer, they felt that they had sufficient help from within the family. As one parent put it 'We're a pretty secure family and needed no other support.' The danger here is that parents may refuse support which the children themselves may very well have welcomed. The remaining two-thirds of the families of direct child victims accepted a visit from a volunteer. As a function of the way in which indirect child victims were identified for the purposes of this research, all the families of indirect child victims in our sample had been visited by the local Victim Support Schemes and had accepted their help. This necessarily creates a somewhat distorted sample, since indirect child victims are those least likely to be identified by support agencies.

Victim Support volunteers often make unsolicited visits to victims' homes. Only 2 of the 51 families (direct and indirect) who were visited by a volunteer unannounced expressed surprise or annoyance that the police had divulged their names to Victim Support without first consulting them. Most of them did not mind at all and were pleasantly surprised by the visit. Even the few who said they were initially annoyed were not necessarily unappreciative. One mother said she was 'a bit annoyed because nobody had asked us would we like her [a volunteer] to turn up' and because 'the police had told someone else without consulting us at all. However, it was nice to know that someone cared.' In all but 8 of the initial visits made to direct victims, the volunteer talked to the child, and usually with their parents present. However, in 5 cases the volunteer saw the child privately. Where no children were at home when the volunteer called, the parents were seen by the volunteer alone. In just under half the indirect cases (and in over three-quarters of burglaries) no children were at home when the volunteer called, and so it was the parents alone who were seen. This could have been a reflection of the fact that Victim Support volunteers were not told in advance of the presence of children in families and it was therefore impossible to plan visits with the child in mind. Even if volunteers are made sensitive to the desirability of talking to children, the difficulty remains that there is no way of ensuring that they will be present when the volunteer calls round. During the daytime the children may be in school, whilst in the evening they may be out or already in bed. These petty difficulties in making contact with children may act as an effective bar to their receiving any support at all.

Where victims received little or no help from their family or friends, Victim Support's role could be especially important. Half of those who said they had received no informal support were visited by Victim Support.[22] All of these children, whether direct or indirect victims, were appreciative of the help they had been given. Gratitude was especially marked in those cases of sexual assault where Victim Support offered long-term support. As has become clear, taboos surrounding incest and sexual assault make these crimes particularly difficult to talk about especially to other members of the family. In such cases, outside help could play a vital role. In a couple of instances involving teenagers, Victim Support volunteers gave help to the child personally. More often, where children were being assisted by social workers in the local authority Social Services Department, Victim Support volunteers focused their energies on the parents. Their work here was primarily intended to help the parents cope with their own distress, but it was also valuable in helping parents to support their children. For example, one mother of an incest victim was persistently contacted by the accused (her husband) throughout the period he was on remand, a fact which greatly distressed both mother and daughter. A Victim Support volunteer attended the committal proceedings at the magistrates court with the mother and also the Crown Court trial. This was much appreciated by both mother and child. Another parent of a girl who had been sexually assaulted by their neighbour and family friend, and where it was thus particularly dificult to share their problems with outsiders, said of Victim Support: 'they have been very helpful and have not been intrusive but have telephoned often'.

In the 4 cases in the sample where the mother had been raped or sexually assaulted, the children were at home when the volunteers called. Given that these women were far too distressed to cope, the volunteers played a vital role in helping to look after the children. In one case the volunteer 'came out first thing, stayed for the whole day, and was very helpful; played with the children (though didn't talk to them about what had happened) and was very patient'. In all these cases the support extended over a period of time and in 3 of them was provided by volunteers working in pairs over several months. They mainly provided emotional sustenance but also gave advice on police and court procedures. One rape victim observed: 'Victim Support

---

[22] One-third of the direct victims and all the indirect victims.

have kept in touch ever since it happened nearly two years ago and I very much appreciated this. I could not have got through the court without them. The only real support the children have is from Victims Support—they took them on picnics and outings. The quality of support they gave was very good.' Even simple help like looking after children to allow their parents some free time alone could be vital in reducing stress and holding the family together. Clearly, then, where effective familial support is lacking, an outside agency like Victim Support can play an important role in helping child victims and their parents to recover.

A similar proportion (just over a half) of the victims (direct and indirect) who claimed that they had received much help from their immediate family and friends had also been visited by Victim Support. One might expect that outside intervention is less likely to be necessary where informal help and support is already available. However, the targeting of resources to take account of those who may be less in need of support is hindered by the fact that volunteers have no information about the composition of the family or the degree of support available to them before they arrive on the doorstep. This did not mean that the external help was unwelcome: on the contrary, all of the Victim Support visits seem to have been appreciated to some degree. For example, one teenage boy who had suffered a severe physical assault asked for help from Victim Support via the Citizens Advice Bureau, even though his family were supportive. He explained: 'it was good to talk to an independent person who sat and listened. They also helped with the Criminal Injuries Compensation form and did everything to do with it.' His mother, who had been upset at the reaction of the police—'it was as if they weren't interested', was also reassured by the support her son received from Victim Support. It made her feel that 'something was being done at last'.

Even when the visit had not proved to be strictly necessary, the fact that Victim Support had come to offer help could provide additional reassurance. The mother of a 10-year-old boy, again the victim of a physical assault, said 'it's nice they are there. It was very nice that they bothered. Another person might have needed their support.' Another teenager who had responded to Victim Support's letter by telephone said that she had been 'reassured and got the impression that had I needed help it would have been there. It was important to talk to someone who was not emotionally involved and who just listened.' Similar views were expressed by several victims who had strong family support, which would seem to suggest that the offer of help is rarely wasted.

In cases of indirect victimization, of which burglary was by far the largest category, the parents interviewed tended to evaluate the help they had been given by Victim Support in terms of their own response rather than that of their children. The volunteers had only been able to talk to children in those burglary cases (one-quarter) where they had been at home when they visited. In half of the cases where they were not present, parents reported that the volunteer had asked whether the children needed help. Some parents voiced disappointment that the volunteer had not come at a time when she or he could talk to the children. One father commented: 'I felt it might have been helpful if the children had talked to the volunteer. She came over as having a very pleasant soothing personality. She was an outsider and the children would perhaps have talked to her more than to us.' Another couple said they 'would have liked someone to have come to explain to P what had happened in language he could understand as he was so upset by the crime'.

Although these parents had identified an unfulfilled need for support, it is significant that only 1 in 10 of those visited by a Victim Support volunteer said that they would have appreciated more help than they had received. Those families dissatisfied with the support they were given tended not to have any very clear idea of how they or their children could have been helped further. To take one example, the family of a child who had been a victim of sexual assault said that they were impressed with what Victim Support had to offer. But they added: 'It would be nice to know what they could do to be more useful . . . when you've been a victim of this type of crime, you don't know the obstacle course you've got to go through. Our daughter ain't mad and don't need a shrink, but what do you do?' These parents said that they would like to have been provided with more information, for example about the availability of groups catering for girls who were abused or assaulted sexually. Such families were clearly looking to Victim Support to provide something more substantial than merely a sympathetic ear. However, the other nine-tenths were generally satisfied with the service which Victim Support provided. Indeed, the vast majority of families where a child had been a direct or indirect victim of sexual assault went on to say that Victim Support was the best, and often the only, help they had received. One mother declared that 'family and friends were very supportive, but Victim Support was the most important source of help for our family'. A single parent of a teenage victim of assault told us: 'they [Victim Support] really filled a gap and really helped us through a crisis when we had no one else to turn to'. There is one further important point: only 1 of the 27 direct victims was referred by Victim Support to another agency.

Thus, it was to the family that all but a handful of the child victims in the study sample turned initially for support. Indeed, emotional help was the prime need of these children. It would be quite wrong, however, to assume that the family is always able to provide for all the child victim's needs. Three-quarters of the child victims and their families in the study sample, while continuing to use the family network of support, voiced the need for more help. In fact, half the children and families actually sought or were offered help from community-based organizations such as Social Services, schools, general practitioners, hospital casualty departments, helplines, and Victim Support Schemes. Help was received from these agencies with varying degrees of satisfaction expressed by the children and their families. The only group of children who were consistently referred to other more specialist agencies for support were children who had been sexually abused or assaulted: they were referred to specialist agencies such as the child psychiatric service. Indeed, it was only in the area of child sexual abuse or assault that there was evidence of interagency cooperation.

In their dealing with children who were victims of other crimes, all agencies worked in isolation rather than in collaboration with each other and there was a lack of communication between them, each working within the limits of its own field of knowledge. At times there was almost a kind of rivalry. A report of the British Association of Social Workers which was published in 1987 drew attention to the important role played by volunteers, self-help groups, and informal carers in helping and supporting people in the community. It highlighted the importance of 'Social workers and other helping professionals [being] willing to work alongside and in partnership with them thus acknowledging that, however much money is spent on health and personal social services we can never legislate for friendships, relationships, neighbourhood interactions and local concerns'.[23] This advice does not appear to have been heeded.

---

[23] British Association of Social Workers, *Towards a Better Partnership*, p. v.

Conclusion

There are a considerable number of agencies—statutory, professional, and voluntary—which are able to provide emotional help, information, and advice for child victims and their families. In practice, the focus of the statutory and professional agencies at present is on the identification of child abuse and the referral of such children to Social Services. None of these agencies has seriously considered the problem of children who are victims of other crime, nor are they aware of agencies to which these children can be referred for help. The statutory responsibility of Social Services for investigating allegations of abuse has obscured the role of other agencies in identifying children who are victims of other crimes and providing support for them and referring them to appropriate agencies. What help there is for such children is provided by the voluntary sector—by helplines, women's refuges, and Victim Support Schemes.

Although the family was the major, and generally the most important, source of support for child victims in the study sample, it was significant that children and their families in three-quarters of the cases needed help beyond the family. The help required—emotional help, advice, and information—was that which could well have been provided by the community-based organizations described above. Assistance was given to half the children and families by Social Services, hospital casualty departments, family doctors, and helplines, schools, and Victim Support Schemes. Children who were victims of sexual abuse or assault were referred to more specialist agencies for help.

The concentration of interest amongst policy-makers, academics, and welfare professionals on the impact of sexual abuse on children has clearly tended to obscure the plight of the wider population of child victims. Yet children and their families who are victims of other crimes also have a diversity of needs. Whilst it is generally assumed that the family itself will furnish support, this assumption overlooks a number of factors. First, the family may not be able to recognize or identify their child's needs. Secondly, where they are aware of the child's need for support, the parents themselves may, for a variety of reasons, be unable to respond appropriately, not least in the case of lone parents. Finally, even if parents do recognize that outside help is needed for either themselves or their children, they may not know where to turn for it. Whilst an array of emotional, informational, and financial support is potentially available for children, at present provision is piecemeal and unco-ordinated, and largely dependent on local initiative. There appears to be only limited liaison between agencies and a profound lack of knowledge about the kinds of help which other professional or voluntary bodies might be called upon to provide. In particular, there is very little awareness of the services which Victim Support Schemes can offer. One rare example of what might be achieved was the Family Help Unit set up after the Hungerford shootings in 1987 referred to in the Appendix.

If the problems highlighted in this chapter are to be effectively alleviated, greater awareness of the needs of child victims, better publicity about possible sources of support, improved interagency liaison, and easier accessibility for child victims and their parents seeking help for themselves are necessary.

8

Conclusion

Child victimization has traditionally been seen solely in terms of child abuse. There can be no doubt that child abuse in its various forms is a serious social problem. However, the focus of public and professional attention on abuse has obscured the problem of children who are the victims of other, often no less serious crimes. Children are far more likely to be thought of as potential offenders than as victims of crime. Yet, as we have seen, they can be victims of a whole range of crimes. They may also be witnesses to crimes committed against other members of their families. The most serious types of personal assault, rape, and even murder often take place in the presence of children or in circumstances of which they are aware. More commonly, they may be present in households where a burglary occurs. Where an offence is committed against a member of a child's family or against the household in general the child is unlikely to be seen as a victim. None the less, children's experiences may be such that they ought properly to be recognized as victims in their own right.

Many agencies can provide services for child victims and their families, whether children are central or marginal to their concerns. Although these agencies could provide support for children who are victims of all crime, there is very little awareness of the needs of such children. Clearly, the preoccupation of all agencies with child abuse, particularly sexual abuse, has overshadowed the needs of other child victims. As yet, no specialist response has been worked out for children who are victims of other crimes.

Very few children escape the experience of victimization unaffected. Children who are the direct victims of sexual or physical assault suffer the highest levels of psychological distress. However, children who are victims of other, less intrusive crimes, such as theft, are also often upset in the immediate aftermath. For many children and their families, the response of the criminal justice system causes additional stress. In our study areas, satisfaction with the initial response by the police declined in the longer term, not least because of the lack of information provided by the police about the progress of their cases. Although very few children were required to appear at witnesses in court, those who were warned to appear were often badly affected by their experiences.

Child victims and their families have a diversity of needs. Many of them could best be met by the development of child-centred assistance. It is important that children be given a voice to express their feelings, needs and wishes. Listening to child victims themselves will allow criminal justice and support agencies to take greater account of their needs and, in doing so, to respond more effectively. Undoubtedly, the best source of support for children is their families, and parents should be enabled to understand and help their children in the aftermath of crime. But it should be recognised that, for a variety of reasons, the family may be unable to cope alone. Existing sources of psychological help, information and financial aid need to be made more accessible to child victims and their families, therefore. There should be far greater public awareness of the needs of child victims, better publicity about possible sources of support, improved interagency co-operation, and easier accessibility for victims seeking help for themselves. It is to be hoped that this study will assist this process, and that a change in public perceptions may result.

Summary of Issues Raised and Implications for Policy

The profile of children who are victims of all crimes, especially of those who are indirectly affected by crimes against their family, must be raised. It should be recognized that the experience of child victims extends far beyond the narrow definition of the abused child, and the concept of a child as an 'indirect' victim needs to be clarified.

Those concerned with the welfare of children should be aware that children may not only be severely affected by assaults against themselves, but may also be affected in a variety of ways by lesser offences, such as theft. Attention also needs to be paid to children who are sexually assaulted by persons outside their own family. Under the present procedures relating to child abuse they are too often overlooked.

In order to build up a better picture of the extent and nature of children's experiences of crime, questions directed at children should be included in any future national or local victimization surveys. More specialized studies are also needed of specific areas of victimization which impinge particularly on children—violence, bullying, racial harrassment, and the experience of witnessing or living with domestic violence or marital rape. All are areas least likely to come to the attention of the criminal justice system.

The Helping Agencies

The statutory responsibility of local authority Social Services Departments for the welfare and protection of children has to a considerable extent obscured the possibility of other agencies providing support for child victims of crime. All professional, statutory, and voluntary agencies who deal with children should institute specific training in the identification of child victims, in the effects of crime on children, and in their likely needs and how help may be given to them. Better information about the effects of crime on children is required, along with the behavioural problems that might result. Agencies will then be in a stronger position to advise parents on what reaction to expect from their child and how to cope with it. Liaison between agencies should be encouraged in order to ensure that available expertise, particularly that of Victim Support, is well publicized and made readily accessible to victims according to their needs.

The attention of all agencies needs to be drawn to the fact that child victims may be eligible for compensation from the Criminal Injuries Compensation Board. Co-operation should be encouraged among police, social workers, and other agencies, including Victim Support Schemes, so that children who are eligible for compensation can be identified and, where appropriate, helped to make an application. The agencies should concern themselves not just with cases likely to occur in the future but with those overlooked in the past. Even if over three years has passed since the offence, the Board is likely to waive the time limit on a late application on behalf of a child.

The Police, the CPS, and the Courts

The police are heavily dependent upon offences being brought to their attention. In order for the criminal justice system to succeed in its objectives, the police need the co-operation of child victims and their families in reporting offences and in investigating crimes. In turn, child victims and their families are dependent upon the police to take their complaints seriously, to investigate them, and to provide information about the progress of the case. The police and other criminal justice agencies need to be aware that children are consumers of the system as victims as well as offenders. The police should, therefore, develop a more sensitive approach to children who are victims of all crime. The specialist response which has been developed in relation to child abuse victims may have a wider application to children who are victims of other crimes.

At present, no agency has clear responsibility for providing information to child victims and their families about the progress of their case, the court, and the outcome of any trial. Since the introduction of the Crown Prosecution Service in 1986 the police may no longer be in possession of such information. Victims should be provided with information about the distinction between the role of police and the CPS. Equally importantly, the recommendation made by Newburn and Merry in relation to victims generally should also be applied to child victims. They called for a reliable system for keeping victims informed of the progress of their case, both by the automatic provision of information on the discontinuance of inquiries, court dates and results, and by responding to *ad hoc* inquiries by the victims themselves. Since children are generally less able to initiate inquiries themselves, the automatic provision of information would seem to be all the more important in cases where they have been victims.[1]

Police awareness of the availability of compensation and Victim Support for child victims should also be raised. The importance of informing families about the emotional help and financial services available for children should be emphasized in police training. The likelihood that children may be indirectly affected by crime needs to be publicized. The police ought routinely to record the presence of children who may be indirect victims in households where a crime has occurred or where a parent or sibling has been assaulted.

The relationship between the police and Victim Support is crucial in ensuring that support is given to child victims. Referral policies need to be reviewed to take account of child victims who come to the attention of the police but who, for recording purposes, do not appear on a crime report. These include children who are the victims of incidents of suspicious behaviour and offences of indecent exposure,

---

[1] Newburn and Merry, *Keeping in Touch*, 41.

and children who are present in families in which crimes have occurred such as burglaries or assaults on parents. Furthermore, if agencies such as Victim Support are to allocate resources effectively, they need far more information about the circumstances of families than they are at present provided with by the police. Consideration needs to be given of how the police could collect and disseminate this information.

It would be extremely helpful if the Crown Prosecution Service were to designate an officer with specialist knowledge of child victims to oversee all such cases.

A number of procedures for improving the situation of children who appear at court, which have not required a change in the law, have recently been introduced. These initiatives such as separate waiting-rooms, derobing, rearrangements of seating in court, and allowing a support person to be present in court are intended to alleviate stress on child witnesses. Guide-lines are needed to help courts know how best to use these procedures. At present they are used on an *ad hoc* basis and are applied to sexually abused or assaulted children. Recently enacted legislation has aimed to make the process of giving evidence easier for children. The Criminal Justice Act, 1988, abolished the requirement that the unsworn evidence of a young child be corroborated before it could be used to support a conviction, and contains provisions for the setting up of a video link to make it easier for abused children to give evidence. The Criminal Justice Act of 1991 has been analysed on pp. 117–18 above. It is to be hoped that the courts will make use of the full scope of the powers available to them under these Acts. While these changes are welcome, however, it is regrettable that no provision has been made for a designated support person to prepare and accompany children when they are required to appear in court. An appropriate agency should be mandated to provide information to all child victims and their families about the progress of the case and about the court process; to liaise with other agencies about the child's needs; to arrange for the orientation of the child witness to give evidence (such as making an advance visit to the court and going over the statement with the child); to support the child in court; and to explain the court verdict and debrief the child after the court hearing.

Victim Support

Referrals to Victim Support of child victims from agencies other than the police, such as doctors, schools, women's refuges, and helplines, should be encouraged. This is because the children with whom they deal often do not come to the notice of the police. This is another reason why close liaison between such agencies and Victim Support is so desirable.

Similarly, the level of awareness both of Victim Support Scheme co-ordinators and of volunteers of the various agencies to which child victims might be referred needs to be raised. Schemes would be helped if a directory of agencies which might be capable of helping child victims were made available. Professional supervision and support needs to be provided at all Victim Support Schemes for staff and volunteers engaged in the difficult task of helping child victims.

Whenever the police refer a case of sexual assault to Victim Support they should inform the scheme of whether or not the child has also been referred to the Social Services Department. The different responsibilities of Victim Support and Social Services in these cases need to be clarified.

All Agencies

Greater interagency co-operation between police, social workers, and other agencies, including Victim Support Schemes, would both improve the quality of response to child victims and minimize the danger of children 'falling through the net'. In order that they may help children, all statutory, professional, and voluntary agencies which deal with children should devise training packages about the victimization of children. These agencies should be fully informed about the particular service which Victim Support Schemes can provide for child victims.

In sum, much greater interaction between agencies and a new strategy for the centralization of information, perhaps in the form of a directory of agencies who might help child victims, are urgently required if their needs are to be adequately met.

Finally, it must be emphasized that none of these implications for policy require any change in the law and they have relatively few financial implications. What we recommend is a better use of existing resources by the formulation and implementation of national policy guide-lines on how agencies should respond to child victims of all forms of crime.

Appendix

The Hungerford Family Help Unit

The formation and work of the Hungerford Family Help Unit is an example of the provision of a co-ordinated community response to a very serious crime in which a considerable number of children were either witnesses or indirect victims. We interviewed the Divisional Director of Newbury Social Services and the co-ordinator of the Hungerford Family Help Unit (a recently retired senior social worker with Berkshire Social Services) to establish how the community response was co-ordinated and their assessment of how it worked in practice.

The shooting of a number of people at Hungerford took place in the school holidays in the summer of 1987, two weeks before the start of term. A local man, Michael Ryan, was solely responsible for the massacre, in which 16 people were killed. The long siege of the area was a large part of the trauma. Police could not allow people to move around and telephones were out of commission. Children were out of their homes. A number of them witnessed the crimes and were unable to communicate with their parents for several hours. As a result each did not know whether the other was safe. Seven young children aged 6 or under were bereaved: of these, four were also witnesses to the death of one of their parents. In one of the cases, two children witnessed the shooting of their mother in Savernake Forest; in the other, two children, a boy aged 6 and a girl aged 3, witnessed the death of their father, who was shot at the wheel of the family car. Many other children were also affected in some way. Three houses adjacent to the primary school were burnt down, so that children going to the school were constantly reminded of the events. The perpetrator of the killings had shot himself in the senior school, and all the children knew exactly where this had happened as it was shown on the television news. One of the members of the youth centre next to the school, who had moved away from the area but who had returned for a visit, was killed. Thus, the schools were a central part of what had happened.

On the day following the shooting, a meeting brought together the statutory and voluntary agencies, local government councillors, and clergy. Some had already been involved in rescue work on the day of the shooting. The meeting agreed to distribute a booklet called *Coping with a Major Personal Crisis* based on an Australian publication. It was printed over the following weekend and distributed to every household. The meeting also agreed that all the statutory caring agencies and voluntary agencies would collaborate to set up the Family Help Unit, which would provide 'a co-ordinated and confidential service under the auspices of Berkshire Social Services Department'. The agencies worked as part of the Unit under the supervision of the co-ordinator and not as part of their own organizations.

Referrals to the Unit were mainly of whole families, very few children being referred in their own right. At first referrals came from GPs or from families seeking help themselves, but soon other agencies made referrals. Staff on the Unit were given a sheet of questions to ask about children when handling calls, but it was hard to assess whether individual staff could cope. The majority of referrals involving children were dealt with initially by social workers, but they worked with very few children directly as a planned exercise. Home visits were made to many families and a great deal of advice was actually given to parents about coping with the needs of their children. Where children were concerned, support involvement lasted a matter of weeks, then tailed off. Usually, the contact period was one or two visits at the most by social workers for the purposes of reassurance; voluntary groups then provided longer-term contact in the form of a befriending service. A number of referrals were made to specialist agencies such as Child Guidance and Child Psychiatry, but problems arose over which service should accept referrals of teenagers. The Unit also gave advice to playgroups, nursery schools, and scout and guide troops, and an educational psychologist gave advice to teachers.

Victim Support Schemes in the area were part of the Hungerford Family Help Unit, and according to the Divisional Director of Newbury Social Services, they played an invaluable part. They were experienced in offering help to victims, often contacting them unannounced and the Unit used this method of contact with the majority of families in Hungerford. Social workers, used to working with an appointments system, received advice from Victim Support about offering 'outreach' help. The Victim Support co-ordinator at Hungerford wrote an account of the work of Victim Support within the Hungerford Family Help Unit:

> It was very different from our usual way of working but the tragedy was on such an enormous scale that it was essential we all worked together as one unit. . . . Inevitably, because Social Services were in charge, they tended to send their own workers who were known to them to what they considered 'difficult' cases. However, Newbury VSS soon gained their confidence and were well used.[1]

Overall, the co-ordinator of the Hungerford Family Help Unit and the Divisional Director of Newbury Social Services felt that a number of issues

---

[1] *Victims Support*, National Association of Victims Support Schemes Newsletter, Apr. 1988.

emerged from the working of the Unit. It was impossible to assess the effects of the shooting without knowing what the person was like beforehand. Many descriptions of children's behaviour and fears could not be separated from their previous behaviour. Children's poor adaptation was also a reflection of parents' poor adaptation, and parents voiced concern for children to express their own anxieties. Social workers were deeply suspicious that in some cases the problems presented as being caused by the shootings were in fact long-standing, but they recognized that it was extremely difficult for all agencies to identify children's problems and needs.

Overall, the Unit co-ordinators agreed that the experience provided an extremely useful lesson in working with voluntary agencies, particularly Victim Support. However, they felt that it raised an important issue about the appropriate role for a volunteer, voicing concern about children being dealt with by volunteers. They did not think that volunteers could be expected to provide help for children without the assistance of other agencies.

Bibliography

Place of publication London unless otherwise mentioned.

OFFICIAL PUBLICATIONS

Barclay, G. C. (ed.), *A Digest of Information on the Criminal Justice System*, Home Office Research and Statistics Department (1991).

Chambers, G., and A. Millar, *Investigating Sexual Assault* Scottish Office, Central Research Unit (Edinburgh, 1983).

Cook, R. F., B. E. Smith, and A. V. Harrell, *Helping Crime Victims: Levels of Trauma and Effectiveness of Services* (Washington, DC, 1987).

Crisp, D., *The Police and the Public*, Home Office Research and Statistical Department Bulletin, No. 29 (1990).

Criminal Injuries Compensation Board, *Annual Reports*.

Criminal Law Revision Committee, *Fifteenth Report: Sexual Offences*, Cmnd. 9213 (1984).

Crown Office and Procurator Fiscal Service, *Going to Court* (1989).

DHSS, *Review of Child Care Law* (1985).

—— *Child Protection: Guidance for Senior Nurses, Health Visitors and Midwives* (1988).

—— *Diagnosis of Child Sexual Abuse: Guidance for Doctors* (1988).

—— and Welsh Office, *Working Together: A Guide to Arrangements for Inter-agency Co-operation for the Protection of Children from Abuse* (1988).

Director of Public Prosecutions, *Code for Crown Prosecutors*, repr. in *Law Society Gazette*, 83(28) (23 July 1986), 2308–13.

Gibson, E., and S. Klein, *Murder 1957–68*, Home Office Research Study, No. 3 (1969).

Graham, J., *Schools, Disruptive Behaviour and Delinquency: A Review of Research*, Home Office Research Study, No. 96 (1988).

Hedderman, C., *Children's Evidence: The Need for Corroboration*, Home Office Research and Planning Unit Paper, No. 41 (1987).

Home Office, *Crime, Justice and Protecting the Public: the Government Proposals for Legislation* (1990).

—— *Victim's Charter: A Statement of the Rights of Victims of Crime* (1990).

Hough, M., and P. Mayhew, *The British Crime Survey: First Report*, Home Office Research Study, No. 76 (1983).

—— —— *Taking Account of Crime: Key Findings from the 1984 British Crime Survey*, Home Office Research Study, No. 85 (1985).

Mayhew, P., D. Elliott, and L. Dowds, *The 1988 British Crime Survey*, Home Office Research Study, No. 111 (1989).

Metropolitan Police and Bexley Social Services, *Child Sexual Abuse: Joint Investigative Programme: Final Report* (1987).

Newburn, T., *The Use and Enforcement of Compensation Orders in Magistrates Courts*, Home Office Research Study, No. 102 (1988).

—— *The Settlement of Claims at the Criminal Injuries Compensation Board*, Home Office Research Study, No. 112 (1989).

—— and S. Merry, *Keeping in Touch: Police–Victim Communication in Two Areas*, Home Office Research Study, No. 116 (1990).

Report of the Inquiry into Child Abuse in Cleveland 1987, Cm. 412 (1988).

Russell, J., *Home Office Funding of Victim Support Schemes: Money Well Spent?*, Home Office Research and Planning Unit Paper, No. 58 (1990).

Scottish Law Commission, *Report on the Evidence of Children and Other Potentially Vulnerable Witnesses*, Scottish Law Commission Study, No. 125 (Edinburgh, 1990).

Smith, L. J. F., *Concerns about Rape*, Home Office Research Study, No. 106 (1989).

—— *Domestic Violence: An Overview of the Literature*, Home Office Research Study, No. 107 (1989).

The Child, the Family and the Young Offender, Cmd. 2742 (1965).

United States Department of Justice, *Teenage Victims: A National Crime Survey Report* (Washington, DC, 1986).

West Yorkshire Police, *Going to Court* (1989).

Williams, K., *Community Resources for Victims of Crime*, Home Office Research and Planning Unit Paper, No. 14 (1983).

REPORTS, PAMPHLETS AND CIRCULARS

Bedfordshire Area Review Committee, *Child Abuse: Manual of Procedure* (Bedford, 1986).

Bedfordshire Police, 'Report of Force Working Party – Rape and Child Abuse' (Bedford, 1988).

Bedfordshire Victim Support, *Coping with Burglary: Your Child's Reactions* (Bedford, 1989).

British Association of Social Workers, *Towards a Better Partnership: Social Workers and Volunteers* (Birmingham, 1987).

Children's Legal Centre, *Being a Witness* (1989).

Commission for Racial Equality, *Learning in Terror: A Survey of Racial Harassment in Schools and Colleges* (1988).

Finer, M., *Report of the Committee on One-Parent Families*, Cmnd. 5629 (1974).

Home Office, *Report of the Advisory Group on Video Evidence* (1989).

London Borough of Greenwich, *A Child in Mind: Protection of Children in a Responsible Society*, Report of the Commission of Inquiry into the Circumstances Surrounding the Death of Kimberley Carlile (1987).

NACRO (National Association for the Care and Resettlement of Offenders), *The Future of the Juvenile Court in England and Wales* (1986).

National Association of Victims Support Schemes, Annual Reports.

—— *The Victim in Court: Report of a Working Party* (1988).

Oxfordshire Joint Child Protection Committee, *Child Protection Procedures* (Oxford, 1987).

Plotnikoff, J., *The Child Witness* (1989).

Telephone Guidelines Working Party, *Telephone Helplines: Guidelines for Good Practice* (1989).

Thames Valley Police and Oxfordshire Social Services, Joint Statement regarding the Investigation of Child Sexual Abuse (Oxford, Dec. 1987).

West Yorkshire Police, *Going to Court* (1989).

Whitcomb, D., E. R. Shapiro, and L. D. Stellwagen, *When the Victim Is a Child* (Washington, DC, 1985).

Department of Education and Science Circular 4/88.

Home Office Circulars 25/83, 69/86, 20/88, 52/88, 7/89.

Local Authority Circular 10/88.

NEWSPAPERS

The Independent.
The Guardian.
The Times.

BOOKS

Ariès, P., *Centuries of Childhood* (1962).

Bagley, C., and K. King, *Child Sexual Abuse: The Search for Healing* (1990).

Bailey, V., *Delinquency and Citizenship: Reclaiming the Young Offender 1914–1948* (Oxford, 1987).

Banks, O., *Faces of Feminism: A Study of Feminism as a Social Movement* (Oxford, 1981).

Besag, V. E., *Bullies and Victims in Schools: A Guide to Understanding and Management* (Milton Keynes, 1989).

Bottomley, A. K., *Decisions in the Penal Process* (1973).
—— and K. Pease, *Crime and Punishment: Interpreting the Data* (Milton Keynes, 1986).
Bray, M., *Susie and the Wise Hedgehog* (1989).
Bridenthal, R., C. Koonz and S. M. Stuard (eds.), *Becoming Visible: Women in European History* (Boston, Mass., 1977).
Bridge, J., S. Bridge, and S. Luke, *Blackstone's Guide to the Children Act 1989* (1990).
Bristow, E. J., *Vice and Vigilance: Purity Movements in Britain since 1700* (Dublin, 1977).
Burgess, A. W., and L. L. Holstrom, *The Victims of Rape: Institutional Reactions* (Boston, Mass., 1978).
Calam, R., and C. Franchi, *Child Abuse and its Consequences: Observational Approaches* (Cambridge, 1987).
Conroy, S., N. G. Fielding, and J. Tunstill, *Investigating Child Sexual Abuse: The Study of a Joint Initiative* (1990).
Dale, P., M. Davies, T. Morrison, and J. Waters, *Dangerous Families: Assessment and Treatment of Child Abuse* (1986).
Davies, G., and J. Drinkwater (eds.), *The Child Witness: Do the Courts Abuse Children?* (Leicester, 1988).
Dingwall, R., J. Eekelaar, and T. Murray, *The Protection of Children: State Intervention and Family Life* (Oxford, 1983).
Dobash, R. E., and R. Dobash, *Violence against Wives* (Shepton Mallet, 1980).
Donzelot, J., *The Policing of Families: Welfare versus the State* (1979).
Dorne, C. K., *Crimes against Children* (New York, 1989).
Elliott, M., *Keeping Safe: A Practical Guide to Talking with Children* (1986).
—— *The Kidscape Primary Kit* (1986).
—— *The Willow Street Kids* (1986).
—— (ed.), *Bullying: A Practical Guide to Coping for Schools* (1990).
—— *Kidscape: Stop Bullying* (1990).
—— *Teenscape: A Personal Safety Programme for Teenagers* (1990).
Emmins, C. J., and G. Scanlan, *Blackstone's Guide to the Criminal Justice Act 1988* (1988).
Fattah, E. A. (ed.), *From Crime Policy to Victim Policy* (1986).
Finkelhor, D. (ed.), *A Sourcebook on Child Sexual Abuse* (1986).
Freeden, M., *The New Liberalism: An Ideology of Social Reform* (Oxford, 1986).
Freeman, M. D. A., *The Rights and Wrongs of Children* (1983).
Garland, D., *Punishment and Welfare: A History of Penal Strategies* (Aldershot, 1985).
Gill, M. L., and R. I. Mawby, *Volunteers in the Criminal Justice System* (Milton Keynes, 1990).

Gottfredson, G. D., and D. C. Gottfredson, *Victimization in Schools* (New York, 1985).

Hanmer, J., and M. Maynard (eds.), *Women, Violence and Social Control* (1987).

—— J. Radford, and E. A. Stanko, *Women, Policing and Male Violence: International Perspectives* (1989).

Harris, R., and D. Webb, *Welfare, Power and Juvenile Justice: The Social Control of Delinquent Youth* (1987).

Hood, R. (ed.), *Crime, Criminology and Public Policy* (1974).

Horley, S., *Love and Pain: A Survival Handbook for Women* (1988).

Housden, L. G., *The Prevention of Cruelty to Children* (1955).

Humphries, S., *Hooligans or Rebels?* (Oxford, 1981).

Johnson, K., *Trauma in the Lives of Children* (Basingstoke, 1989).

Jones, D., J. Pickett, M. R. Oates, and P. Barbor, *Understanding Child Abuse*, 2nd edn. (Basingstoke, 1987).

Jones, D. P. H., and M. McQuiston, *Interviewing the Sexually Abused Child* (1988).

Jones, T., B. Maclean, and J. Young, *The Islington Crime Survey: Crime, Victimization and Policing in Inner-City London* (1986).

Kelly, L., *Surviving Sexual Violence* (Oxford, 1988).

King, M. (ed.), *Childhood, Welfare and Justice: A Critical Examination of Children in the Legal and Childcare Systems* (1981).

—— and C. Piper, *How the Law Thinks about Children* (Aldershot, 1990).

Lacey, N., C. Wells, and D. Meure, *Reconstructing Criminal Law* (1990).

Lee, C. M. (ed.), *Child Abuse: A Reader and Sourcebook* (Milton Keynes, 1978).

Lloyd-Bostock, S. (ed.), *Children and the Law* (1984).

—— *Law in Practice* (1988).

Lurigio, A., W. G. Skogan, and R. C. Davis (ed.), *Victims of Crime: Problems, Policies and Programs* (Newbury Park, Calif., 1990).

McCabe, S., and F. Sutcliffe, *Defining Crime: a study of Police Decisions* (Oxford, 1978).

—— and P. Treitel, *Juvenile Justice in the United Kingdom: Comparisons and Suggestions for Change* (1984).

Maguire, M., *Burglary in a Dwelling: The Offence, the Offender and the Victim* (1982).

—— and C. Corbett, *The Effects of Crime and the Work of Victims Support Schemes* (Aldershot, 1987).

—— and J. Pointing (eds.), *Victims of Crime: A New Deal?* (Milton Keynes, 1988).

Martin, F. M., S. J. Fox, and K. Murray, *Children out of Court* (Edinburgh, 1981).

Martin, J. P. (ed.), *Violence and the Family* (1978).

Masson, J., *The Children Act 1989: Text and Commentary* (1990).

Mawby, R. I., and M. L. Gill, *Crime Victims: Needs, Services and the Voluntary Sector* (1987).

Morris, A., and H. Giller (eds.), *Providing Criminal Justice for Children* (1983).

—— *Understanding Juvenile Justice* (1987).

—— and M. McIsaac, *Juvenile Justice? The Practice of Social Welfare* (1978).

Mrazek, P. B., and C. H. Kempe (eds.), *Sexually Abused Children and their Families* (New York, 1987).

Munthe, E., and E. Roland, *Bullying: An International Perspective* (1989).

O'Moore, M., *Report of the Conference on Bullying in Schools, Stavanger, 1987*, Strasbourg Council for Cultural Co-operation (Strasbourg, 1988).

Pagelow, M. D., *Woman-Battering: Victims and their Experiences* (Beverly Hills, Calif., 1981).

Parker, H., M. Casburn, and D. Turnbull, *Receiving Juvenile Justice: Adolescents and State Care and Control* (Oxford, 1981).

Parsonage, W. H. (ed.), *Perspectives on Victimology* (Beverly Hills, Calif., 1979).

Parton, N., *The Politics of Child Abuse* (Basingstoke, 1985).

Pinchbeck, I., and M. Hewitt, *Children in English Society*, i (1969).

Platt, A. M., *The Child Savers: The Invention of Delinquency* (Chicago, Ill., 1969).

Prochaska, F. K., *Women and Philanthropy in Nineteenth Century England* (Oxford, 1980).

Radzinowicz, L., and R. Hood, *A History of English Criminal Law*, v (1986).

Roberts, A. R. (ed.), *Battered Women and their Families* (New York, 1984).

—— *Helping Crime Victims: Research, Policy and Practice* (Newbury Park, Calif., 1990).

Rock, P., *Helping Victims of Crime: The Home Office and the Rise of Victim Support in England and Wales* (Oxford, 1990).

Russell, D., *The Secret Trauma: Incest in the Lives of Girls and Women* (New York, 1986).

Salter, A. C., *Treating Child Sex Offenders and Victims: A Practical Guide* (Newbury Park, Calif., 1988).

Shapland, J., J. Willmore, and P. Duff, *Victims in the Criminal Justice System* (Aldershot, 1985).

Shorter, E., *The Making of the Modern Family* (1976).

Sparks, R., H. Genn, and D. Dodd, *Surveying Victims* (1977).

Spencer, J. R., and R. H. Flin, *The Evidence of Children: The Law and the Psychology* (1990).

—— G. Nicholson, R. Flin, and R. Bull, *Children's Evidence in Legal Proceedings: An International Perspective* (Cambridge, 1990).

Stanko, E. A., *Intimate Intrusions: Women's Experiences of Male Violence* (1985).

Tattum, D. P., and D. A. Lane (eds.), *Bullying in Schools* (Stoke-on-Trent, 1988).

Vicinus, M., *A Widening Sphere: Changing Roles of Victorian Women* (Bloomington, Ind., 1977).

Violence Against Children Study Group, *Taking Child Abuse Seriously* (1990).

Walker, L. E., *The Battered Woman* (1979).

Walklate, S., *Victimology: The Victim and the Criminal Justice Process* (1989).

ARTICLES

Adler, Z., 'Prosecuting Child Sexual Abuse: A Challenge to the Status Quo', in M. Maguire and J. Pointing (eds.), *Victims of Crime: A New Deal?* (Milton Keynes, 1988), 138–46.

Anderson, S., R. Kinsey, I. Loader, and C. Smith, 'Cautionary Tales: A Study of Young People and Crime in Edinburgh: A Summary of Findings', Edinburgh, 1990.

Asquith, S., 'Justice, Retribution and Children', in A. Morris and H. Giller (eds.), *Providing Criminal Justice for Children* (1983), 7–18.

Bailey, V., and S. Blackburn, 'The Punishment of Incest Act 1908: A Case Study of Law Creation', *Criminal Law Review* (1979), 708–18.

Baker, A. W., and S. P. Duncan, 'Child Sexual Abuse: A Study of Prevalence in Great Britain', *Child Abuse and Neglect*, 9 (1985), 457–67.

Black, D., and T. Kaplan, 'Father Kills Mother: Issues and Problems Encountered by a Child Psychiatric Team', *British Journal of Psychiatry*, 153 (1988), 624–30.

Blagg, H., and P. Stubbs, 'A Child Centered Practice? Multi-agency Approaches to Child Sexual Abuse', *Practice* 2(1), 1987, 12–19.

Blom-Cooper, L., 'Legal Lessons from Cleveland', *New Law Journal*, 138(6365) (July 1988), 492.

Bottoms, A. E., 'On the Decriminalization of English Juvenile Courts', in R. Hood (ed.), *Crime, Criminology and Public Policy* (1974).

Byrne, K., and N. Patrick, 'Bexley Bounces Back', *Social Work Today*, 24 May 1990.

'The Children Act, 1989', *Childright*, 66 (May 1990), 7–18.

Conte, J. R., 'The Effects of Sexual Abuse on Children: A Critique and Suggestions for Future Research', *Victimology*, 10 (1985), 110–30.

Corbett, C., and K. Hobdell, 'Volunteer based services to Rape Victims: Some recent develoments', Maguire and Painting (eds.), *Victims of Crime: A New Deal?* (Milton Keynes, 1988).

Cornick, B., 'Proceeding Together', *Community Care*, 17 Mar. 1988.

Crewdson, R., and C. Martin, 'The Great Ormond Street Policy on Video Recordings', *Family Law*, 19 (1989), 161–2.

Davis, L. V., and B. E. Carlson, 'Observations of Spouse Abuse: What Happens to the Children?' *Journal of Interpersonal Violence*, 2(3) (Sept. 1987), 278–91.

Decker, D. L., R. M. O'Brien, and R. M. Schichor, 'Patterns of Juvenile Victimizations and Urban Structure', in W. H. Parsonage, *Perspectives on Victimology* (Beverly Hills, Calif., 1979), 88–98.

Duff, P., 'Criminal Injuries Compensation and "Violent" Crime', *Criminal Law Review* (1987), 219–30.

Elbow, M., 'Children of Violent Marriages: The Forgotten Victims', *Social Casework*, 63(8) (Oct. 1982), 465–8.

Feyerherm, W. H., and M. J. Hindelang, 'On the Victimization of Juveniles: Some Preliminary Results', *Journal of Research in Crime and Delinquency*, 11 (Jan. 1974), 40–9.

Flin, R., 'Child Witnesses: The Psychological Evidence', *New Law Journal*, 138(6371) (26 Aug. 1988), 608–10.

—— and R. Bull, 'Child Witnesses in Scottish Criminal Proceedings', in J. R. Spencer *et al.* (eds.), *Children's Evidence in Legal Proceedings: An International Perspective* (Cambridge, 1990), 193–200.

Freeden, M., 'Eugenics and Progressive Thought: A Study in Ideological Affinity', *Historical Journal*, 22(3) (Sept. 1979), 645–72.

Giller, H. 'Is there a role for a Juvenile Court?', *Howard Journal*, 25 (1986), 161–71.

Glaser, D., and J. R. Spencer, 'Sentencing, Children's Evidence and Children's Trauma', *Criminal Law Review* (1990), 371–82.

Goodman, G. S. (ed.), 'The Child Witness', *Journal of Social Issues* 40(2) (1984), 1–194.

—— 'The Child Witness: Conclusions and Future Directions for Research and Legal Practice', *Journal of Social Issues*, 40(2) (1984), 157–75.

—— and D. P. H. Jones, 'The Emotional Effects of Criminal Court Testimony on Child Sexual Assault Victims: A Preliminary Report', in G. Davies and J. Drinkwater (eds.), *The Child Witness: Do the Courts Abuse Children?* (Leicester, 1988).

—— C. Aman, and J. Hirschman, 'Child Sexual and Physical Abuse: Children's Testimony', in J. S. Ceci, D. F. Ross, and M. P. Toglia (eds.), *Children's Eye-Witness Memory* (New York, 1987).

Grusznski, R. J., J. C. Brink, and J. L. Edleson, 'Support and Education Groups for Children of Battered Women', *Child Welfare*, 67(5) (Sept.–Oct. 1988), 431–44.

Hardin, M., 'Guardians *ad litem* for Child Victims in Criminal Proceedings', *Journal of Family Law*, 25(4) (1986–7), 687–728.

Hepburn, J. R., and D. J. Monti, 'Victimization, Fear of Crime and Adaptive

Responses among High School Students', in W. H. Parsonage (ed.), *Perspectives on Victimology* (Beverly Hills, Calif., 1979), 121–32.

Hershorn, M., and A. Rosenbaum, 'Children of Marital Violence: a Closer Look at the Unintended Victims', *American Journal of Orthopsychiatry*, 55(2) (Apr. 1985), 260–6.

Holdaway, S., 'Police and Social Work Relations: Problems and Possibilities', *British Journal of Social Work*, 16 (1986), 137–59.

Jaffe, D. A., S. Wolfe, and L. Zak, 'Emotional and Physical Health Problems of Battered Women', *Canadian Journal of Psychiatry*, 31 (1986), 625–9.

Jervis, M., 'Detached amid the Clamour', *Social Work Today* (30 June 1988), 18–19.

Jones, D. P. H., 'The Evidence of a Three-Year-Old Child', *Criminal Law Review* (1987), 677–81.

—— and J. Melbourne McGraw, 'Reliable and Fictious Accounts of Sexual Abuse to Children', *Journal of Interpersonal Violence*, 2(1) (1987), 27–45.

Kaufman, I., 'Child Abuse: Family Victimology', *Victimology*, 10 (1985), 62–71.

Kelly, L., 'What's in a Name? Defining Child Sexual Abuse', *Feminist Review*, 28 (Spring 1988), 65–73.

—— and L. Regan, 'Flawed Protection', *Social Work Today* (19 April 1990), 3–5.

King, M., 'Welfare and Justice', in M. King (ed.), *Childhood, Welfare and Justice: A Critical Examination of Children in the Legal and Childcare Systems* (1981).

Lindberg, F. H., and L. J. Distad, 'Survival Responses to Incest: Adolescents in Crisis', *Child Abuse and Neglect*, 9 (1985), 521–6.

Lynch, M. A., 'Child Abuse before Kempe: An Historical Literature Review', *Child Abuse and Neglect*, 9 (1985), 7–15.

McEwan, J., 'Child Evidence: More Proposals for Reform', *Criminal Law Review* (1988), 813–22.

—— 'In the Box or on the Box: The Pigot Report and Child Witnesses', *Criminal Law Review* (1990), 363–70.

Maguire, M., 'The Impact of Burglary upon Victims', *British Journal of Criminology*, 20(3) (1980) 261–75.

—— 'Victims' Needs and Victim Services: Indications from Research, *Victimology: An International Journal*, 10(1–4) (1985), 539–59.

—— and J. Shapland, 'The "Victims Movement" in Europe', in A. J. Lurigio, W. G. Skogan, and R. C. Davis, *Victims of Crime: Problems, Policies and Programs* (Newbury Park, Calif., 1990), 205–25.

Malamquist, C. P., 'Children who Witness Parental Murder: Post Traumatic Aspects', *Journal of the American Academy of Child Psychiatry* 25(3) (1986), 320–5.

Mawby, R. I., 'The Victimization of Juveniles: A Comparative Study of

Three Areas of Publicly Owned Housing in Sheffield', *Journal of Crime and Delinquency*, 16 (1979), 98–114.

May, M., 'Violence in the Family: A Historical Perspective', in J. P. Martin (ed.), *Violence in the Family* (1978).

Miers, D., 'The Criminal Justice Act: The Compensation Provisions', *Criminal Law Review* (1989), 32–42.

Morgan, J., 'Children as Victims of Crime', in M. Maguire and J. Pointing (eds.), *Victims of Crime: A New Deal?* (Milton Keynes, 1988), 74–82.

—— and J. Plotnikoff, 'Children as Victims of Crime: Procedure at Court', in J. R. Spencer, G. Nicholson, R. Flin, and R. Bull (eds.), *Children's Evidence in Legal Proceedings: An International Perspective* (Cambridge, 1990), 189–92.

Morris, A., 'Interspousal Violence: A Review of Research', *Cambrian Law Review*, 20 (1989), 7–16.

Naylor, B., 'Dealing with Child Sexual Assault: Recent Developments', *British Journal of Criminology*, 29(4) (1989), 395–407.

Pfouts, J., *et al.*, 'Forgotten Victims of Family Violence', *Social Casework* 27(4), 1982, 367–8.

Phipps, A., 'Ideologies, Political Parties and Victims of Crime', in M. Maguire and J. Pointing (eds.), *Victims of Crime: A New Deal?* (Milton Keynes, 1988), 177–88.

Pope, B. C., 'Angels in the Devil's Workshop', in R. Bridenthal, C. Koonz, and S. M. Stuard (eds.), *Becoming Visible: Women in European History* (Boston, Md., 1979).

Pratt, J., 'Corporatism: The Third Model of Juvenile Justice', *British Journal of Criminology*, 29(3) (1989), 236–54.

'Prosecuting Child Abuse', *Prosecutors' Perspective*, 2(1) (Jan. 1988).

Pynoos, R. S., and S. Eth, 'Children Traumatized by Witnessing Acts of Personal Violence: Homicide, Rape and Suicidal Behaviour', in S. Eth and R. S. Pynoos (eds.), *Posttraumatic Stress Disorder in Children* (Washington, DC, 1985).

—— —— 'The Child Witness to Homicide', *Journal of Social Issues*, 40(2) (1984), 87–108.

—— —— 'Witnessing Violence: Special Intervention. Programs for Child Witnesses to Violence', in M. Lystadt (ed.), *Violence in the Home* (New York, 1986), 193–216.

—— —— 'Witness to Violence: The Child Interview', *Journal of the American Academy of Child Psychiatry*, 25(3) (1986), 306–19.

—— and K. Nader, 'Psychological First Aid and Treatment Approach to Children Exposed to Community Violence: Research Implications', *Annals of the Institute of Psychiatry*, forthcoming.

—— —— 'Children who Witness the Sexual Assaults of their Mothers', *Journal of the American Academy of Child Psychiatry*, 27 (1988), 567–72.

Riggs, D. S., and D. G. Kilpatrick, 'Families and Friends: Indirect Victimization by Crime', in A. J. Lurigio, W. G. Skogan, and R. C. Davis, *Victims of Crime: Problems, Policies and Programs* (Newbury Park, Calif., 1990), 120–38.

Rosenbaum, A., and D. K. O'Leary, 'Children: The Unintended Victims of Marital Violence', *American Journal of Orthopsychiatry*, 51(4) (Oct. 1981), 629–99.

Schechter, M. D., and L. Roberg, 'Sexual Exploitation' in R. E. Hefler and C. H. Kempe (eds.), *Child Abuse and Neglect: the Family and the Community* (1986)

Shapland, J., and D. Cohen, 'Facilities for Victims: The Role of the Police and the Courts', *Criminal Law Review* (1987), 28–38.

Silvern, L., and L. Kaersvang, 'The Traumatized Children of Violent Marriages', *Child Welfare*, 68(4) (July–Aug. 1989), 421–36.

Smith, D., 'The Limits of Inter-agency Co-operation', in A. Harrison and J. Gretton (eds.), *Crime UK 1988* (Newbury, 1988), 55–60.

Soloway, R., 'Counting the Degenerates: The Statistics of Race Deterioration in Edwardian England', *Journal of Contemporary History*, 17(1) (Jan. 1982), 137–64.

Spencer, J. R., 'Child Witnesses and the Criminal Justice Bill', *New Law Journal*, 137, 6330 (6 Nov. 1987), 1031–3.

—— 'Reforming the Competency Requirement', *New Law Journal*, 138(6346) (4 Mar. 1988), 147–8.

—— 'Children's Evidence: How Not to Reform the Law', *New Law Journal*, 138, 6365 (15 July 1988), 497–9.

—— and P. G. Tucker, 'The Evidence of Absent Children', *New Law Journal* 137(6320) (28 Aug. 1987), 816–17.

Stanko, E. A., 'Hidden Violence against Women', in M. Maguire and J. Pointing (eds.), *Victims of Crime: a New Deal?* (1988), 40–6.

Steele, B. F., 'Notes on the Lasting Effects of Early Child Abuse throughout the Life Cycle', *Child Abuse and Neglect*, 10 (1986), 283–91.

Stone, C., 'Public Interest Case Assessment and Diversion from Prosecution', Vera Institute of Justice, New York (1987).

Temkin, J., 'Child Sexual Abuse and Criminal Justice: 1', *New Law Journal*, 140(6447) (16 Mar. 1990), 352–5.

—— 'Child Sexual Abuse: 2', *New Law Journal*, 140(6448) (23 Mar. 1990), 410–11.

Thane, P., 'Childhood in History', in M. King (ed.), *Childhood, Welfare and Justice* (1981), 6–25.

Children's Legal Centre, 'The Children Act 1989', *Childright*, 66 (May 1990), 7–18.

Tunnard, J., 'Countdown to the Children Act', *Magistrate*, 46(10) (Nov. 1990), 186.

Vizard, E., M. Tranter, and A. Bentovim, 'Interviewing Sexually Abused Children', *Adoption and Fostering* 11(1) (1987), 20–25.

White, R., 'Child Abuse and Compensation', *New Law Journal*, 139(6437) (22 Dec. 1989), 1758–9.

—— 'The Pigot Report', *New Law Journal*, 140(6445) (2 Feb. 1990), 300–1.

Whitcomb, D., 'When the Victim Is a Child: Past Hope, Current Reality and Future Promise of Legal Reform in the United States', in J. R. Spencer, G. Nicholson, R. Flin, and R. Bull (eds.), *Children's Evidence in Legal Proceedings: An International Perspective* (Cambridge,. 1990).

Wilkinson, C., and R. Evans, 'Police Cautioning of Juveniles: The Impact of Home Office Circular 14/1985', *Criminal Law Review* (1990), 165–76.

Williams, G., 'Videotaping Children's Evidence', *New Law Journal*, 137(6290) (30 Jan. 1987), 108–12.

—— 'More about Videotaping Children', *New Law Journal*, 137(6300) (10 Apr. 1987), 351–2.

—— 'More about Videotaping Children: 2', *New Law Journal*, 137(6301) (17 Apr. 1987), 369–70.

Williams, J., 'Family Courts: Justice for the Children?', *Social Work Today*, 10 Nov. 1988, 17–19.

Woodcraft, E., 'Child Sexual Abuse and the Law', *Feminist Review* 28 (Spring 1988), 124–32.

Index